Celestial Messengers

An In-depth Biblical Study of Angels

Exploring the Roles, Symbolism, and Significance of Angels in Scripture

By
Gary E. Risenhoover

Published by Kinetic Digital Publishers
www.kineticdigitalpublishers.com
For permissions, inquiries, or other correspondence, please visit our website.
ISBN eBook: 979-8-90235-129-0
ISBN Paperback: 979-8-90235-130-6
ISBN Hardcover: 979-8-90235-131-3
LCCN: 2026909186

TABLE OF CONTENTS

Hello Adventurous Reader!

Hey there, incredible soul! Buckle up, because you're about to dive into a book like no other. This creation was sparked by an insatiable desire to explore the unknown, to unravel mysteries, and to share stories that ignite your imagination. Months of tireless research, countless late-night brainstorming sessions, and a heart full of passion led to the birth of these pages.

Every chapter was meticulously crafted, blending the thrill of discovery with the warmth of human experience. I wanted to build a bridge connecting curious minds to the vibrant tapestry of ideas hidden just beyond the horizon. Each word is a stepping stone on your personal adventure.

Behind the scenes, this book breathed life from fascinating studies, vivid interviews, and moments of pure inspiration snatched from everyday life. It's a cocktail of dedication, curiosity, and a sprinkle of magic that I hope you'll savor with every turn of the page.

I poured my soul into weaving narratives that don't just inform, but captivate and challenge you to think differently. It's about sparking a fire, encouraging you to question, to dream bigger, and embrace the exhilarating unknown.

So, as you flip through these chapters, prepare to feel inspired, energized, and perhaps a little transformed. This isn't just a book; it's your ticket to a rollercoaster of ideas and emotions. Let's dive deep, laugh often, and maybe even stumble upon a few surprises along the way.

You're not just a reader here—you're an explorer. Ready to embark on this thrilling expedition? The pages await your curious mind!

Remember, the journey is just as important as the destination. Soak in every bit, challenge every notion, and let your imagination run wild.

Stay curious, stay bold, and don't forget—this is just the beginning. Together, we're about to make magic. Happy reading, friend!

Gary E. Risenhoover

With boundless excitement and gratitude

Gary E. Risenhoover

Whispers from the Heavens: The Origins of Angels

Creation and Cosmic Beginnings

From the very beginning of Scripture, angels are intimately woven into the tapestry of creation, portrayed not as afterthoughts but as primordial beings brought forth alongside the cosmos itself. The biblical narrative invites readers to glimpse angels as integral participants in the divine act that set the universe into motion. In this subchapter, we journey to the dawn of time, exploring the origins of these celestial messengers through the lens of Genesis and other early scriptural texts, while drawing upon theological insights that illuminate their nature as luminous bridges between heaven and earth. This exploration unfolds through a rich interplay of scripture, symbolism, and spiritual reflection, aiming to reveal the radiant essence of angels as foundational figures within the unfolding story of creation.

The opening verses of Genesis provide a profound starting point in understanding the cosmic beginnings of all things, including angelic beings. Genesis 1:1 declares, "In the beginning, God created the heavens and the earth," setting the stage for a creation that is orderly, intentional, and brimming with divine purpose. Though angels are not explicitly named in this text, the references to "heavenly hosts" and the imagery that follows suggest the presence of spiritual beings fashioned by God during the initial act of creation.

The concept of angels as part of the created order is borne out in several passages throughout the Old Testament. Consider Psalm 148:2, which commands, "Praise him, all his angels; praise him, all his heavenly hosts!" This verse situates angels within the cosmic order, alongside the sun, moon, and stars, praising God in a celestial chorus. The heavens themselves, sparkling with countless lights, become a symbolic backdrop for understanding angelic beings as radiant inhabitants of a realm threaded between the divine and human spheres.

The Genesis account is silent on many details of the angelic nature, yet by examining parallel biblical motifs and theological reflections, a richer picture emerges. Angels appear frequently in the Old Testament as messengers, warriors, and worshipers. Their origins, therefore, transcend a simple "created being" designation; they embody the vast mystery of God's creative word manifested in living, radiant forms. These forms are often described with an emphasis on light and brilliance—symbols pointing toward their divine mission and origin.

The motif of light, intimately linked to angels, is not incidental. In biblical thought, light is a primary symbol of God's presence and holiness. In Genesis 1:3, God commands, "Let there be light," and light bursts forth before the creation of sun and stars, emphasizing its primordial and divine quality. Angels, as bearers of light, reflect God's glory and function as vessels through which divine illumination reaches the created world. The apostle John, in the prologue to his gospel (John 1:1-5), poetically identifies Jesus as the "true light" that shines in the darkness, a theme echoed in the radiant nature of angels, who serve as heralds of that light.

The depiction of angels as beings of light finds further biblical support in passages such as Daniel 10, where the angelic figure appears "clothed in linen, with a body like chrysolite, his face like lightning, his eyes like flaming torches" (Daniel 10:5-6). The vivid description connects angels to a celestial luminosity that is awe-inspiring and distinctly otherworldly. The imagery of lightning and fire captures both their power and their proximity to divine holiness.

Beyond explicit descriptive texts, the overarching biblical narrative embraces the cosmic and symbolic significance of angels through allusions to the starlit sky and celestial landscapes. The psalmist's majestic praise in

Psalm 19 declares, "The heavens declare the glory of God; the skies proclaim the work of his hands." Stars, seen as fixed points of radiant light suspended in the vast firmament, evoke thoughts not only of the physical universe but of spiritual realities. Angels, like these luminaries, illuminate the space between God and creation, embodying radiance and conveying divine messages with clarity and authority.

Ancient Jewish literature further deepens the framework within which angels' origin is understood. Books such as the Book of Enoch—though not canonical in most Christian traditions—offer extensive angelologies that reflect early ideas about angelic beings as primordial, vast in number, and powerful in their cosmic function. Enoch portrays angels as created beings who existed before the flood and played roles in both guidance and judgment in the human realm. While some fallen angels introduced sin and chaos, the majority remained faithful servants of God's cosmic order.

The affirmation of angels as created beings—still utterly dependent on God—is a cornerstone of both Jewish and Christian theology. Unlike God's self-existing and eternal nature, angels partake in existence as contingent beings with beginnings rooted in God's creative will. Their luminous form denotes their participation in the divine light but does not equate them with deity. This distinction is crucial in early theological reflections, which protect God's uniqueness while recognizing angels' elevated status above ordinary creatures.

Christian theology draws upon scriptural foundations to further explicate angels' cosmic origins and roles. The New Testament, while not focusing extensively on angelic creation, reaffirms their presence at the cosmic crossroads of God's redemptive plan. For example, Colossians 1:16 states, "For by him all things were created: things in heaven and on earth, visible and invisible ... all things have been created through him and for him." The phrase "things in heaven" encompasses angelic beings, situating their creation within the all-encompassing creative work of

Christ, the Logos. This ties angels intimately to the divine Logos, through whom the cosmos was woven into existence.

The Gospel of John, too, reveals the cosmic significance of Jesus as the "Word" through whom all things were made, including the spiritual realm inhabited by angels. This theological insight places the origin of angels within a divine economy characterized by purpose and relationality, not random emergence. Angels as "luminous messengers" are thus participants in the divine plan that commences at creation's dawn and continues throughout salvation history.

The symbolism of light that permeates biblical descriptions of angels carries profound spiritual implications. Light not only represents God's holiness but also conveys truth, purity, and guidance. Angels' radiant quality, therefore, signifies their role in illuminating God's will to humanity, acting as beacons that reveal and protect. This symbolism finds a poetic resonance in Isaiah's vision of seraphim—literally "burning ones"—surrounding God's throne, calling to one another, "Holy, holy, holy is the Lord Almighty; the whole earth is full of his glory" (Isaiah 6:3). These fiery beings, ablaze with divine radiance, reflect the core essence of angelic nature as fiery conduits of holiness.

Furthermore, Ezekiel's vision of cherubim (Ezekiel 1) depicts them as complex beings of light, movement, and intricate form. The "wheel within a wheel" and "eyes all around" imagery conveys a cosmic intelligence and vigilance consistent with their function as guardians and intermediaries. The cherubim's radiant presence serves as a vivid image of angels' dual role—both as servants of divine mystery and protectors of sacred spaces.

Poetic meditations on the nature of angels deepen this understanding. In contemplating angels as "whispers sent from the heavens," one might envision them as the living breath of God's creative word, shimmering across the expanse of creation. Their luminous essence reflects not only divine holiness but also a dynamic energy that inspires awe and reverence.

They are not static entities but vibrant expressions of God's ongoing involvement in the cosmos.

This luminous nature also conveys a paradoxical closeness and transcendence. Angels embody a radiant brightness that dazzles yet does not blind, a holy presence that approaches human reality while remaining distinctly other. Their light serves as a metaphor for divine revelation—illuminating the darkness of human experience with glimpses of God's glory, truth, and love. They act as liminal beings standing at the boundary of the seen and unseen, bridging the eternities with the temporal.

Early Christian thought built upon these scriptural and symbolic foundations, offering nuanced reflections on angels' origins and purposes. Church Fathers such as Augustine, Gregory the Great, and Aquinas synthesized biblical exegesis with philosophical inquiry to clarify angels' nature as pure spirits created by God. For Augustine, angels were "immortal spirits" endowed with intellect and will, created to serve God and minister to humanity. This understanding emphasizes angels not only as messengers but also as rational beings, capable of choice and activity.

Aquinas, in his *Summa Theologica*, elaborates that angels are simple, immaterial substances created without bodies, possessing sublime intellect and will. Their creation precedes that of human souls, situating angels as original inhabitants of the spiritual realm. Their luminous form, therefore, is not physical light as humans experience but a spiritual radiance reflecting their pure nature and proximity to the divine.

The role of angels as intermediaries between God and creation underlines their fundamental purpose within the cosmic order. Their origin at creation's dawn is not a mere historical footnote but the foundation of their ongoing ministry. They serve as custodians of God's law, warriors against cosmic chaos, worshipers in the heavenly courts, and guides to human souls navigating earthly existence.

Theologically, angels embody the interface between the infinite and the finite, the eternal and the temporal. Their radiant beginning at creation affirms their role as conduits through which divine presence and power flow into the world, sustaining the delicate balance between heaven and earth.

Moreover, the diverse classifications and hierarchies of angels found in biblical passages express the manifold ways in which their primordial origin manifests in function and rank. Passages in Isaiah, Ezekiel, and Revelation depict varied angelic orders such as seraphim, cherubim, thrones, powers, and principalities—each reflecting a distinct dimension of angelic participation in God's cosmic governance. These classifications affirm that from creation onward, angels are organized in ways that reveal the complexity and grandeur of the divine kingdom.

In conclusion, the biblical portrayal of angels as primordial beings fashioned at creation's dawn invites readers into a profound encounter with the mystery of God's cosmic artistry. Angels emerge not as abstract supernatural entities but as vibrant, radiant vessels, made to bridge the divine and terrestrial realms. The symbolism of light and radiance associated with angels encapsulates their essence as luminous messengers—beings of holiness, power, and intimate participation in God's unfolding plan. Scriptural exegesis, enriched by poetic meditation and theological reflection, reveals the angels' origins as fundamental to understanding their enduring significance within the biblical narrative.

As we proceed through this study, appreciating angels' creation and cosmic beginnings will provide the foundational tone for comprehending their multifaceted roles throughout Scripture. They stand at the threshold of divine revelation and human experience, eternal witnesses to the mystery of God's creative word. Thus, the story of angels begins not in isolated incidents but in the very first breath of creation—a testament to their enduring place in the celestial hierarchy and the unfolding drama of salvation.

Names and Natures: Defining Angelic Identity

The biblical concept of angels, though often perceived as straightforward messengers from the divine, unfolds into an intricate tapestry of linguistic roots, symbolic titles, and theological nuances upon closer examination. To fully grasp the identity of these celestial beings, it is essential first to explore the origins and meanings embedded in the very words used to describe them in Scripture. This journey into semantics and etymology reveals not only the essential nature of angels but also the rich layers of their spiritual reality as portrayed in biblical texts.

At the heart of the biblical portrayal lies the term "angel" itself, a word whose roots and evolution frame much of our understanding of these mysterious figures. Derived from the Greek word ἄγγελος (angelos), which literally means "messenger," the term is rooted in the cultural and linguistic milieu of the New Testament and Hellenistic Judaism. This Greek designation is uniquely capable of conveying the primarily functional role attributed to angels: emissaries sent forth from God to communicate messages, execute divine will, or protect the faithful. The Greek verb ἀγγέλλω (angellō), meaning "to announce" or "to tell," highlights this active, communicative role. Thus, the title "angel" inherently underscores the purpose-driven aspect of these beings—they are not merely passive presences but agents dispatched with intent and mission.

Yet the concept of angelic beings predates the Greek terminology. In the Old Testament's original Hebrew context, the term most commonly translated as "angel" is מַלְאָךְ (mal'akh), which similarly means "messenger." Like its Greek counterpart, mal'akh roots the identity of these entities in their role as divine envoys. However, Hebrew Scriptures imbue the term with additional connotations that intertwine with angelic nature, function, and status. The root of mal'akh suggests one who is sent or dispatched—literally a "one sent forth"—and is applied to human messengers as well as divine, underscoring a shared function but divergent source of authority.

This dual use can initially blur the distinctiveness of angels in the biblical narrative, but a closer study shows that when mal'akh refers to heavenly beings, specific attributes and contexts clarify their supernatural identity. For instance, mal'akh YHWH—"the messenger of the LORD"—often appears with divine authority, sometimes even identified as a theophany or a pre-incarnate appearance of God Himself. Hence, while the term fundamentally denotes a messenger, it also carries embedded theological implications about divine presence and power. The interchangeability in Hebrew between "messenger" and "angel" points to a conceptual fluidity that invites scrutiny: angels are not merely couriers but extensions of God's will and agents of His sovereign action.

Beyond mal'akh, other Hebrew terms enrich our understanding of angelic identity. The word שַׂר (sar), often translated as "prince" or "ruler," appears in conjunction with angelic beings in certain passages, signifying a hierarchical dimension within the angelic host. For example, in Daniel 10 and 12, the term "Prince of Persia" and "Prince of Greece" indicates angelic figures associated with earthly nations, suggesting a celestial administration or governance. This link between angelic beings and earthly realms complicates their role beyond mere messengers, casting them as cosmic participants in human history and divine providence.

In Greek texts beyond the New Testament, additional terms like δαίμων (daimon), meaning "spirit" or "divine power," and πνεῦμα (pneuma), meaning "spirit," further illustrate the complex landscape of spiritual beings. While Christian Scripture makes clear distinctions between angels as created spiritual beings and other entities like demons or human spirits, the ancient world often conflated these categories. The New Testament writers, therefore, navigate linguistic and cultural challenges, carefully delineating figures such as angels (angeloi), spirits (pneumata), and demons (daimonia), each with distinct attributes and roles within the cosmic order.

This tapestry of terminology invites us to consider the multifaceted nature of angels as both messengers and mighty beings, transcending simple classification. Scriptural descriptions frequently emphasize distinctive attributes that illustrate the heavenly essence of angels—attributes that go beyond function to reveal their spiritual composition and role in the divine economy. One such recurring motif is the radiance or brightness of angels. The Hebrew term for "brightness," זֹהַר (zohar), evokes the luminous glory often associated with divine presence. Biblical narratives regularly portray angels surrounded by dazzling light or "the glory of the LORD" (Hebrew: כְּבוֹד יְהוָה, kavod Yahweh), reflecting their proximity to God's holiness.

For instance, when the angel Gabriel appears to Daniel (Daniel 8:15–17), he is described as a figure "clothed in linen, with a belt of fine gold" and having a "face like lightning," highlighting an otherworldly brilliance that sets him apart from mortal beings. Similarly, in the New Testament, the angel at Jesus' tomb in Matthew 28:3 is said to have an appearance like lightning and clothing as white as snow. Such radiant depictions symbolize their pure and holy nature, signaling their direct association with God's sanctity and power.

Strength and awe-inspiring presence form another dimension of angelic identity. Angels are often described as warriors or mighty executors of God's will, underscoring their role not only as messengers but as agents of divine intervention. Michael, the archangel, displays this martial character as a heavenly prince engaged in spiritual warfare (Revelation 12:7–9), a defender of God's people against demonic forces. This martial aspect entangles angels with the cosmic struggle between good and evil, situating them as divine champions who possess overwhelming power far exceeding human capability.

Yet, alongside their might and radiance, angels are inherently spiritual and invisible to the naked eye, capable of manifesting in various forms as the divine mission demands. Often, they assume human appearance, indistinguishable from ordinary men, enabling direct interaction with people. The three visitors to Abraham in Genesis 18, for instance, appear as travelers, their angelic identity only revealed by their words and actions. This fluidity of form hints at a dimension of angelic existence that is not bound to physicality yet can temporarily adopt such to fulfill God's purposes. It also emphasizes the relational nature of angels, bridging the divine and human spheres.

Theologically, understanding the nature of angels requires delineating their position relative to other heavenly beings. Scripture presents a hierarchy of spiritual entities, with distinctions that are sometimes subtle but significant. For instance, cherubim and seraphim, often associated with temple worship and divine throne-room imagery, differ in function and form from the more commonly portrayed angelos/mal'akh. Cherubim, described in Ezekiel's visionary account (Ezekiel 1 and 10), possess multiple wings, faces of various creatures (man, lion, ox, eagle), and are bearers of God's glory and mobility. Their multifaceted form symbolizes complex divine attributes, including wisdom, strength, holiness, and judgment.

Seraphim, found in Isaiah 6, are six-winged beings who proclaim God's holiness, covered with wings to signify reverence and readiness to serve. Their name, often understood to mean "burning ones," conveys a fiery purity, spotlighting their role in purification and worship. Unlike the more interactive and mission-driven angels, cherubim and seraphim occupy specialized roles within the divine presence, emphasizing holiness and the cosmic order of heaven.

In contrast to these exalted orders, angels functioning as messengers or guardians engage more directly with human affairs, as seen in Gabriel's annunciation to Mary or guardian angels mentioned in Matthew 18:10.

This spectrum from throne guardians to earthly messengers illustrates a layered angelic cosmos, where identity varies according to function, rank, and proximity to God.

Such distinctions illuminate common theological misunderstandings. One frequent confusion arises in equating angels with spirits more generally or attributing to them roles reserved for God. Though angels are spiritual beings, the Bible consistently emphasizes their created nature. Hebrews 1:14 describes angels as "ministering spirits sent to serve those who will inherit salvation," distinctly marking them as servants rather than objects of worship. Unlike God, they possess no divine essence or sovereign authority, and the Bible warns against angelic worship, as seen in Revelation 19:10 where the apostle John is corrected for bowing to an angel.

Another area of confusion lies in conflating angels with demons or evil spirits. While demons are fallen angels or malevolent spirits opposed to God's purposes, biblical texts draw sharp lines between these hostile entities and the holy angels. Their names, attributes, and functions are poles apart: angels embody obedience, light, and protection, while demons represent rebellion, darkness, and destruction. This contrast is crucial for a proper understanding of spiritual reality in biblical thought.

To deepen this understanding, biblical visions provide vivid portrayals of angelic forms that surpass everyday descriptions—visions that combine symbolic and poetic elements. These prophetic glimpses into the heavenly realm underscore the majestic and awe-inspiring nature of angels, often layered with theological meaning.

Ezekiel's vision (Ezekiel 1:4–28) remains one of the most detailed biblical descriptions, revealing creatures with human and animal features, multiple wings, and eyes covering their bodies and wheels alongside them. The multiplicity of eyes symbolizes divine omniscience and vigilance, while the wheels suggest mobility and omnipresence. These attributes signify the angels' role as dynamic agents of God's will, constantly active in the universe. The prophet's struggle to capture their overwhelming brilliance crowns these descriptions with a sense of mystery and reverence.

Similarly, John's vision in Revelation 4 and 5 offers a heavenly court scene with four living creatures around God's throne, resembling lion, calf, man, and eagle—echoing Ezekiel—each covered in eyes and engaged in ceaseless worship. These creatures, sometimes understood as exalted angelic beings or symbolic representations of creation, further expand the cosmic tapestry in which angels function. Their roles reflect the holistic participation of angels in the worship and governance of creation, moving beyond individual missions to cosmic order.

These poetic visions serve dual purposes: they represent theological truths with vivid imagery and inspire awe at the divine grandeur. The symbolism of multiple faces, wings, eyes, and fire conveys layers of meaning about angelic attributes—holiness, knowledge, swiftness, purity, vigilance—that transcend literal description. Poetic imagery thus becomes a theological language, revealing the depth and breadth of angelic identity within God's universal reign.

These biblical accounts position angels firmly within the cosmic hierarchy introduced earlier in this study. Angels occupy a tier between God and humanity, bridging the infinite divine with finite creation. Their identity as created, spiritual beings entrusted with divine authority reflects a cosmos ordered by holiness, power, and purpose. They relate vertically—serving God—and horizontally—interacting with the human realm—acting as intermediaries who uphold God's covenant and engage in spiritual warfare.

This cosmic order also reflects angelic distinctions by rank and function, indicating an organized and purposeful celestial host. Terms like "archangel" denote leading angels with specific authority, while seraphim and cherubim fulfill specialized liturgical and protective functions. The plural use of angelos in the New Testament emphasizes a multitude, a "heavenly host," reflecting both the vastness and diversity of these beings, each contributing to God's overarching plan.

In summary, the biblical semantics and etymology of "angel" and related terms open a window into the complex identity of these celestial messengers. The interplay between their titles—messenger, prince, spirit—and attributes—radiance, strength, sacred mission—draws a portrait of beings who are simultaneously powerful yet subordinate, radiant yet approachable, awe-inspiring yet service-oriented. Their forms as glimpsed through Scripture and visions reveal spiritual realities clothed in poetic symbolism, inviting deeper contemplation and reverence.

By clarifying the distinctions between angels, spirits, and other heavenly beings, the biblical narrative provides a coherent theology of angelic identity that undergirds their role in the cosmic order. Far from vague or mythical figures, angels emerge as integral components of God's interaction with the world, participating in divine governance, worship, and the unfolding of salvation history. This understanding enriches our appreciation of biblical angelology and prepares us to explore further the roles and missions of these heavenly messengers within the divine drama.

Building on this foundational comprehension of angelic identity, subsequent chapters will delve into their specific functions—from guardianship and guidance to judgment and worship—illustrating how the biblical witness presents angels as dynamic participants in God's sovereign plan. Through careful reflection on names, forms, and nature, the celestial identity of angels shines brightly as a profound testament to the breadth and depth of the heavenly realm described in Scripture.

Angelic Functions at Creation

From the very dawn of existence, when the cosmos was but a formless void awaiting the breath of divine command, the presence and purpose of angels begin to shimmer into view. These luminous beings, often glimpsed at the periphery of creation's grand narrative, emerge not as mere bystanders but as essential participants in the unfolding of divine will. To consider the angelic functions at creation is to delve into the sacred orchestration behind all that is seen and unseen—a realm where heavenly messengers weave the fabric of eternity with threads of obedience, might, and reverent fervor.

The biblical tapestry, rich with poetic imagery and profound theological depth, offers glimpses of angels as more than spiritual entities; they are God's emissaries, bearers of divine intent, and agents upon whom the Creator entrusts the delicate and marvelous tasks that undergird all existence. Their origin is intrinsically linked to their appointed purpose— each angel a purposeful note in the celestial symphony, harmonizing with the sovereign voice that called creation from chaos.

To embark on this exploration, one must first attune the heart to the scriptural echoes that affirm angels' roles at the threshold of creation. In the opening lines of Genesis, God's Spirit hovers over the waters, and the word of the Lord brings forth light, land, and life. While the text is silent on angels' direct involvement at this precise moment, subsequent scriptural and theological reflections reveal that they stand as guardians and ministers throughout the creative process, participating as divine agents in the governance and sanctification of the newly formed cosmos.

One of the most striking scriptural windows into angelic functions at creation appears in the Psalms, where angels are described as "ministering spirits sent out to serve for the sake of those who are to inherit salvation" (Hebrews 1:14). While this passage refers to angels' role in salvation history, it illuminates a broader truth: angels are commissioned servants, acting continually within God's unfolding plan. This service, viewed in the light of creation, suggests angels function as custodians of divine order, maintaining the balance and sanctity of God's handiwork.

In the rich imagery of Job 38, when God interrogates Job from the whirlwind, the "morning stars" sing together, and all the "sons of God" shout for joy. These "sons of God" have long been understood by many biblical scholars as referring to angelic beings rejoicing at the dawn of creation. Their jubilant presence at this cosmic inception bears witness to their integral connection to the creative act itself—as beings who not only witness God's power but participate in its manifestation by offering praise that resonates throughout the universe.

Furthermore, the prophet Ezekiel's vision of the cherubim reveals angelic beings as bearers of God's throne, full of eyes and incomparable mobility, underscoring their role as divine guardians and bearers of glory (Ezekiel 1:4-28). While this vision appears well into the biblical narrative, it reflects an angelic reality deeply rooted in creation: angels uphold the very presence and majesty of God, traversing the created realms as extensions of divine authority and sanctity. The cherubim's depiction as guardians echoes the role assigned to angelic beings at the gates of Eden (Genesis 3:24), where they stand sentinel to preserve the sacred boundary between heaven and earth, guarding the way to the tree of life after humanity's fall.

In the intricate design of creation, angels carry out distinct but overlapping functions, each reflecting an aspect of God's sovereign will. From protecting the integrity of creation to delivering the divine word, to manifesting God's presence in tangible ways, angels act as intermediaries between the transcendent God and the temporal realm. This mediatory function is no mere convenience but a deliberate aspect of the divine plan whereby God's holiness and justice permeate the cosmos without being compromised by direct and overwhelming divine intervention. Angels become the conduits through which heavenly authority touches the earthly domain.

One of the earliest impressions of angelic function at creation comes from theological reflections on God's command that the heavens "declare the glory of God" and the firmament "show forth His handiwork" (Psalm 19:1). In many Jewish and Christian traditions, it is held that the angelic host participates in this cosmic praise, giving voice to creation's glory and serving as embodiments of God's order and majesty in the unseen realm. This celebration is not a passive act but an active participation in creative worship, wherein angels harmonize with all of creation in acknowledging God's sovereign artistry.

Beyond praise and protection, angels act decisively as messengers—heralding divine decrees that shape and govern the cosmos and human history alike. Their role as messengers, or "malakim" in Hebrew, highlights their primary function as communicators of divine will, bridging the ineffable holiness of God with the mutable affairs of creation. From the divine commands to Isra'el through the angelic host to the unfolding salvation history revealed in the New Testament, angels execute God's instructions with unwavering precision.

Throughout the biblical narrative, stories depict angelic beings intervening at key moments to initiate, sustain, and complete God's creative and redemptive purposes. In Exodus, the angel of the Lord descends to deliver Israel from slavery, guiding them through the wilderness and embodying divine presence amid their journey. While the exodus story speaks more directly to salvation history, it simultaneously reflects angels' primordial function as custodians of order and agents of God's plans within the created world.

The Psalms provide abundant reference to angelic protection over creation's inhabitants, reinforcing the theme of divine guardianship. Psalm 91:11 proclaims, "For He will command His angels concerning you to guard you in all your ways." This promise, though often applied in personal spiritual contexts, evokes the fundamental role of angels as protectors—appointed at creation to watch over the integrity and flourishing of life itself. This protective duty aligns with the broader concept of cosmic stewardship, where angels, though supernatural, remain oriented toward the preservation and flourishing of the created order under God's dominion.

Engaging with the rich theological tradition, early Church Fathers such as Augustine, Aquinas, and others elaborated on the idea that angels were created before the material universe, existing in a primordial realm of spirit that interfaces with the physical cosmos. They saw angels as the first fruits of creation, created good and imbued with intellect and will, designed to assist and govern the material cosmos in accordance with God's eternal purpose. This understanding deepens the biblical narrative, situating angels at the very inception of all that is, linking their origin to their ongoing role in governance, worship, and mediation.

The motif of angelic mediation threads its way through Scripture with profound clarity: angels facilitate encounter between the infinite God and finite creation while ensuring that each sphere maintains its holy boundaries. This is witnessed most vividly in the incarnation narrative, where angelic announcements herald the birth of Christ, signifying a new chapter in God's engagement with the world. Yet, even before this redemptive climax, angels fulfill their creative functions by maintaining the balance of heavenly and earthly realms, reflecting the divine harmony established at the universe's inception.

Another dimension of angelic function at creation is their role as executors of divine judgment and purifiers of creation when it diverges from God's plan. Though this function becomes more explicit in later biblical episodes involving the judgment of nations or the fall of rebellious angels, it hints at an ongoing maintenance role assigned to angelic beings—upholding the sanctity of creation by removing or restraining what threatens its ordered flourishing. Their capacity to wield power— both merciful and judicial—is intrinsic to their originating purpose as servants aligned with God's righteous will.

The angelic function of revealing divine mysteries further manifests in biblical texts where angels serve as guides to prophetic understanding. For example, the Book of Daniel describes an angelic figure providing interpretation and insight into complex heavenly visions, a role that underscores angels' intimate knowledge of the heavenly realm that transcends human comprehension. This enlightenment function suggests that from the beginning, angels bridge not only spatial divides between heaven and earth but also the cognitive gulf between divine wisdom and human understanding.

In contemplating the full scope of angelic functions at creation, one discerns a seamless integration of roles—protectors, messengers, worshipers, executors of judgment, and mediators of divine presence. Each function reveals a facet of God's relational design for the cosmos—a cosmos not left to chance or impersonal forces but crafted and sustained through personal, purposeful agency. Angels, therefore, are not autonomous powers but are thoroughly dependent upon and responsive to God's command, existing to enact a will greater than themselves and a plan that embraces all of reality.

This celestial choreography invites readers to perceive the created world as a luminous tapestry where heaven and earth interlace through angelic ministry. The presence of angels at creation signals that the divine does not seek isolation but longs for engagement, relationship, and stewardship. It also primes the believer to understand angelic intervention in their own life not as accidental or extraordinary, but as a continuation of this age-old pattern of divine care and communication woven into the cosmos since its first breath.

Moreover, pondering angels at creation nurtures a reverent awe toward the cosmos itself, inspiring a deeper appreciation for the interconnectedness of all things. The cosmic dance of light, spirit, and matter invites an awareness that humans are participants within a grander story, watched over and aided by celestial beings who derive their very being and mission from God's creative decree. It is a summons to humility and trust—to recognize that the invisible realms abound with guardians and guides acting as partners in God's redemptive and sustaining work.

This subchapter, therefore, is more than an account of angelic origins and functions; it is a window into the heart of God's creative purpose. Angels embody the truth that creation is not random or chaotic but ordered, cherished, and perpetually engaged by divine hands and heavenly messengers. Their existence from the earliest moments points toward a cosmos that is inherently relational, a cosmos in which spiritual and earthly realities intermingle under the sovereign gaze of God.

As the narrative of Scripture unfolds, this foundational understanding of angels—rooted in creation—prepares readers to grasp their enduring significance throughout salvation history and theological reflection. It situates angels not as distant mythic figures but as living participants in a dynamic and ongoing divine drama that embraces all existence. In this way, the angelic functions at creation serve as a guiding prism, illuminating the multifaceted nature of these celestial messengers and inviting a deeper engagement with the sacred story in which all are called to partake.

In the final analysis, to contemplate angels at creation is to glimpse the profound mystery of a God who wills that His invisible glory be enacted through visible beings and deeds. It is to recognize that the heavens do not remain silent but praise and protect, mediate and manifest, guiding both cosmos and creature according to the flawless wisdom of their Creator. Herein lies a sacred trust—a trust that angels carry as they fulfill their ordained functions from the moment of their inception and throughout the eternal unfolding of God's redemptive plan.

Gary E. Risenhoover

Echoes of Light: Angelic Appearances in the Old Testament

Visions and Visitations: Angelic Manifestations

Throughout the Old Testament, angels appear not as mere background figures but as vivid, dynamic messengers—profound conduits between the divine and human realms. Their visitations are moments pregnant with awe, mystery, and transformative potential, marked by sensory impressions of brilliant light, consuming fire, and powerful voices that speak beyond ordinary human experience. This subchapter invites readers into these ancient narratives, reanimating the angelic encounters recorded in Scriptures, and unpacking their theological and symbolic weight while maintaining a storytelling cadence that evokes the emotional and spiritual atmosphere of these divine visitations.

Abraham's Encounters: The Threshold of Divine Promise One of the earliest and most striking angelic manifestations occurs in the life of Abraham, the patriarch with whom God establishes a covenant that shapes the destiny of Israel and beyond. In Genesis 18, Abraham is visited by "three men" at the oaks of Mamre. The narrative, rich with sensory detail, portrays these figures as more than ordinary travelers. The text states that Abraham "lifted his eyes and looked, and behold, three men stood in front of him." Though called men, the supernatural nature of their appearance quickly becomes evident.

The imagery here is vivid: the scorching afternoon sun beats down on the tent, while the sudden arrival of these figures brings a palpable shift in atmosphere. The reader senses the tension between the ordinary— hospitality to strangers in the desert—and the extraordinary—the unfolding of God's promises through angelic agents. Abraham's immediate response is one of reverent hospitality, "Let a little water be fetched, and wash your feet, and rest yourselves under the tree." This reaction signifies the awareness of sacredness implied in the encounter.

The dialogue that follows is no less remarkable. One of the visitors declares that Sarah will bear a son within the year, an announcement causing Sarah to laugh within herself, reflecting human incredulity in the face of divine mysteries. The inclusion of all three visitors shifts as one "LORD" reveals Himself speaking from the midst of the angelic visitors (Yahweh), indicating that the angelic beings act as representatives or messengers of God's sovereign will.

Throughout the encounter, sensory details accentuate the celestial quality: the heat of the day, the shade beneath the oak, the aroma of food prepared, and the intimacy of the conversation. These elements anchor the story in human experience even as they reveal the profound presence of heavenly messengers. The angels serve several functions here—announcers of God's promise, witnesses to Abraham's faith, and agents who later proceed to Sodom, linking human intercession with divine judgment.

Yet, even beyond Genesis 18, angelic mediation pervades Abraham's narrative. In Genesis 22, the "angel of the LORD" intervenes at the climactic moment when Abraham is about to sacrifice Isaac. Here again, the angel speaks with divine authority, halting the sacrifice and providing a ram as a substitute offering. The sensation of urgency, the dramatic tension heightened by natural sounds and Abraham's heavy breathing, and the sudden exclamation of the angel bring this visitation to life, encompassing human obedience, divine testing, and merciful provision.

Jacob's Dream and Angelic Ladder: A Vision Between Heaven and Earth Moving from Abraham to Jacob, another profound angelic experience unfolds—one that embodies the symbolic role of angels as connectors between heaven and earth. In Genesis 28:10-17, Jacob's dream beside a lonely stone becomes a mystical window into the celestial realm.

As Jacob lies on the ground, the biblical account describes "behold, a ladder was set up on the earth, and the top of it reached to heaven; and behold, the angels of God were ascending and descending on it." The sensory and symbolic language here is vivid: the ladder or stairway serves as a cosmological bridge, a vertical axis mundi where divine beings freely traverse between God's presence and the earthly realm.

The dream's quiet setting—the night's stillness, the solitude—amplifies the awe of the vision. In his waking awareness, Jacob confesses, "Surely the LORD is in this place, and I did not know it... How awesome is this place! This is none other than the house of God..." The revelation is salvific, infusing the ordinary landscape with sacred significance, a holiness created through angelic presence.

Theologically, the angels ascending and descending represent the ongoing connection between God and Jacob's descendants, a reassurance that divine oversight and protection encircle the chosen covenant community. This vision foreshadows later angelic guardianship and signals the dynamic interplay between earthly faith and heavenly reality.

Moses and the Burning Bush: Fire Without Consumption The encounter between Moses and God through the medium of the burning bush in Exodus 3 is perhaps one of the most iconic theophanies in Scripture, where angelic presence is implied within the divine manifestation. Although the text does not explicitly name an angel in this episode, the "angel of the LORD" is strongly associated with manifestations of God's presence elsewhere in Exodus, suggesting that angelic agency undergirds this encounter.

Moses, tending sheep in the wilderness, notices a bush "that was burning with fire, yet the bush was not consumed." The sensory impact of this phenomenon—fire's intense heat, light, and motion contrasted with unconsumed vegetation—creates a startling paradox that grabs

Moses' attention and signals the supernatural. This fire symbolizes God's holiness and presence, a consuming yet sustaining energy that points beyond itself to the God of Israel.

The voice that calls Moses from the bush commands his attention: "Do not come near; take your sandals off, for the place on which you are standing is holy ground." The voice carries authority and sanctity, echoing the otherworldly nature of the angelic herald. The command to remove sandals recalls the ancient recognition of sacred space, a threshold marked by humility and reverence.

This setting encapsulates the angel's role as mediator: bringing God's word, commissioning Moses, and revealing divine intention within an earthly moment. The visual spectacle of fire paired with audible command invites the reader into a heightened spiritual atmosphere that is at once terrifying and life-giving.

The Pillar of Fire and Cloud: Guidance in Wilderness The presence of angels guiding and protecting Israel as a collective can be discerned in Exodus, where the "pillar of cloud by day and a pillar of fire by night" leads the Israelites out of Egypt. In Exodus 13:21-22, the text describes: "The LORD went before them by day in a pillar of cloud to lead them along the way, and by night in a pillar of fire to give them light..." Scholars often interpret these pillars as manifestations of angelic presence or the "angel of the LORD" acting as God's protective escort. The sensory elements are striking: the burning column lighting the darkness, the cloud hiding the intense brightness during daylight, the movement leading a vast multitude through treacherous terrain. The imagery evokes both awe and reassurance.

This angelic guidance emphasizes relational themes: God's care, presence, and ongoing accompaniment amid uncertainty and danger. The soundscapes of the wilderness—the crackling of fire, the murmur of moving hosts, the whisper of wind—surround the Israelites and the reader, creating an immersive atmosphere of divine escort framed by the celestial messenger.

The Angel at Sinai: The Mountaintop Encounter During the Sinaitic covenant event, angelic presence remains integral to the divine revelation. In Exodus 23:20-23, God promises Israel, "Behold, I send an angel before you to guard you on the way and to bring you to the place that I have prepared."

This angel serves as a protector and mediator, embodying God's holiness and authority. The text warns of strict obedience to the angel's words, "for my name is in him," implying the angel's role as a visible and audible extension of God's presence.

The sensory descriptions associated with Sinai—thunder, lightning, fire, smoke, the sound of a trumpet—heighten the reverence and terror of the encounter. The angel becomes the face of divine communication, a bridge between the infinite God and finite humanity.

Here, the atmosphere is thick with both awe and fear, emotions captured in the trembling of the people and Moses' intercession. Such manifestations remind the reader that angelic beings inspire both comfort and reverence as they carry God's holy will.

Gideon's Divine Visitor: Fire, Voice, and Assurance In the time of the Judges, angelic visitations continue to catalyze pivotal moments. Judges 6 recounts Gideon's encounter with "the angel of the LORD," described initially as "a man" appearing while Gideon is threshing wheat in a winepress to hide it from Midianites.

The sensory environment is filled with tension—the low hum of threat from Midian, the secretive labor, and then the sudden disruptive presence of the angel. The text notes that "the angel of the LORD appeared to him and said, 'The LORD is with you, O mighty man of valor.'"

This greeting, combining divine authority and personal empowerment, imbues Gideon with courage. The angel's presence is accompanied by fire, as later Gideon's offering is consumed by a flame from the angel. The crackling fire and rising smoke become symbols of divine acceptance and powerful confirmation.

Gideon's response—"Alas, O Lord GOD! For now I have seen the angel of the LORD face to face"—expresses a mixture of fear, humility, and awe, emphasizing the intense emotional and spiritual impact of such visitations.

Prophetic Encounters: Angels as Heralds and Agents of Judgment The prophetic literature of the Old Testament offers some of the most dramatic and symbolic angelic encounters, where visions blend heavenly imagery with urgent, often unsettling messages.

In Isaiah 6, the prophet Isaiah recounts a vision in the temple wherein seraphim, fiery six-winged angelic beings, surround the throne of God. The account is rich in sensory detail: "Above him stood the seraphim. Each had six wings: with two he covered his face, and with two he covered his feet, and with two he flew." Their voices are thunderous, proclaiming "Holy, holy, holy is the LORD of hosts; the whole earth is full of his glory."

The soundscape and the fiery glow of their wings create an immersive scene of celestial worship that overwhelms Isaiah's senses and conscience. The seraphim's role includes the purification of Isaiah, touching his lips with a burning coal—fire here representing divine cleansing and commissioning.

This complex vision reveals angels not only as messengers but as participants in cosmic worship and agents of transformation. The emotional undertone is one of humility, reverence, and awe before the holiness of God and the mediatory function of angels.

Similarly, in Ezekiel 1, the prophet describes a vision of "living creatures" with multiple faces and wings, often identified with cherubim or angelic beings, surrounded by wheels and a dazzling expanse of crystalline brightness. The overwhelming sensory details—sight of flashing lightning, sound of rushing waters and fire—underscore their otherworldly power and sacredness.

In Daniel 10, the angelic visitation takes on the form of an overpowering figure whose appearance causes Daniel to faint and fall sick. His garments shine like lightning, his face is like glowing bronze, and his voice is like the sound of a multitude. This angel delivers revelations of future events, battling spiritual opposition on behalf of God's purposes.

Through these prophetic visions, the angelic becomes a vehicle for divine revelation, judgment, and encouragement—engaging the prophet's whole being through sensory encounter and spiritual vision, confirming the angel's role as God's emissary in the revelation of the divine plan.

Angels as Avenging Agents and Protectors: The Duality of Divine Messengers Throughout the Old Testament narratives, angels fulfill dual functions: delivering comfort and protection to the faithful, while also serving as agents of judgment and wrath. This dual role is apparent in episodes such as the destruction of Sodom and Gomorrah (Genesis 19) and the plague that struck the Assyrians (2 Kings 19).In Genesis 19, two angels visit Lot, warning him of imminent destruction. Their arrival is marked by urgency and authority, their glowing presence underscored by Lot's instinctive hospitality and fear. The vivid sensory details—knocking at the door, the sway of the city's dark impending doom, the eventual fiery rain that consumes Sodom—are interspersed with the angels' protective actions, guiding Lot and his family to safety while executing divine judgment.

The emotional atmosphere is charged: fear, tension, salvation, and destruction intertwine. The angels here reveal the sober reality of the divine will—both merciful and just—and their role as executors of God's decisions.

Similarly, in 2 Kings 19, an angel strikes down 185,000 Assyrian soldiers encamped against Jerusalem, an act of sudden and overwhelming divine intervention. The narrative's brevity intensifies the impact, while the sudden silence and morning realization paint the angel as a swift, invisible agent of God's deliverance.

These episodes demonstrate the multifaceted nature of angels: protectors for the covenant community, instruments of divine justice, and bearers of both hope and warning.

Angelic Voices: Communication Beyond Words Across these narratives, a defining element of angelic manifestations is communication—primarily auditory, but often transcending human language's limits. Angels speak with authority, clarity, and urgency, their voices stirring human hearts and moving historical events.

Abraham, Sarah, Gideon, and Daniel all hear the angelic voice as a direct message from God, yet the emotional tone varies: gentle reassurance, stern command, comforting promise, or ominous warning. The sound is sometimes described metaphorically—as the roar of many waters, the sound of trumpets or thunder—intensifying the sensory experience.

This auditory dimension serves to heighten both the credibility of the message and the emotional impact on the recipient, bridging divine transcendence with human reception.

Visual and Sensory Symbolism: Light, Fire, and Movement The manifestations are frequently accompanied by powerful visual symbols— blazing fire, radiant light, flying movements—that mark angels as otherworldly. Light often signifies holiness, purity, and God's presence, evident in Moses' burning bush, the pillar of fire, and the glowing appearance of the angel in Daniel.

Fire conveys purification, judgment, but also presence and invitation, as in Isaiah's seraphim or Gideon's consuming flame. Movement—

ascending and descending stairways, flight with many wings—symbolizes angelic freedom between celestial and earthly realms.

These sensory elements embed the encounters in the experiential world while simultaneously pointing beyond it, inviting readers to envision the meeting point of heaven and earth.

The Emotional and Spiritual Atmosphere: Awe, Fear, and Hope The narratives subtly but unmistakably transmit an atmosphere charged with emotional and spiritual intensity. Recipients often respond with fear or trembling (Moses at Sinai, Gideon's fear), humility and repentance (Isaiah's cleansing), or joyous hope and assurance (Abraham's promised seed, Jacob's awakening).This emotional dimension plays a crucial role in shaping biblical theology of angels: they are not mere messengers but intermediaries who evoke responses of praise, obedience, and transformation.

Conclusion: Angels as Bridges in Old Testament Visions and Visitations The Old Testament presents angels as multifaceted beings— manifesting in dazzling light, consuming fire, majestic voices, and powerful interventions—who move across the threshold between God's invisible presence and human history. Their visitations are marked by rich sensory detail and profound emotional resonance, underscoring their role as bridges connecting the divine mystery with everyday human experience.

From Abraham's hospitable reception, through Jacob's visionary ladder, Moses' burning bush, to the prophetic seraphim and warrior angels, these narratives paint a panorama where angels are not simply emissaries delivering information but are dynamic participants in the unfolding redemptive story.

In experiencing the awe, fear, comfort, and hope inspired by these celestial messengers, biblical readers are invited into deeper reflection on the intersection of the earthly and the divine—a meeting place where

God's mysterious will unfolds through the glorious, often terrifying, presence of His angels.

Angels as Protectors and Warriors

Throughout the Old Testament, angels emerge not only as messengers bearing divine revelation but also as formidable protectors and warriors. Their roles transcend mere communication; they embody the tangible presence of God's power actively engaged in the defense and preservation of His people. This subchapter explores these martial and protective dimensions of angelic activity, particularly focusing on key scriptural narratives that reveal angels standing as God's shields and instruments of judgment in the midst of spiritual and earthly conflict. Central to this exploration is the figure of Michael the Archangel, whose character encapsulates the luminous might and vigilance of heavenly guardianship.

The Old Testament is replete with vivid depictions of angels intervening on behalf of Israel and, by extension, on behalf of divine justice. These accounts reveal an intricate portrayal of angelic beings who operate under God's sovereign command, executing divine will in ways both awe-inspiring and terrifying. By examining prominent episodes of angelic protection and combat, we gain insight into the cosmic battle unfolding behind Israel's historical narrative—a battle where angels serve as God's warriors, defenders, and enforcers of divine law.

One of the earliest and most dramatic depictions of an angel acting as protector occurs in the story of Hagar in the wilderness (Genesis 16). Here, an angel of the Lord appears to Hagar amidst her desperation, offering not only solace but a divine assurance that her son Ishmael will become a great nation. While this episode is often noted for the angel's role as a messenger and comforter, it also carries the theme of divine protection. The angel's intervention prevents Hagar's perilous journey from ending in death, serving as a guardian presence in a harsh and hostile environment. This initial glimpse subtly foreshadows the more overtly militant functions angels assume as the biblical narrative progresses.

As Israel's history unfolds, the protective character of angels becomes significantly pronounced, especially in contexts of national crisis or divine retribution. Notably, in the account of the Exodus, angelic guardianship assumes a more explicit martial dimension. While the text does not detail angels battling the Egyptian oppressors directly, God's deliverance of Israel is often understood to involve angelic forces acting as divine agents of protection. The pillar of cloud and fire that leads Israel through the wilderness can be symbolically interpreted as an angelic presence, a visible manifestation of God's guardianship over His covenant people during their vulnerable flight from bondage.

Further, the narrative of the Passover points to angelic involvement in judgment and protection. In Exodus 12, the "destroyer" (Hebrew: מַכַּת מַכְּתֵי־מַכָּה or simply the angel of death) is sent forth to execute God's judgment on the Egyptian firstborn, underscoring an angelic role as an executor of divine justice. Simultaneously, the blood on the Israelite doorposts signifies God's protection wrought by this angelic agent, safeguarding those under covenant from harm. The dual aspect of angels as protectors of the faithful and as warriors against enemies vividly emerges here, intertwined with the very fabric of salvation history.

The Book of Numbers provides an even clearer instance of angelic protection, where an angel confronts Balaam's donkey and Balaam himself (Numbers 22:22-35). The "angel of the Lord" stands as a heavenly sentinel restraining Balaam from cursing Israel, demonstrating angelic oversight in guarding God's promises and people from external threats. This account highlights the angel's role not merely as a passive observer but as a combatant who halts nefarious intentions, underscoring the angel's function as a divine protector who intervenes decisively to uphold divine will.

Perhaps one of the most dramatic illustrations of angelic militancy and protection appears in the episode of the destruction of the Assyrian camp (2 Kings 19:35; Isaiah 37:36). When the Assyrian army, under King Sennacherib, besieges Jerusalem, the narrative recounts how an angel of the Lord strikes down 185,000 Assyrian soldiers overnight, effectively rescuing the city without human battle. This profound demonstration of angelic warfare vividly affirms that the defense of Israel is fundamentally a divine endeavor, often enacted through invisible yet devastating warrior angels. The sudden and overwhelming nature of this intervention emphasizes the omnipotence of God's heavenly hosts and their instrumental role in divine deliverance.

This motif of angels as divine warriors is further elaborated in the concept of spiritual warfare, which emerges more explicitly in prophetic and apocalyptic literature. While later texts, such as Daniel and Zechariah, expand this symbolism, even earlier writings contain hints of an ongoing cosmic battle behind human history. Daniel 10 offers a remarkable portrayal of angelic combat wherein an angel describes contending "with the prince of the kingdom of Persia" and being aided by Michael, "one of the chief princes" (Daniel 10:13, 21). This passage unveils angelic engagement in spiritual conflict on behalf of God's people, where celestial beings wrestle against spiritual powers that seek to undermine Israel's destiny.

Michael the Archangel, in particular, emerges as the quintessential angelic warrior, protector, and leader. His presence is especially prominent in texts that emphasize the militant and protective roles of angels. Identified as "your prince" and "the great prince who stands watch over the sons of your people" (Daniel 12:1), Michael represents the embodiment of God's luminous, fearsome protector. Unlike many other angelic figures described simply as "messengers" or "angels of the Lord," Michael's name—meaning "Who is like God?"—suggests a unique standing: a heavenly champion who mirrors divine authority in the cosmic struggle against evil.

The Old Testament gives Michael a singular role in guarding Israel during times of spiritual crisis and conflict. His leadership over angelic armies and his engagement in celestial battles underscore the reality that the nation's protection is not merely political or military but fundamentally spiritual and theological. Michael's decisive interventions ensure that God's covenantal promises to Israel are safeguarded amid cosmic disruption and human threats.

The role of angels as divine warriors also intersects the theme of divine justice. Angels are not only guardians but executors of God's righteous judgment against wickedness and injustice. Their military actions are expressions of divine holiness, wrath, and sovereignty, serving to uphold divine order. In this light, angelic warfare is not a violent rebellion but a sanctified mission carried out under God's authority to defend truth and punish evil.

This understanding is further reinforced by angelic appearances to key biblical figures, where protectiveness accompanies a readiness to do battle on behalf of God's will. For instance, the angelic visitor who wrestles with Jacob (Genesis 32:22-32) symbolizes the struggle between human vulnerability and divine power, culminating in Jacob's blessing and name change to Israel. This mysterious combatant can be understood as an angelic figure who both tests and protects the patriarch, illustrating the complex interaction of protection, trial, and spiritual confrontation embedded in angelic activity.

The Book of Psalms also contains numerous references that illuminate the protective and militant nature of angels. Psalm 91:11-12 states, "For he will command his angels concerning you to guard you in all your ways; they will lift you up in their hands, so that you will not strike your foot against a stone." This poetic assurance portrays angels as vigilant guardians assigned to watch over the faithful during their journey, lifting them above harm. Such imagery emphasizes angels as divine sentinels who shield believers from danger and actively intervene to preserve life.

In addition, Psalm 103:20-21 praises "Bless the Lord, you his angels, you mighty ones who do his bidding, who obey his word," recognizing their powerful agency in executing God's commands. Here, angels are exalted as mighty warriors in God's service, highlighting their readiness to act with force and authority as defenders and ministers of justice.

Another poignant example appears in the story of the angel who stymies King Herod's plans in the New Testament, but whose roots can be traced back to Old Testament portrayals of protectors fighting the enemies of God's people. Though the New Testament develops these themes further, the foundation laid in the Old Testament presents angels as fearsome spiritual warriors charged with safeguarding the covenant and executing divine judgment.

From a theological perspective, the protective and militant roles of angels in the Old Testament invite reflection on the nature of divine justice and cosmic order. Angels act as instruments of God's holiness, charged to maintain the boundaries between good and evil, covenant and chaos. Their involvement in Israel's history testifies to a universe not governed solely by chance or human might but overseen by divine powers who engage directly in the affairs of humanity to fulfill God's redemptive purposes.

Historically, Jewish thought has embraced the notion of angelic protectors and warriors. In the Second Temple period, literature such as the Book of Enoch and other apocryphal texts expands upon these images, portraying angels as leaders of heavenly armies confronting evil forces. These traditions, while not canonical, reflect the development of angelology and underscore the enduring fascination with angels as cosmic defenders.

Within Christian theology, the Old Testament depictions of angelic protectors and warriors contribute to a broader understanding of spiritual warfare, divine providence, and the conflict between good and evil. The figure of Michael continues to resonate as a protector of the faithful and leader of angelic hosts, echoed in New Testament and later Christian writings. Such views affirm that the angelic realm is an active, dynamic partner in the unfolding spiritual drama that encompasses human history.

Ultimately, the Old Testament's portrayal of angels as protectors and warriors invites believers to recognize the ongoing reality of spiritual conflict and divine guardianship. These heavenly beings are neither distant abstractions nor mere symbols but vividly depicted participants in God's plan to protect, judge, and redeem. Through their luminous presence and wondrous deeds, angels affirm the God of Israel's power and care, reinforcing faith in a God who fights on behalf of those who belong to Him.

In conclusion, the narrative threads woven throughout the Old Testament testify to the multifaceted roles that angels fulfill as protectors and warriors. From the wilderness appearance beside Hagar to the fiery destruction of the Assyrian camp, from the spiritual battles narrated in Daniel to the protective leadership of Michael, these accounts collectively affirm that angels act as God's luminous champions—fearsome, vigilant, and relentless in securing divine justice and the well-being of His chosen people. The theological significance of these depictions lies not only in their historical context but in their enduring call to recognize the depth and intensity of the cosmic struggle for righteousness in which God's people are engaged, guarded always by celestial messengers amidst the echoes of light that resound throughout Scripture.

Messengers and Heralds in Covenant History

In the vast tapestry of covenant history woven throughout the Old Testament, angels emerge not merely as ethereal beings but as luminous messengers—a radiant conduit through which the divine will is articulated, promises are proclaimed, and the sacred trajectory of God's unfolding plan is disclosed. These celestial heralds, shimmering with the brilliance of lightning and echoing with voices as resplendent as a choir of stars, stand at pivotal junctures of God's covenantal engagement with humanity. Their appearances are not incidental; rather, they signify moments charged with divine purpose, where heaven's decrees pierce the veil of earthly silence and announce the dawn of new epochs in the history of redemption.

Angels, in this light, are fundamentally communicators. Their mission transcends mere interaction; they are the living voice of God's intents, the bearers of promises that buoy faith, the conveyors of warnings that redirect wayward paths, and the embodiments of covenantal fidelity. Through them, God's covenant—His solemn agreements with humanity—becomes a dynamic narrative punctuated by radiant intervention. The interplay between the angelic and the human realms creates a sacred dialogue rich with symbolism and theological resonance, shaping the identity and destiny of the people chosen to inherit God's promises.

At the heart of this communicative ministry stands Gabriel, the Herald par excellence, whose appearances in scripture crystallize the angelic role as divine announcer. Gabriel's name, meaning "God is my strength," itself suggests the power and authority vested in this celestial envoy to proclaim God's plans with clarity and gravitas. Unlike other angelic figures who sometimes appear as agents of mystery or warfare, Gabriel's appearances are suffused with the purpose of revelation—he brings forth messages that illuminate the divine blueprint and invite human response in faith and obedience.

One of the most iconic instances of angelic communication is Gabriel's encounter with Daniel, detailed in the Book of Daniel, a text itself steeped in apocalyptic imagery and covenantal themes. In Daniel 8 and 9, Gabriel appears to explain visions that carry deep implications for the future of God's covenant people. The brilliance of the angelic messenger, described metaphorically as a figure clothed in shining linen with a glorious countenance, serves as a beacon breaking through Daniel's anxious quest for understanding. Gabriel's words not only unravel mysteries but reaffirm God's sovereign control over history, reinforcing the covenantal promise amidst trials and tribulations.

This revelation is no mere exchange of information; it is an unveiling bathed in celestial light. The imagery surrounding Gabriel's communication evokes the natural phenomena of lightning—sudden, brilliant, and awe-inspiring—a metaphor for how divine truth pierces human obscurity. His voice, resonating with authority and gentleness alike, embodies the paradox of heavenly communication: both thunderous in significance and tender in invitation. Through Gabriel, the narrative coherence of covenant faithfulness is maintained, even as the unfolding events appear uncertain or ominous.

Notably, the role of angels as covenantal messengers is not confined to future prophecy but extends to the affirmation of God's ongoing relationship with His people. Throughout the Old Testament, angelic appearances frequently accompany covenant milestones—moments when the divine-human bond is sealed, tested, or renewed. Consider the angel who wrestles with Jacob at Peniel (Genesis 32). This encounter is suffused with covenantal symbolism: Jacob, the bearer of the covenant promises, engages bodily with the angel, emerging with a new name—Israel—which signifies his transformed identity and the continuation of God's covenant through his descendants. The angelic figure here functions as both challenger and affirming presence, a communicator of divine blessing through struggle.

The voice of the angel at Peniel, described in biblical poetry as "like the voice of a man," yet enveloped in otherworldly radiance, represents the voice of covenantal confirmation. The wrestling match itself, suffused with physicality and heavenly mystery, conveys the deep intertwining of human struggle and divine purpose. The messenger's role here is not purely verbal; it is enacted through encounter—illuminating the manifold ways angels communicate God's covenant, sometimes through words, sometimes through presence, sometimes through challenge.

Similarly, in Exodus, when the angel of the Lord appears to Moses in the burning bush, the angel's communicative function is profound. The imagery of fire—an emblem of divine holiness and transformative power—combined with the angelic presence, signals a pivotal covenant moment. Here, the angel announces God's commitment to redeem Israel from Egypt, rendering visible the invisible presence of God in covenant action. The angel's voice, thunderous yet intimate, is a clarion call to liberation, intertwined with covenant promises that shape Israel's identity as the chosen people.

This communicative motif reappears as the angel who guides Israel throughout the wilderness journey—a presence described in Exodus 23:20-23 as a "messenger" sent to guard and lead the people. The passage explicitly connects this angel with the establishment and preservation of the covenant, underscoring the angelic role in faithfully transmitting God's promises, commands, and warnings. The angel's instruction often carries the tone of divine authority tempered by care, reinforcing the inseparability of covenant mercy and justice.

Within this framework, the radiant imagery that often accompanies angelic appearances emerges as a theological symbol of God's glory (Hebrew: kabod), His manifest presence among His people. The continuity of motifs—lightning, fire, radiant faces—links angelic messengers to the divine glory that both conceals and reveals God's transcendent holiness. This luminous presence is not merely decorative but functional, clarifying the serious and sacred nature of the message delivered. The brilliance strikes awe and demands attentive listening, affirming the words as emanations from the Divine.

Tracing the trajectory of angelic appearances within covenant history also reveals their crucial role in mediating divine warnings—a facet integral to covenant fidelity. The covenant relationship, by its nature, entails conditions and expectations; angels function as the heavenly heralds who communicate both promise and warning, joy and judgment. Their messages often serve as divine wake-up calls, urging repentance and renewal before the covenant is broken. The Book of Judges, for example, depicts angels appearing to leaders and prophets with admonitions that carry covenantal weight, reflecting God's ongoing desire for His people to walk rightly.

Examining the profound dialogue between angels and individuals also highlights the reciprocal dynamic of covenant communication. The angelic messenger speaks with authority but invites human response—faith, obedience, hope. This dialogue echoes the covenant itself, which is relational rather than transactional. Angels do not impose silently; their communications shimmer with an invitation to partake in God's purposes. For example, the angel's announcement to Hagar in Genesis 16, though brief, carries deep covenant implications: God's ongoing care for the marginalized and the promise that Ishmael will become a great nation. The angel's words both assure and commission, bringing God's promises into the broken realities of human life.

In another poignant moment, the angel who appears to Balaam in Numbers 22 serves as a divine mediator between a rebellious prophet and God's covenant will. The radiant messenger's sword drawn for defense, the angel's voice stern yet purposeful, underscore the tension inherent in covenant fidelity and divine communication. Here, the angel's message is not only that of encouragement but also correction—emphasizing the role of angels as custodians of the covenant order.

These angelic interventions inevitably bring the human and the heavenly into dialogue, uniting the earthly narrative with the divine purposes. Their appearances coincide with the unfolding story of God's redemptive plan, marking temporal boundaries where promises move from potential into fulfillment. Each encounter adds a luminous thread to the covenant's rich fabric, affirming God's unchanging commitment while revealing new dimensions of His holiness and grace.

Moreover, angelic communications are integral to the cultivation of faith and hope, qualities core to the covenant relationship. The dazzling radiance, the voice like rushing waters or the crackle of lightning, serve to awaken trust in God's promises even when their fruition seems distant or improbable. The angel's appearance becomes an ephemeral yet indelible imprint on the human spirit, a reminder that God's voice remains steadfast amidst the flux of history.

The dual capacity of angels to both soothe and challenge is central to their communicative power. Their messages nurture hope through the annunciation of God's plans and yet demand accountability, reflecting the covenant's call to holiness. The oscillation between promise and warning, light and shadow, forms the rhythm of their appearances, reinforcing the layered complexity of the covenant itself.

Significantly, angelic heralds function as more than mere messengers; they are heralds of God's presence, corporeal signs of the divine promise fulfilled or soon to be actualized. Their radiant personhood—clothed in light and majesty—embodies the transcendent nature of the covenant, which cannot be fully grasped in human terms alone but is glimpsed in the brilliance of heaven's emissaries. This poetic interweaving of light and voice invites recognition that covenant communication is a multifaceted encounter, engaging human senses and souls alike.

While Gabriel remains the principal figure in prophetic annunciations, other angelic figures contribute to this communicative enterprise, each adding nuance and texture to the unfolding divine message. The "angel of the Lord," a figure sometimes indistinguishable from God Himself, serves as a recurring symbol of the intimate communication between Creator and creation within covenant history. His various appearances, whether as protector, guide, or judge, underscore the holistic nature of covenant mediation through angelic presence and speech.

Further, angels function within the grand orchestra of covenant history as both individual emissaries and representatives of a heavenly council, situating their messages within the broader cosmic governance that undergirds God's covenantal plan. Their voices ripple beyond single encounters, resonating across the tapestry of scripture and history, continually reaffirming that God's promises transcend immediate circumstances and are upheld by divine agency.

As one moves toward the climax of the Old Testament narrative, angelic messengers prepare the way for the ultimate covenant fulfillment. Their radiant announcements anticipate the coming of the Messiah, the incarnate Word who will embody perfectly God's covenant with humanity. The angelic heralding foreshadows this great revelation, linking past covenant milestones with future hope.

In sum, the role of angels as messengers and heralds in covenant history is profound and multifaceted. Through dazzling appearances suffused with imagery of light and thunder, through voices that command attention and invite faith, angels mediate God's promises and warnings with a clarity that pierces the shadows of human doubt. Their interventions mark the hinge points of covenant milestones—announcements of promise, clarifications of divine plans, confirmations of God's presence and commitment. They reveal a God deeply invested in relationship, communicating not only through prophetic words but through the living, radiant presence of His celestial messengers. This dynamic communication, at once brilliant and tender, illuminates the path of covenant faithfulness and shapes the narrative of salvation history as a continual dialogue between heaven and earth.

Thus, the angelic mission of communication within covenant history beckons readers to listen deeply—to the thunderous voices and the luminous revelations, to the challenges and consolations that embody God's enduring covenantal love. As echoes of light resounding across the ages, these celestial messengers reinforce the divine promise: that amid changing times and human frailty, God's word stands sure, radiant with the glory of His eternal faithfulness.

Symbolic Interpretations and Spiritual Lessons

Angelic appearances in the Old Testament are more than mere historical or narrative events; they carry profound symbolic weight and spiritual significance that resonate deeply within the biblical worldview. To understand these manifestations solely at a surface level would be to overlook the intricate layers of meaning they convey. Throughout this subchapter, we will explore the rich tapestry of symbolism and spiritual lessons embedded in these encounters, appreciating how angels serve as bridges between the divine and human realms, apocalyptic heralds, protectors, and mysterious messengers of God's will.

At the heart of Old Testament angelology lies a paradoxical duality—angels appear as both powerful and tender, terrifying and comforting. This dual nature mirrors the broader theological framework of God's relationship with humanity, where justice and mercy, grandeur and intimacy, wrath and grace exist side by side. This subchapter reflects on these paradoxes and the subtle messages woven within the narratives, encouraging readers to approach angelic appearances not just as historical facts but as divine manifestations rich with spiritual insight.

The figure of the angel functions on multiple levels—historical, theological, symbolic, and existential. By exploring the various dimensions of angelic symbolism in Old Testament scripture, we deepen our understanding not only of these celestial beings but also of God's own nature and His ongoing interaction with His people.**The Angel as Divine Mediator: Bridging Heaven and Earth**One of the primary roles angels occupy in Old Testament accounts is that of mediators between the divine and human spheres. Angels are often portrayed as messengers (from the Hebrew "mal'akh"), serving as agents who convey God's commands, guidance, judgments, and encouragement to individuals or entire nations. Yet their role extends beyond the mere transmission of information; angels embody the principle that the divine can and does intervene in human history, often in ways that are both subtle and overwhelming.

This mediatory function is emblematic of the profound mystery of God's transcendence juxtaposed with His immanence. Angels represent how the infinite God reaches into the finite world without compromising either divine sovereignty or human freedom. Through visions of angels, the biblical text invites believers to contemplate the reality of God's presence—even when unseen and unexpected—and the possibility of encountering the sacred in moments of crisis, bewilderment, or worship.

Consider the angel of the LORD who appears to Hagar in Genesis 16. Here, the angel does more than deliver a message; he reveals God's attentive care for the marginalized and oppressed, declaring blessings and naming the place "Beer Lahai Roi," the well of the Living One who sees me. The angel's appearance signals that God's oversight extends to the most desolate and desperate circumstances. Symbolically, this encounter teaches that divine mediation is not confined to grand cosmic events but intimately touches individual human suffering and hopes.

Similarly, when the angel Gabriel visits Daniel or when the angelic host appears to the patriarchs, they stand as emissaries of divine purpose and agents of revelation—gateways through which God's plan unfolds. These portrayals encourage readers to discern that God's agency, while direct, often lapses through a network of divine messengers who communicate not only commands but also comfort and assurance.**Power and Tenderness: The Ambiguity of Angelic Presence**A striking feature of angelic appearances in the Old Testament is their simultaneous capacity to inspire awe and dread, reassurance and alarm. They often deliver messages of judgment or warnings and yet provide protection and consolation. This duality captures the tension inherent in the character of God Himself as revealed throughout scripture.

For instance, the terrifying angel of death who passes over Egypt in Exodus 12 serves as an instrument of divine judgment, yet the same act hastens the liberation of Israel, ultimately embodying deliverance. The cherubim guarding the entrance to Eden are awe-inspiring guardians, wielding fiery swords that bar human access, yet their role reflects God's holiness and justice in a tender desire to preserve sanctity.

This ambivalence underscores the multifaceted nature of divine interaction. Angels symbolize God's power to execute justice and to protect, illustrating that sacred encounters are rarely neutral. They invoke reverence and responsibility, reminding believers of the consequences that arise when covenantal fidelity falters and the mercy extended to those who turn back to God's ways.

The story of Jacob wrestling with the "man," often interpreted as an angelic figure, poignantly captures this duality. The experience is at once a struggle, marked by physical exertion and spiritual conflict, and also a moment of blessing and transformation. Jacob's subsequent renaming as Israel signals the passage from human striving into divine purpose. Here, angelic symbolism conveys the complexity of spiritual encounter—an encounter that may challenge, unsettle, and at times distress, but ultimately leads to deeper self-understanding and divine affirmation.**Angelic Symbolism as a Reflection of Divine Attributes**Angels in the Old Testament also symbolize key attributes of God's character, making the invisible visible and the ineffable tangible. Their depiction frequently highlights themes of holiness, sovereignty, justice, mercy, and mystery.

Cherubim and seraphim, for example, represent aspects of God's holiness and overwhelming glory. Their descriptions in books such as

Ezekiel and Isaiah employ rich, symbolic imagery: multiple wings, eyes, and fiery appearances—all motifs that transcend human comprehension and suggest divine omniscience and omnipresence. Through these celestial beings, the text invites readers to glimpse the perfection and majesty of God in forms both symbolic and sacramental.

Moreover, angels' roles in delivering prophetic messages and enacting divine will amplify the theme of God's unwavering sovereignty. No earthly power or human authority supersedes God's plans, and angels serve as visible signs of this ultimate control, reminding humanity of their place within a divine order.

Yet even in their grandeur and otherworldliness, angelic figures display qualities of compassion and tenderness, reflecting God's mercy and concern. The angelic assistance given to figures such as Elijah during times of physical and emotional exhaustion reveals that God's care extends beyond spiritual principles into tangible acts of kindness.

These opposing yet complementary traits embodied by angels encourage believers to internalize a more holistic understanding of God— one that is both transcendent and immanent, just and merciful, powerful and loving.**Themes of Faith and Wonder: Responding to Angelic Encounters**Angelic appearances in scripture frequently elicit responses of fear, reverence, wonder, and faith. The initial reaction to an angelic presence often entails trembling or falling prostrate, highlighting humanity's natural response to divine revelation and presence. These reactions are not merely emotional but deeply spiritual, reflecting an acknowledgment of God's overwhelming holiness and the profound mystery of the divine-human encounter.

The theme of faith permeates these encounters. Individuals such as Abraham, Moses, and Daniel exhibit trust in God's messengers even when the messages themselves portend uncertainty or upheaval. Faith emerges as the appropriate response to angelic revelation, requiring openness to the unknown and willingness to follow divine guidance.

Wonder also plays a vital role in angelic symbolism. Angels are embodiments of God's otherness, evoking a sense of awe that transcends rational understanding. Their presence invites believers to cultivate a spiritual disposition marked by openness, humility, and a longing for the sacred. Wonder, in this sense, serves as a threshold into deeper spiritual realities, encouraging readers to contemplate the mysteries of God's working in the world.

The repeated emphasis on faith and wonder throughout angelic encounters underscores a vital spiritual lesson: trust in God's providence amid uncertainty and marvel at His creative power amidst the mundane are essential to a vibrant and resilient spiritual life.**Angels as Symbols of Divine Protection and Deliverance**Throughout the Old Testament narratives, angels frequently originate as agents of divine protection, rescuing God's people in perilous situations and delivering them from danger. This protective symbolism reinforces the theme that God's care is active and present, embodied in sentinels that guard and intervene.

The account of the angel who defends Daniel in the lions' den illustrates this vividly—the angel's presence communicates God's deliverance in the face of mortal threat and serves as an assurance that faithfulness will be rewarded with divine safeguarding. Similarly, the angelic encampments described in Psalm 34:7 portray a celestial host as a protective army around the righteous.

Symbolically, this protection transcends physical safety. The angel as protector also signifies spiritual guardianship, standing watch over the soul's journey and providing strength in moments of trial. Such imagery reassures believers that they do not walk alone amid life's struggles and that divine help is both near and accessible.

This motif also highlights a broader theological assertion: that God's providence extends into the most vulnerable and contested spaces, and that believers' faith is intertwined with the reality of angelic guardianship. Recognizing this can inspire confidence and peace in the midst of personal and communal challenges.**The Angelic Call to Holiness and Covenant Faithfulness**Angels in the Old Testament often appear not only as messengers of God's will but also as reminders and enforcers of the covenantal relationship between God and His people. Their appearances frequently coincide with moments that demand renewed fidelity, repentance, or obedience, making them symbolic figures exhorting holiness and covenant faithfulness.

The angelic visitations to prophets and patriarchs consistently urge attention to divine commandments and encourage perseverance in the face of opposition. In this way, angels function as divine heralds of accountability and hope, calling the people back to the covenant path.

This call to holiness is reflected in the awe-inspiring presence of seraphim in Isaiah 6, whose proclaiming "Holy, holy, holy" echoes the heart of Israel's covenantal identity. The transcendent radiance of these beings invites those who witness or contemplate them to recognize the inviolable sanctity of God and, by extension, to pursue a life marked by holiness.

The spiritual lesson here is powerful: angelic encounters challenge believers to examine their own commitments and to respond with renewed dedication to God's covenant. Angels symbolize the divine standard and serve as catalysts for inner transformation, urging faithful obedience.**Angels and the Mystery of Divine Will**The enigmatic quality of angels in the Old Testament serves as a reminder of the mysteries inherent in God's will and governance of the cosmos. Often, angelic actions and messages are difficult to fully discern or comprehend, demanding patience, humility, and spiritual discernment from those who encounter them.

This dimension of mystery is especially significant because it invites believers into a posture of trust in God's unfathomable wisdom. The complexity and sometimes contradictory nature of angelic encounters underscore that divine purpose is not always immediately apparent and may require faith to embrace the unknown.

For example, the angel who wrestles with Jacob remains a mysterious figure, open to multiple interpretations and charged with symbolic resonance that transcends simple explanation. The mixture of blessing and struggle in this encounter invites readers to appreciate the complexity of God's guidance and the often paradoxical nature of spiritual growth.

Acknowledging this mystery is, in itself, an important spiritual lesson. It guards against presumption and hubris while fostering a deeper reliance on God's timing and revelation. Angels, as bearers of divine inscrutability, encourage believers to cultivate a humble openness that is essential for genuine spiritual maturity.**Conclusion: Integrating Narrative and Spiritual Reflection**The symbolic interpretations and spiritual lessons embedded in Old Testament angelic encounters reveal a profound dialogue between the divine and human worlds. Angels serve as celestial messengers, divine agents of mediation, and embodiments of God's complex nature—powerful yet tender, terrifying yet comforting.

By reflecting on these multi-layered meanings, readers embark on a journey that transcends historical events and ventures into the realm of spiritual insight. Angelic narratives invite us to dwell in faith, to stand in awe before divine mysteries, and to respond with trust and obedience. They remind us of God's constant presence and involvement in human affairs, even when unseen.

Moreover, these reflections prepare the foundation for the broader biblical understanding of angels developed throughout this book. They introduce recurring themes of divine mediation, covenant faithfulness, protection, holiness, and the interplay between mystery and revelation.

Ultimately, angelic symbolism in the Old Testament calls believers to a deeper awareness of the sacred—urging us to recognize that no encounter with these celestial beings is ever merely incidental. Each visitation echoes

God's light, illuminating paths of faith, wonder, and transformation in the unfolding story of salvation.

50

Harbingers of Glory: The New Testament Angelic Portrait

Annunciations and Birth Narratives

The story of Christ's birth is among the most celebrated and profound moments within the Christian tradition, and the presence of angels in these narratives serves as both a divine herald and a bridge between heaven and earth. Angels, as spiritual messengers of God's glory and will, play a crucial role in the unfolding of this sacred event, illuminating the arrival of the incarnate Word with radiant hope and assurance. This subchapter delves deeply into the angelic appearances that punctuate the birth narratives in the New Testament, with a particular focus on the annunciations to Mary and the shepherds. Through a detailed examination of these accounts, sacred storytelling is enriched with theological insights, revealing the multifaceted roles angels embody as bearers of divine truth and agents of redemptive history.

The Gospel of Luke provides the most extensive angelic interactions surrounding the nativity, offering beautiful and vivid images of those heavenly messengers appearing at moments of critical divine intervention. It begins with the Archangel Gabriel's visitation to the virgin Mary in Nazareth, where the extraordinary unfolds amid the simplicity of an ordinary day. Gabriel's entrance is swift and purposeful, carrying news that will turn the course of history. The scene hums with a tension that balances earthly apprehension and celestial certainty. Gabriel greets Mary with words that embody grace—"Hail, favored one! The Lord is with you" (Luke 1:28)—a salutation that echoes beyond linguistic politeness into a profound recognition of divine favor and destiny. The angel's message reveals not only the impending miraculous conception but also the fulfillment of ancient promises, framing Mary's role within the mystery of the Incarnation.

This annunciation scene is not just an isolated encounter but a theological fulcrum upon which subsequent events rest. The angel's words carry the weight of God's initiative—"You will conceive and bear a son, and you shall name Him Jesus" (Luke 1:31)—unfolding the mystery of a new covenant embodied in the Messiah. Gabriel further explains the significance of the child's name and mission, describing Him as "great" and the "Son of the Most High" (Luke 1:32). As the narrative unfolds, the theological depth of the encounter becomes apparent. The angel's message embodies divine promise and mercy, the dawn of salvation, and the bridging of the heavenly and earthly realms. Gabriel's presence vividly illustrates the angel's role as a mediator of divine revelation, entrusted with announcing God's plan to a young woman whose faith and obedience will pivot the story of human redemption.

Beyond the announcement to Mary, angels continue to weave through the birth narrative, underscoring the cosmic importance of this event. Luke's Gospel recounts another stunning angelic visitation—this time to shepherds tending flocks in the fields near Bethlehem. Here, angels appear in a "sudden" and "glorious" fashion, their presence marking an eruption of heavenly light into the darkness of night (Luke 2:9). The narrative richly describes the "angel of the Lord" appearing to the shepherds with a message that fills the surrounding atmosphere with awe: "Do not be afraid; for see—I am bringing you good news of great joy for all the people: to you is born this day in the city of David a Savior, who is the Messiah, the Lord" (Luke 2:10-11).The angelic announcement to the shepherds is suffused with profound theological and symbolic significance. Unlike the private revelation to Mary, this proclamation is public and communal, aimed at humble pastoral workers who symbolize the marginalized and those on the periphery of society. The choice of shepherds as recipients highlights the inclusive reach of Christ's redemptive mission, affirming the message that salvation is a gift to all humanity, especially the lowly and oppressed. The brightness of the angels' message reverberates as a beacon of hope and a herald of peace on earth, uniting heaven's glory with earth's longing.

What follows the angelic message is no less extraordinary: suddenly a "multitude of the heavenly host" burst forth in celestial chorus, praising God with words that echo through generations: "Glory to God in the highest heaven, and on earth peace among those whom he favors!" (Luke 2:13-14). This scene of angelic worship moves beyond mere communication into divine liturgy, where heaven's praise becomes interwoven with human history. The angels function as heavenly worshippers and divine heralds, their proclamation affirming the incarnation as the fulfillment of divine fidelity and the dawn of peace.

Both angelic episodes—Gabriel's annunciation to Mary and the shepherds' heavenly visitation—are deeply interconnected signposts within the biblical drama of salvation. Together, they reveal the dual nature of the angels' role: as messengers of personal calling and cosmic proclamation, bearer of intimate grace and universal hope. The two stories also frame the Incarnation with rich theological symbolism— Mary's encounter embodies the mystery of obedience and divine selection, while the shepherds' experience conveys the joy and peace that Christ's birth infuses into a fractured world.

The Gospel of Matthew offers a complementary angelic perspective in the birth narrative through the figure of an angel who appears in dreams to Joseph. While Gabriel's annunciations in Luke emphasize proclamation and revelation, Matthew's angelic visitations focus on guidance, protection, and reassurance. In Matthew 1:20, the angel encourages Joseph not to fear taking Mary as his wife, affirming the divine origin of the child: "Joseph, son of David, do not be afraid to take Mary as your wife, for the child conceived in her is from the Holy Spirit." This angelic reassurance preserves the integrity and dignity of Mary within her social context and ensures that Joseph will act faithfully within God's plan.

Later, after the birth, an angel again appears to Joseph in a dream to direct the family's escape from King Herod's murderous intent (Matthew 2:13). In this interdiction, angels shift roles—from announcers of joyous news to protectors ensuring the safety of the Christ child. This angelic intervention underscores a theme woven deeply into the New Testament: angels are not only bearers of divine revelation but also guardians of divine promises and providence. Their presence signifies that the salvation story is under celestial watch, unfolding under God's careful care.

Throughout these birth narratives, angels are portrayed with luminous imagery and language that conveys their otherworldly presence and spiritual significance. The texts often emphasize their brilliance, inspiring awe and reverence in those who behold them. The radiant light surrounding the angels serves as a metaphor for divine holiness, illuminating the darkness that closes in upon humanity apart from God's intervention. In this way, angels become visible symbols of the glory and majesty of God, shattering fears with their announcements and offering reassurance with their presence.

The theological implications of these angelic encounters ripple beyond the immediate narratives. The Incarnation—the mystery of God becoming flesh—is inaugurated through an angelic lens, indicating that even in the most human of moments, the divine intersects with creation. Angels, as messengers, make visible the invisible reality of God's kingdom breaking into the world. They attest to the profound truth that Jesus is "God with us" (Emmanuel), signaling a new era in salvation history. This revelation challenges the original hearers and readers to contemplate the depths of divine love and humility that undergird the nativity.

Moreover, the hopeful and joyous character of the angels' messages invites ongoing reflection on the nature of divine communication. Angels do not merely inform; they inspire faith, courage, and praise. Their words summon responses that shape history and individual lives alike. Mary's "yes" to Gabriel's announcement will lead to the birth of the Savior, while the shepherds' immediate obedience to the angel's message results in their becoming the first human witnesses to the newborn Christ. Through these responses, the angelic messages transcend time, calling every believer into participation with the unfolding story of redemption.

Imagining these sacred moments anew enriches our understanding of the angelic presence and invites readers into an intimate contemplation of divine mystery. Picture Gabriel's luminous form standing gently before Mary—the quiet strength in his declaration, the tenderness mingled with heavenly authority. The air thick with expectancy, a young woman whose heart is poised between fear and faith. Then shift to the dark fields near Bethlehem where shepherds watch their flocks beneath a star-laden sky. Suddenly, the sky explodes with blinding light, and angels pour forth like streams of silver fire, singing a song that quivers with eternal joy. The shepherds' astonishment melts into adoration, their hearts ignited by a message that will ripple through all generations.

These narrative reenactments, infused with theological depth, help modern readers transcend mere historical curiosity and enter the sacred space where heaven touches earth. They remind us of the angelic dimension present in moments of divine encounter—messengers who carry God's glory, who herald the fulfillment of ancient promises, and who beckon humanity toward hope and renewal.

In the final analysis, the annunciations and birth narratives reveal angels as indispensable figures within the New Testament's portrayal of the Incarnation. They are not peripheral characters but central participants in the divine drama. Through their radiant presence and reverent words, angels illuminate the profound truth of God's intervention in human history—a truth that continues to resound with transformative power. Their appearances invite believers to stand in awe, to receive the message of salvation with humble joy, and to recognize the new dawn heralded by the birth of Christ.

As we reflect on these angelic encounters, we confront the mystery of God's love made manifest. The brilliance of the angels who announce Christ's birth points us to a light shining in the darkness, a light that darkness cannot overcome. Their voices echo through the centuries, calling humanity to embrace the promise of redemption and to live within the luminous hope of new beginnings. In this sacred interplay of heaven and earth, the celestial messengers fulfill their eternal mission, bridging divine glory with human longing, and inviting all who listen into the embrace of God's unfolding kingdom.

Angels Amid Resurrection and Ascension

The New Testament presents a vivid and compelling portrait of angels as celestial agents intimately involved in the defining moments of Christ's resurrection and ascension. These events stand at the very heart of Christian faith — the triumphant conquest of death and the glorification of the Savior — and angels emerge not merely as passive witnesses but as active heralds and participants. Their presence at the empty tomb and during the ascension serves both a theological and symbolic function, emphasizing divine victory, offering assurance to believers, and pointing forward to the ultimate restoration of creation. This subchapter explores the multifaceted role of angels amid these profound moments, unpacking their scriptural significance and illuminating their enduring impact on the Christian imagination.**Angelic Presence at the Empty Tomb: Witnesses and Messengers of Resurrection**The resurrection narratives in the Gospels are marked by the startling and awe-inspiring appearances of angels at the tomb of Jesus. The tomb, once sealed and guarded, is found empty, a silent yet powerful testimony to Christ's triumph over death and decay. However, it is the angelic beings who provide the explicit confirmation and interpretation of this event, guiding and comforting the women and disciples who arrive in astonishment and mourning.

In the Gospel of Matthew (28:2-7), an angel of the Lord descends from heaven, causing the stone to roll away with an earthquake. The description is dramatic and filled with divine authority: "His appearance was like lightning, and his clothing white as snow." This image of radiant brilliance, evoking purity and heavenly power, underscores the angel's role as a messenger of divine intervention. He proclaims to the women, "He is not here; for he has risen, as he said." The angel's words not only announce the empty tomb but also affirm the fulfillment of Jesus' own predictions of resurrection. Here, the angel functions as the liberator of hope, transforming despair into joy and confusion into clarity.

The Gospel of Mark (16:5-7) similarly recounts the presence of a young man in white who speaks to the women: "You seek Jesus the Nazarene, who was crucified. He has risen; he is not here." The white garment symbolizes purity and resurrection life, and the figure's calm instruction represents divine order replacing human chaos. Luke's narrative adds a layer of solemn reassurance, with two men in dazzling apparel who remind the women of Jesus' earlier declarations about his suffering, death, and rising (Luke 24:4-7). The presence of two angels may symbolize the witness of divine testimony, reinforcing that the resurrection is no illusion or human fabrication but a divine reality confirmed from heaven.

John's Gospel, though differing in emphasis and detail, nonetheless includes the striking image of angels within the tomb. Two angels are described sitting where Jesus' body once lay, one at the head and the other at the feet (John 20:12). This positioning recalls the care and attention given to Jesus' body and resonates with ancient burial customs, suggesting both honor and heavenly vigilance. Their purpose, while not accompanied by direct speech in this instance, frames the encounter between the risen Christ and Mary Magdalene, who turns from the angels to recognize the living Lord.

The repeated mention of angels clothed in white, radiant and commanding yet compassionate, underscores their symbolic role as intermediaries between God's transcendent glory and human frailty. They serve as visible proof that death has been overcome by divine power — the luminous bearers of the hope that the resurrection perfectly embodies.**Angels as Pillars of Hope and Justice**Beyond their role as messengers, angels at the resurrection functions represent pillars of hope and divine justice in the cosmic drama of salvation. The resurrection is not merely an event but a profound declaration that God's justice prevails over human injustice and that God's hope is a steadfast reality beyond human despair.

The visitation of angels at the tomb confronts the darkness of crucifixion—the apparent triumph of evil—with a brilliant light. Their arrival shatters the finality of death and challenges the power of sin. This theological dimension is critical, for the resurrection is the keystone of Christian hope: through Christ, the ultimate judgment on sin and death has been overturned.

Additionally, angels at the tomb can be interpreted as witnesses to the moral victory of God. Just as the High Priest and the scribes once accused Jesus of blasphemy and insurrection, the angelic announcement declares a divine verdict of innocence and divine vindication. The resurrection vindicates Jesus' mission and identity as the Son of God, a truth angels have proclaimed consistently throughout Scripture.

Moreover, the positioning of angels as guardians or keepers of the tomb—illustrated by references such as in Matthew 27:62-66 regarding the sealing and guarding of the tomb by Roman soldiers—inverts earlier expectations. While the guards were meant to secure Jesus in death, the angel's presence signifies God's greater authority, breaking through human attempts to suppress the divine plan. Angels, therefore, symbolize divine justice that cannot be thwarted by earthly powers.**The Ascension: Angels as Divine Witnesses and Guides**Following the resurrection appearances, the New Testament takes us to another pivotal moment: the ascension of Jesus into heaven. It is an event that completes the earthly ministry of Christ and inaugurates his exalted reign at the right hand of God. Angels again appear, this time serving as witnesses and guides who illuminate the spiritual significance of the ascension and its implications for the Church and the world.

Acts 1:9-11 provides the most detailed account of the ascension, explicitly highlighting angelic presence. As Jesus is lifted up, a cloud receives him out of the sight of the Apostles, and two men in white stand beside them. These men, understood as angels, address the bewildered disciples, telling them that Jesus "will come in the same way as you saw him go into heaven." This statement serves both as reassurance and prophecy — angels confirm the ongoing narrative of divine redemption and anticipate the Second Coming.

The angels at the ascension perform an essential theological function by bridging the earthly and heavenly realms. They interpret the mysterious "cloud" that surrounds Jesus, a symbol often associated with the manifestation of divine glory (see Exodus 13:21-22; 1 Kings 8:10-11). Their presence validates that Jesus has returned to the heavenly throne, glorified and exalted, and they emphasize the continuing work of Christ in heaven.

In addition to their role as celestial spectators and heralds, angels in the ascension narrative serve as models for Christian hope and perseverance. Their assurance that Jesus will return "in the same way" nurtures an expectancy among believers, encouraging faith amid uncertainty and expectancy amid waiting. The angelic message links the resurrection victory to the future consummation of God's kingdom, inspiring the Church's mission and endurance.**Symbolic Dimensions: Light, White Garments, and Heavenly Authority**Throughout the resurrection and ascension accounts, angelic imagery is saturated with symbolism that reinforces their roles as divine agents. The consistent depiction of angels clothed in dazzling white garments evokes purity, holiness, and the victorious light of the risen Christ. This motif recalls Old Testament depictions of heavenly beings and the glory of God's presence, signaling that the events at the tomb and on the Mount of Olives are intersections of heaven and earth.

Light functions as a key symbolic element, representing life, truth, and the dispelling of darkness. The angel's appearance "like lightning" (Matthew 28:3) or in "dazzling apparel" (Luke 24:4) captures the overwhelming brilliance of God's victory over death and sin. This radiant imagery invites believers into a spiritual encounter that transcends the physical realm, drawing attention to the mystical and transformative nature of the resurrection event.

Furthermore, angels embody heavenly authority. They have been sent from God's throne to enact God's will, to announce divine mysteries, and to maintain the order of salvation history. Their bold proclamations and commanding presence evoke that authoritative dimension, reminding the faithful that the resurrection is not merely a human experience or metaphor but a cosmic, divine act witnessed and affirmed by the heavenly host.**The Transformative Power of the Resurrection and Ascension: Spiritual Reflections**The angelic appearances in resurrection and ascension narratives invite deeper spiritual reflection on the transformative power these events hold. They do not merely narrate historical occurrences but open a window into the ongoing reality of God's redemptive work in the world and in the believer's life.

The presence of angels at the empty tomb challenges readers to move from despair to faith, from doubt to hope. The angelic message that "He is not here; He has risen" is an invitation to encounter the living Christ, to embrace the new life ushered in by the resurrection. This encounter is not static; it calls believers to be resurrected spiritually — to leave behind the tombs of sin, fear, and death in their own hearts.

Angels at the tomb emphasize that resurrection is a divine act of liberation, one that cannot be engineered by human strength but is granted as a gift through God's grace. This recognition fosters humility and trust, encouraging the faithful to rely on the power of God rather than their own capacities.

Similarly, the ascension and the angel's promise of Christ's return foster an eschatological hope that shapes Christian living. It calls for active anticipation — to live as people who await the restoration of all things, bearing witness to the resurrection victory in their daily lives. The angels' role thus transcends their historical function; they become spiritual archetypes of divine guidance, hope, and justice that inspire the Church to remain steadfast.**Angelic Ministry as Continuation and Preparation**It is important to understand that angels at the resurrection and ascension do not act in isolation but as part of God's broader heavenly ministry. Their appearances signal the continuity of divine engagement with the world, from creation through covenant history to the new creation inaugurated by Christ's resurrection.

Their ministry highlights a divine order in which angels serve to prepare the way for humanity's participation in God's kingdom. Just as angels announced the birth of Jesus, ministered to him in the wilderness, and strengthened him in Gethsemane, so too do they proclaim his resurrection and instruct the disciples about his exalted status.

The angelic words and presence encourage disciples not only to believe but to bear witness, extending the proclamation of resurrection power throughout the world. Their proximity to pivotal moments signals that angelic beings stand at the intersection of heaven and earth, facilitating the movement of salvation history and bearing witness to God's ultimate purposes.**Theological Implications: Angels as Testaments of Divine Redemption**Engaging these angelic appearances at resurrection and ascension narratives opens profound theological insights. First, angels function as testaments to the reality and certainty of resurrection, serving as divine witnesses who confirm the truth that undergirds Christian faith.

Second, angels reveal the cosmic dimension of salvation. The resurrection and ascension are not confined to human experience but involve the heavens responding to God's redemptive work. The angelic hosts affirm the universal significance of Christ's victory over death, as the defeat of sin ripples through all creation.

Third, the angelic presence informs the understanding of hope and justice in Christian theology. They embody the certainty that God's justice will triumph and that hope is grounded in God's faithfulness. Their role at the end of the earthly ministry of Jesus points to the restored order that believers anticipate and participate in.

Finally, angels demonstrate the personal care of God for humanity. Their comforting reassurances to startled women, their encouragement to disciples, and their ongoing ministry remind believers that resurrection and ascension are not abstract concepts but lived realities accompanied by divine presence and care.**Conclusion: Illuminating Christ's Triumph with Luminous Authority**Angels amid resurrection and ascension narratives emerge as multifaceted agents illuminating the profound victory of Christ. They are not ornamental details but essential participants and heralds of God's saving work. Their radiant presence, authoritative proclamations, and comforting ministry testify to a divine victory that transforms death into life and heaven into accessible reality.

As luminous pillars of hope and justice, angels invite all believers to enter the mystery of resurrection, to live transformed by the power of Christ's triumph, and to uphold the promise of his return. The scriptural symbolism surrounding their appearances beckons readers beyond historical curiosity into spiritual wonder and active faith.

Thus, angels at the empty tomb and the ascension stand as celestial messengers bearing witness to the heart of the Gospel: that through Christ, death is conquered, hope restored, and humanity invited to share in the eternal glory of God's kingdom. In embracing these truths, the faithful are called forward — nourished in wonder, sustained in hope, and empowered to bear radiant witness to the living Christ until his return.

Guides and Companions on the Christian Journey

Throughout the unfolding narrative of the New Testament, angels emerge not merely as distant, awe-inspiring emissaries of the divine but as intimately involved companions in the believer's journey of faith. This continued and deepening role of angels—as guides, protectors, and encouragers—infuses the early Christian experience with both concrete help and profound spiritual meaning. As the nascent Church moved through times of trial, transformation, and triumph, angelic presence remained a subtle yet vital lifeline, weaving through individual stories and communal memory. This subchapter explores this enduring angelic involvement, focusing on well-attested episodes such as the encounter on the road to Emmaus and the manifold protections afforded to the early Christian community. By interlacing scriptural witness with theological reflection and human experience, we seek to illuminate the warmth and nearness of angels as fellow travelers on the path of discipleship.

In the Gospel of Luke, one of the most touching depictions of angelic companionship comes not in a grand celestial vision but in the quiet revelation to two disciples walking the road to Emmaus. The story unfolds on that first Easter afternoon, a time heavy with grief, confusion, and shattered hope. Two followers of Jesus, their hearts burdened by the crucifixion, walk together, recounting the astonishing and troubling news of the empty tomb. Then a stranger joins them, a traveler who engages them patiently, listening to their doubts and fears, and finally, in the breaking of bread, reveals himself to be the risen Christ. While Luke never explicitly identifies this traveler as an angel, the wider biblical and theological tradition embraces the interpretation that this presence functions in the angelic role of guide—leading the disciples from despair to understanding, from blindness to sight.

This moment on the Emmaus road beautifully illustrates one dimension of angelic activity: that of spiritual accompaniment in moments of uncertainty and spiritual blindness. Here, the angelic figure—whether understood as a literal heavenly being or a divinely appointed mediator—shares in the human experience, walking alongside the disciples and gently opening their eyes to the truth. It is a model of angelic care that combines closeness with revelation, proximity with mystery. The guide is not a distant sentinel but a companion, deeply invested in the transformation of the human heart. This intimacy is crucial, for faith is not merely intellectual assent but a journey of the whole person, involving emotions, memories, and the slowly unfolding comprehension of God's purposes.

From this luminous example, the New Testament narrative unfolds a broader picture of angels as protectors and advocates during the birth and growth of the early Church. The Acts of the Apostles offers several striking instances where angelic intervention directly aids the fledgling Christian community. In one dramatic episode (Acts 12), Peter, imprisoned by Herod Agrippa, faces imminent execution. The text recounts a vivid angelic rescue: a radiant presence appears in the night, His light piercing the gloom, His touch awakening the apostle from sleep, guiding him past guards and locked gates, and leading him to freedom. This narrative not only signals divine care for Peter personally but underscores the sustaining role of angels in protecting the Church's leadership against forces of persecution. Here, angels function as both guardians and liberators, their activity affirming the in-breaking power of God into hostile human circumstances.

The lesson woven through these stories is that angelic protection is neither abstract nor automatic. Rather, it is an engagement in the fragile interplay between divine sovereignty and human responsibility. Angels do not override human freedom or circumstances arbitrarily; instead, their interventions serve God's larger purposes, often operating in ways that are hidden, unexpected, and deeply personal. The angelic presence challenges believers to recognize that amid suffering, uncertainty, and opposition, they do not journey alone. This recognition brings comfort and courage, transforming fear into trust, vulnerability into hope.

Moreover, angelic assistance is not confined to isolated moments of extraordinary intervention but permeates the everyday spiritual reality of the Christian community. Early Church fathers and Christian tradition commonly acknowledge angels as ministers of grace sent to serve those who will inherit salvation (Hebrews 1:14). These portrayals invite the faithful to an awareness that angels participate quietly in the life of the Church, attending public worship, guarding sacred spaces, and supporting the communal life shaped by faith and prayer. Their ministry, though unseen, remains profoundly connected to the believers' shared experience, a reminder that the invisible world deeply intersects with the visible.

The personal dimension of angelic assistance is equally significant. Throughout Scripture and tradition, angels often appear as encouragers and messengers of hope in moments of despair or decision. For the individual believer navigating the complexities of life and faith, this angelic presence offers a palpable sense of companionship. Like a trusted friend or mentor, the angel accompanies, advises, and sometimes even comforts with words or signs. This relational aspect is vital because the Christian journey is rarely a straightforward ascent. It is marked by setbacks, questions, and periods of spiritual dryness. In such seasons, the awareness of angelic presence nurtures perseverance and trust, cultivating a sense that even in isolation, one remains enfolded in divine love.

The Apostle Paul's writings reflect this reality. Although the New Testament does not offer detailed descriptions of angelic encounters on Paul's missionary journeys, he clearly acknowledges their existence and ministry. In 2 Corinthians 12, Paul speaks of a "thorn in the flesh," a persistent affliction possibly linked to angelic or demonic forces, and he describes receiving visions and revelations—experiences attended by spiritual realities beyond human perception. This complex interplay suggests that angels operate in a spiritual realm that intersects with human struggles in diverse ways, including both assistance and protection against adversarial influences. Paul's life and letters remind us that the angelic role is not only to guide and guard but also to participate in the cosmic battle in which God's people find themselves engaged.

The communal dimension of angelic accompaniment is most clearly seen in the early Christian worship and liturgical life. Angelic presence is woven into the very fabric of worship, echoing biblical imagery from Revelation, where heavenly beings surround the throne of God, offering praise and intercession. This biblical vision informs Christian liturgy, which often recognizes a celestial realm joining in prayer and worship. The sense of being accompanied by angelic hosts enriches the community's spiritual experience, fortifying the congregation with the knowledge that their fellowship transcends earthly bounds. This belief offers a profound source of encouragement, especially in times of persecution or internal challenge.

The pastoral implications of this understanding are deeply reassuring. When believers gather—whether in the majestic splendor of a cathedral or the humble setting of a small house Church—they are enveloped by a cloud of witnesses that includes not only saints and martyrs but also angelic beings. This cosmic solidarity speaks to the unity and universality of the Christian experience. Angels as companions affirm that faith is never an isolated venture but a shared pilgrimage, a communal journey toward God's kingdom.

A further and often overlooked facet of angelic companionship on the Christian journey is their role as witnesses to pivotal moments of individual and corporate transformation. Angels appear at key junctures—births, callings, conversions, deaths—marking these events with divine significance. The Gospel accounts themselves are punctuated by angelic announcements, from the angels who herald the birth of John the Baptist and Jesus to those who attend the resurrection. In these appearances, angels bear witness to God's unfolding story of salvation, inviting participants and readers alike into awe and gratitude.

One particularly poignant example from early Christian tradition relates to the martyrdom of saints, many of whom recount angelic presence in their hour of trial and death. Though martyrdom is a theme more fully developed in post-New Testament writings, the seeds of this understanding lie in the apostolic era. Believers who faced persecution often testified to the comfort and strength they received through angelic affirmation. These stories underscore the intimacy of angelic companionship—an assurance that even in the shadow of death, angels stand nearby, ministering not only protection but also peace and hope.

Theologically, the angelic role as guide and companion underscores the incarnational nature of Christian faith: God reaching into human history, engaging with the full reality of human existence, including its vulnerabilities and struggles. Angels, as messengers and servants of God, bridge the ineffable divine realm and the tangible human world. They embody the truth that divine assistance is not an abstract principle but a lived reality for believers journeying through a world often marked by uncertainty and hardship.

This incarnational dynamic invites reflection on the nature of presence itself. The angels' intimate closeness challenges any notion of God as a remote deity, instead emphasizing God's desire to accompany, instruct, and protect. The presence of angels reassures believers that God's care extends to the minutiae of their daily lives and their deepest spiritual needs. There is a profound tenderness implicit in the message that invisible, holy beings watch over all who seek God, sustaining them with gentle attentiveness.

In this way, angels become models of faithful service and divine hospitality. Their role is neither self-seeking nor distant but utterly oriented toward the well-being of God's people. They welcome, escort, shield, and celebrate the progress of faith, never imposing but always present, ready to assist. For the Christian, this reality offers a profound source of encouragement and hope—a knowledge that the journey of faith, with all its joys and sorrows, is shared with unseen companions whose sole purpose is to guide toward ultimate communion with God.

The integration of angelic presence into the Christian journey also invites a richer appreciation of prayer and spiritual life. Recognizing angels as advocates and ministers encourages believers to engage prayerfully with the heavenly realm, seeking not only divine intervention but also the partnership of the whole communion of creation. This perspective broadens the experience of spiritual companionship beyond the human sphere, inviting a lived awareness of cosmic solidarity.

Moreover, scriptural and traditional teachings on angels remind the Church that spiritual growth occurs within a context of interconnected relationships—between God, angels, and human beings. The angels' presence highlights the continuum of relationships that faith encompasses, extending from the temporal to the eternal. They bear witness to the transforming power of grace that shapes history, communities, and individual hearts.

In synthesizing these insights, it is crucial to balance the transcendent mystery of angels with their immediate pastoral significance. Angels are not merely theological abstractions or mythic figures; they are real participants in God's redemptive work. Their constant companionship is a source of joy, consolation, and courage—particularly in times when the Christian journey feels fraught with difficulty. For those who struggle with doubt, fear, or loneliness, the biblical depictions and theological affirmations of angelic assistance offer a tangible reminder that they are not alone. Faith is a journey at once deeply personal and profoundly communal, traversed with the guidance and protection of divine messengers who walk beside, lighting the way.

The Emmaus road story continues to inspire this conviction. Just as the disciples on that day found hope rekindled through the presence of a guiding companion, so too do believers today find in angels a symbol and reality of God's persistent care. The gentle unfolding of understanding, the shared breaking of bread, the revelation of Christ's love—all these elements speak to the heart of what it means to be accompanied on the Christian journey. Angels embody the tender and sure presence of God in pilgrimage, offering light in darkness, courage in uncertainty, and hope in despair.

Thus, the story of angels as guides and companions is not simply a fascinating biblical motif but a living reality that invites the faithful into deeper trust. It challenges believers to cultivate an awareness of spiritual presence in their daily lives, to embrace the mystery of divine accompaniment, and to find in this companionship the strength to persevere faithfully. Through the veiled ministry of angels, the journey toward glory is marked by a profound and sustaining fellowship—one that echoes the heart of the gospel itself: that we are loved, watched over, and led by God's own messengers on the path to eternal life.

Symbolic Roles in New Testament Theology

Throughout the New Testament, angels emerge not only as literal divine emissaries but also as potent symbolic figures imbued with rich theological meaning. Their presence resonates far beyond simple narratives of heavenly messengers delivering instructions or protection; angels assume a broader, emblematic role that reverberates through the essential themes of Christian doctrine—justice, resurrection, and hope. A contemplation on these symbolic dimensions invites readers to peer into the depths of New Testament theology, where angels serve as conduits of divine glory and cosmic order, heralding an eschatological horizon that beckons a transformed creation. In weaving together scriptural imagery, theological reflection, and poetic meditation, this subchapter seeks to illuminate the profound and multifaceted symbolic weight angels bear within the New Testament canon.

At the heart of New Testament theology lies the tension and promise of eschatology—the unfolding of God's ultimate plan for creation, culminating in divine judgment, renewal, and restoration. Angels are intrinsic to this narrative, functioning as both agents and symbols of the divine economy in the age to come. Their appearances in apocalyptic literature, particularly the Revelation of John, highlight their role as cosmic heralds and executors of divine will. Here, angels move beyond mere emissaries to become living symbols of God's sovereignty over history, embodying the tension between judgment and mercy that defines the eschaton.

Revelation, the climactic book of the New Testament, offers some of the most vivid and symbolically charged angelic portraits. Angels in Revelation function as mediators between heaven and earth, administering divine justice and guiding the faithful through tribulations toward ultimate victory. The seven angels who stand before God's throne (Revelation 8:2) symbolize perfect divine order, entrusted with the seven trumpets that sound the impending judgments upon the earth. Their trumpet blasts act as a metaphor for God's sovereign declaration, awakening humanity to the reality of God's justice and the urgency of repentance.

Beyond their function as heralds of judgment, these angels encapsulate a deeper theological truth: they are embodiments of God's righteous authority and agents of cosmic purification. When the angels pour out the bowls of God's wrath (Revelation 16), they visually represent the outworking of divine justice upon the forces of evil. This imagery transcends the literal, inviting meditation on the moral order God upholds and the ultimate defeat of evil powers. In this light, angels symbolize the enforcement of divine justice, reminding believers that history is not random or futile but undergirded by a purposeful divine governance.

Yet, the angels of Revelation do not only inspire dread; they also illuminate a profound hope. The closing chapters of Revelation depict angels praising God, announcing the New Jerusalem, and inviting the redeemed into the eternal presence of God. These scenes conjure a vision where angels are not agents of fear but messengers of salvation and eternal joy. Their constant worship in heaven shapes them as symbols of unceasing divine praise and the eternal communion between God, angels, and redeemed humanity. These dual roles—judgment and praise— underscore the complex symbolic function of angels as balancing the weight of divine justice with the promise of resurrection and hope.

Moving from apocalyptic literature to the Pauline epistles, angelic symbolism also deeply permeates the doctrines of resurrection and hope that Paul emphasizes. In 1 Thessalonians 4:16, Paul describes the Lord's return accompanied by "the voice of the archangel," signaling the resurrection of the dead in Christ. Here, the archangel's voice symbolizes the cosmic authority and divine confirmation of the eschatological promise. The call to rise from the grave transcends mere physical resurrection; it signifies the restoration of creation and the renewal of life itself. The presence of the archangel, then, serves as a powerful metaphor for God's ultimate victory over death and the ushering in of eternal life.

Further enriching this symbolic portrayal, Pauline theology attributes to angels a role in encouraging the faithful throughout their earthly sojourn. Angels become emblematic of divine reassurance amidst trials, reflecting the hope anchored not in transient worldly realities but in the unshakable promises of God. For instance, in 2 Corinthians 12:7, Paul's reference to a "thorn in the flesh" guarded against by a messenger of Satan could also be read against the backdrop of angelic presence as symbols of spiritual warfare and protection. This tension between forces of good and evil, enacted through celestial beings, metaphorically represents the believer's ongoing spiritual journey, where angelic figures become signposts of divine care and cosmic conflict.

The Gospel narratives themselves teem with angelic symbolism that frames Jesus Christ's mission within the cosmic battle of light and darkness, sin and salvation. The angelic annunciations surrounding Christ's birth are fraught with theological significance that extends beyond mere historical notice. When the angel Gabriel proclaims to Mary the coming Incarnation (Luke 1:26–38), the angel's words symbolize the intersection of heaven and earth, where divine promise breaks into human history. Gabriel's role as the herald of the Messiah points to a divine intervention that transcends time, heralding the dawn of salvation and hope. This announcement becomes a symbol of God's faithfulness to His covenant and the inauguration of a new creation through Christ.

Likewise, angels ministering to Jesus after His temptation in the wilderness (Matthew 4:11; Luke 22:43) symbolize divine affirmation and sustenance amid spiritual struggle. These moments use angelic presence poetically to express God's intimate involvement in the human experience of trial and suffering. Angels become metaphors for divine comfort and strength, confirming that God's glory is not distant but present in weakness and vulnerability.

Beyond individual scenes, angels function collectively in the Gospels as metaphoric manifestations of the heavenly realm breaking into earthly existence. The angelic choir that announces Jesus's birth to the shepherds (Luke 2:13–14) conveys more than joyful news; it symbolizes cosmic rejoicing, the harmonization of creation in the presence of God's glory. The angels sing of "peace on earth," a phrase heavy with eschatological longing that reflects the ultimate healing and reconciliation God intends for the cosmos. Through their song, angels become symbols of the divine peace and hope that Christ's coming initiates.

The Book of Hebrews further enriches this symbolic tapestry by positing angels as ministering spirits sent to serve those who will inherit salvation (Hebrews 1:14). Here, angels stand as representative figures of God's ongoing care for believers, embodying the paternal compassion and protection offered by the divine. The depiction contrasts angels with Christ, who is exalted above them, yet assigns to them a sacred role in God's redemptive plan. This nuanced hierarchy underlines angels not as autonomous beings but as symbols of God's meticulously ordered grace and providence.

The Johannine literature likewise contributes unique symbolic dimensions to angelic portrayals. In the Gospel of John and Revelation, angels often accompany divine revelation and eschatological fulfillment, symbolizing the intersection between divine mystery and human hope. For example, in Revelation 5, angels surround the throne of the Lamb, worshipping and declaring Him worthy to open the scroll. This scene symbolically places angels as celestial witnesses to Christ's redemptive authority, reinforcing the theological motif of Christ as the Lamb who conquers and redeems. Angels, therefore, become icons of obedient submission to God's salvific plan and mirrors of celestial harmony in worship.

Examining these varied scriptural glimpses, we find the symbolic power of angels in the New Testament continually returning to three interrelated themes: justice, resurrection, and hope. These themes form an inseparable triad at the core of Christian theology and find vivid expression through angelic imagery.

Justice, as mediated by angels, reveals the seriousness of divine holiness and the inevitability of judgment for sin. Angels act as instruments of this justice, their activities in Revelation and elsewhere evoking awe and fear, but always within the context of God's faithful commitment to righteousness. They symbolize the divine order that will ultimately prevail and the moral accountability binding all creation.

Resurrection, meanwhile, is symbolically fronted by angels through their role in announcing and facilitating the resurrection event. Their voices awaken the dead, their proclamations conquer the finality of death. Angels thereby become poetic embodiments of life triumphant—a celestial chorus heralding restoration and renewal as central to the Christian hope.

Hope, woven through and beyond justice and resurrection, imbues the angelic symbolism with warmth and assurance. Despite scenes of judgment, angels' presence points toward the possibility of a new creation where peace reigns and God's glory is fully manifested. The angelic praise and worship portrayed in Revelation and the Gospel narratives symbolize the eternal hope God grants to those who trust in Him. Angels become the visual and poetic language through which this hope is communicated, inviting human hearts into deeper longing and trust in divine promises.

From a scholarly perspective, New Testament angelology must be understood as deeply embedded within a worldview suffused with symbolic meaning and cosmic significance. The angelic imagery is not merely ornamental or peripheral but integral to the theological articulation of God's interaction with the world. Contemporary theological studies emphasize how New Testament writers adapted and reshaped existing Jewish angelic traditions—such as those found in intertestamental literature like 1 Enoch—to articulate distinctively Christian truths about Christ's redemptive work and God's unfolding kingdom.

Scholars such as George Ladd and N.T. Wright highlight how angelic figures in the New Testament bridge the gap between the present age and the age to come, serving as tangible signs of God's immediate action in history and future consummation. N.T. Wright, in particular, notes the importance of angelic appearances in reinforcing the truths of resurrection and judgment, underscoring angels as narratological devices that express theological realities too profound to be captured by human language alone.

Moreover, the poetic language employed in the New Testament often leverages angelic imagery to evoke a sense of awe and mystery—a sacred symbolism that invites readers into spiritual reflection. The angels' shining appearance, their trumpet voices, and their worshipful adoration create a multi-sensory vision of the heavenly realm, stirring the imagination and affections toward God's transcendent glory. This symbolic power is not static but dynamic, continually inviting believers to gaze beyond the material and temporal into the eternal.

Theologically, angels function as living metaphors that communicate the presence and purposes of God. They embody qualities such as holiness, purity, authority, and servanthood, while simultaneously acting as signs of God's intervention in human affairs. The interplay between their visible activities and their symbolic resonance allows the New Testament to convey layered meanings—addressing the immediate needs and fears of early Christians while gesturing toward ultimate realities beyond human comprehension.

In closing this examination, one might meditate on the profound eloquence with which angels carry the weight of divine truths within New Testament theology. As harbingers of glory, angels encapsulate the paradox of Christian hope—both a call to sober justice and an encouragement toward joyful resurrection. Their symbolic presence challenges the reader to consider the vastness of God's redemptive plan and the certainty that light will triumph over darkness.

Encountering angels in the New Testament becomes an invitation to participate in the cosmic drama of salvation. They beckon us to be attentive to divine voice amid life's tumult, to embrace the promise of resurrection with unwavering hope, and to live in the light of God's uncompromising justice tempered with mercy. In their shining forms and celestial voices, angels open a window into the divine mystery, encouraging deeper spiritual engagement and worship. Their presence is at once a reminder and a revelation: that behind the veil of history stands the unchanging God whose glory will one day fill the earth.

Thus, angels remain eternal symbols of God's faithful activity—embodied messages whose significance transcends time, culture, and circumstance. In their manifold roles within the New Testament, they reveal not only the heavenly realm's proximity but also the inexhaustible depth of God's plan for humanity. To gaze upon the symbolism of angels is to glimpse a world infused with holiness, justice, and hope, beckoning the believer toward a future where God's glory is fully unveiled, and heaven and earth are reconciled in unspeakable joy.

Celestial Choirs and Hierarchies: Ordering the Divine Host

The Nine Orders of Angels

The celestial hierarchy of angels has long fascinated theologians, scholars, and believers alike, for it offers a glimpse into the ordered, majestic realm of the divine host. Rooted in scripture but largely shaped by early Christian tradition, particularly the influential writings of Pseudo-Dionysius the Areopagite, this system classifies angels into nine distinct orders—known as the "Nine Choirs of Angels"—arranged into three triads according to their roles, proximity to God, and spiritual functions. Each order pulsates with unique characteristics, symbolic meanings, and scriptural echoes that illuminate their purpose in the cosmic order.

Though the Bible itself does not explicitly delineate these nine orders, scattered references—augmented by the interpretive efforts of theologians—have converged into a coherent vision that continues to enrich Christian thought and devotion. In this subchapter, we undertake an expansive survey of these celestial ranks, animating their sacred nature with poetic imagery and theological depth. Through this journey, the shimmering wings, radiant light, and ineffable power of the angelic realm come vividly to life.*****The First Triad: Angels Closest to God's Throne**At the summit of angelic hierarchy stand the highest orders—those closest to the throne of God Himself. Their essence is consumed by an intense, uninterrupted vision of divine glory, and they serve as intermediaries revealing God's will to the lower ranks and ultimately to humanity. This triad consists of the Seraphim, Cherubim, and Thrones.**Seraphim: The Burning Ones**The Seraphim occupy the loftiest place in the celestial hierarchy. Their name, derived from the Hebrew *saraph*, meaning "to burn" or "fiery ones," evokes awe-inspiring images of radiant, consuming fire. The prophet Isaiah's vision in chapter 6 offers the Bible's most distinctive depiction of these beings: "Above him stood the seraphim; each had six wings: with two he covered his face, and with two he covered his feet, and with two he flew" (Isaiah 6:2). This poetic detail encapsulates reverent humility—the covering of face from the full glory of God—paired with dynamic readiness to serve.

Seraphim blaze with pure, divine love, embodying holy passion and zeal. Their flaming presence signifies the purifying fire that sanctifies creation and illuminates divine truth. Like tongues of flame, they incessantly praise God, chanting the ceaseless hymn: "Holy, holy, holy is the Lord of hosts; the whole earth is full of his glory!" (Isaiah 6:3). This triune acclamation underscores the Trinitarian nature of God, echoed perpetually by the Seraphim's worship.

Functionally, Seraphim act as guardians of God's throne and agents of purification. They ignite the prophet Isaiah's lips with coal from the altar (Isaiah 6:6–7), symbolizing the sanctifying power that cleanses sin and prepares human hearts to receive divine revelation. Their transcendent brilliance surrounds the throne room with love's burning intensity, a celestial fire that kindles the relationship between the divine and creation.

In iconography and mystical tradition, Seraphim are often portrayed as flaming wheels or radiant beings engulfed in scintillating light. Their six wings convey powerful symbolism: two to veil their grandeur from God's ineffable splendor, two to cover their feet representing modesty and reverence, and two for swift flight, denoting zeal and readiness to serve. Through the Seraphim, the divine essence—pure love and light in constant motion—is both concealed and revealed.**Cherubim: Keepers of Divine Wisdom**Next in proximity to the divine throne stand the Cherubim, whose name derives from the Hebrew *kerub* and carries connotations of fullness of knowledge and insightful wisdom. Far more than the simplistic Renaissance depiction of winged infants, biblical Cherubim are complex, multi-faced creatures embodying intellect, guardianship, and profundity.

Ezekiel's vision (Ezekiel 1:4–28; 10:1–22) offers the richest biblical source for understanding Cherubim. They emerge as composite beings with four faces—of a man, a lion, an ox, and an eagle—each symbolizing aspects of creation and divine attributes: mankind, strength, servitude, and swiftness. These faces represent the ordered harmony of creation under God's sovereignty. Their form is described as gleaming like burnished bronze, aflame with fiery brightness, and each carries four wings that beat in perfect synchronization.

Functionally, Cherubim serve as guardians of sacred spaces and mysteries. In Genesis (3:24), God places cherubim with a flaming sword to guard the entrance of Eden, keeping humankind from reentering the paradise lost through disobedience. Upon the ark of the covenant, golden cherubim with wings outstretched overshadow God's mercy seat (Exodus 25:18–22), symbolizing their role as divine intermediaries and protectors of sacred covenants.

Cherubim are intimately connected with divine wisdom and knowledge. Their guarded presence around God's throne shapes the transmission of revelation, linking the infinite mysteries of the divine with the finite world. Theologically, they embody the perfect harmony of justice and mercy, intellect and holiness, always attentive to the cosmic order.

Symbolically, their multiple faces evoke a panoramic vision of creation's entirety, reminding believers of God's omnipresence and omniscience. Their dazzling appearance reflects the splendor and complexity of divine wisdom—beyond human comprehension, yet accessible through faith.**Thrones: The Embodiment of Divine Justice**The third angelic order in this highest triad is the Thrones, often described as "wheels" or "galgalim" in Hebrew, symbolizing stability and steadfastness. Thrones are the personification of God's justice, fairness, and authority, the solid foundation upon which divine order rests.

Scriptural allusions to the Thrones emerge primarily from Ezekiel's vision, where wheels within wheels—intersecting in a mysterious pattern—appear alongside the living creatures (Ezekiel 1:15–21). These wheels are said to be full of eyes, symbolizing watchfulness and omniscience, and they move in unison with the cherubic beings, signifying harmony between justice, divine will, and wisdom.

The Thrones' key attribute is impartial judgment, administering the justice of God that sustains righteousness throughout creation. They provide a stable, unshakable base upon which the heavenly government functions, ensuring that divine law permeates the cosmos with order and fairness.

The imagery of rotating wheels suggests both movement and solidity simultaneously—dynamic justice in action that is immovable in principle. Thrones stand as celestial thrones themselves, bearing the presence of God's majesty and dispensing divine authority. Their wings and eyes reflect both responsiveness to divine command and complete awareness of cosmic events.

In holy tradition, Thrones represent humility, carrying the weight of divine justice without interference, silently upholding God's righteous decrees. They remind humanity that true justice springs not from human strength but rests on the righteous and unchanging nature of God's throne.*****The Second Triad: Heavenly Governors and Administrators**Moving outward from the direct presence of God's throne, the second triad of angels serves as heavenly administrators and governors. These orders—the Dominions, Virtues, and Powers—govern the cosmos, directing the created order and acting as agents through which God's purposes are enacted across the universe.**Dominions: Regulators of Angelic Duty**Dominions, also known as "Lordships," hold the reins of authority within the angelic host. Their primary role is to regulate the duties of lower angels, ensuring that divine commands are faithfully executed and that the celestial order remains harmonious.

Scriptural references to Dominions are subtle yet significant. Colossians 1:16 mentions "dominations" in a list of heavenly beings, and their name itself reflects their role as "dominant" or ruling angels overseeing delegated authority. Dominions are portrayed as rulers who do not exercise lordly pride, but rather humble stewardship, acting as wise administrators bridging the nearer angels and God's explicit will.

Theologically, Dominions symbolize divine governance and the orderly arrangement of cosmic affairs. They oversee principalities and powers, coordinating assignments across realms and facilitating communication of divine will. Their presence embodies the disciplined structure that maintains balance in the universe.

Iconographically, Dominions are often depicted holding scepters or orbs, ancient symbols of authority and governance. Their graceful demeanor reflects poised command, blending power with servitude. Their wings shimmer with an aura of regal authority, yet beneath the splendor lies devoted obedience.

Dominions inspire believers to acknowledge order and submission under God's sovereignty, encouraging the faithful to emulate humble leadership founded in divine purpose, not selfish ambition.**Virtues: Bearers of Divine Grace and Wonder**The Virtues compose the middle order of this triad and represent the channel through which God's grace and blessings flow. Their name suggests strength, valor, and miraculous power, emphasizing the efficacious working of God in creation and redemption.

Scriptural references to this order are less explicit but are inferred from passages mentioning "virtues" and "powers" in the context of spiritual blessings (1 Peter 3:22; Ephesians 6:12). The Virtues are seen as agents of miracles, bestowing strength and fostering the growth of faith in humanity.

Traditionally, Virtues are believed to control the elements, seasons, and natural phenomena, orchestrating the rhythms of creation at God's bidding. They inspire awe and wonder through the manifestation of God's sustaining power in the world.

Visually, Virtues are frequently portrayed with radiant light or holding instruments associated with miracles and blessings—such as a radiant chalice or a harp. Their countenance glows with serene energy, portraying the balance of gentle grace with mighty force.

Spiritually, the Virtues encourage believers to recognize the hand of God at work in the ordinary and extraordinary, cultivating trust in divine providence and power amid adversity.**Powers: Warriors Against Darkness**The third order of this triad, Powers, serve as celestial warriors, engaged in the cosmic battle against evil and spiritual disorder. Their name underscores authority exercised through strength to maintain divine law and protect creation.

Biblical references to Powers appear notably in Ephesians 6:12, where Paul delineates the "principalities, powers, the rulers of the darkness of this world," suggesting Powers stand as defenders against demonic forces, sustaining spiritual order.

Powers have the sacred charge to guard the cosmos from malevolent beings, restraining chaos and subjugating rebellious spiritual entities. They wield divine authority to guard the moral fabric of creation and assist humanity in spiritual warfare.

Iconographically, Powers are depicted in armor, brandishing swords or shields—symbols of their martial role. Their countenance is stern yet righteous, embodying both fierce justice and protective vigilance.

By contemplating Powers, believers gain assurance that spiritual battles are waged justly and victoriously by divine agents, fostering courage in personal struggles for righteousness.*****The Third Triad: Angels Close to Humanity**The outermost triad—the Principalities, Archangels, and

Angels—focuses on direct interaction with the created world, especially humanity. These orders serve as messengers, guides, and guardians, operating in conjunction with divine governance to bring God's presence tangibly into human history.**Principalities: Guardians of Nations and Leaders**The Principalities exercise authority over groups of people, nations, and institutions. Their task is to oversee earthly governments, cultural movements, and social structures, guiding leaders and communities toward God's providential plan.

Scripture references to Principalities are found in Paul's writings (Romans 8:38; Ephesians 1:21), where they appear among celestial powers, revealing a spiritual hierarchy influencing worldly affairs. Principalities inspire rulers and societal institutions to act justly and pursue peace.

Imagery of Principalities often involves regal emblems—crowns, scepters, or orbs—but their authority is exercised purely as divine stewards. They encourage governance rooted in justice and care for the vulnerable.

Theologically, Principalities underscore the reality of spiritual influence on earthly realms, reminding believers that political and social life falls under God's sovereign gaze, watched over by faithful celestial advocates.**Archangels: Divine Messengers and Agents of Revelation**Archangels represent the highest rank among angels who directly interact with humanity, functioning as mighty messengers and leaders of the heavenly host in delivering God's revelations and interventions.

The New Testament explicitly names Michael and Gabriel as archangels. Michael, "who is like God," is portrayed as a warrior chief defending God's people (Daniel 10:13, Revelation 12:7), while Gabriel serves as the herald announcing pivotal divine messages, including the birth of John the Baptist and Jesus Christ (Luke 1:19, 26–38).The title "archangel" connotes chief or principal angel, reflecting their authoritative role in leading other angels and orchestrating significant moments of salvation history. They act as both protectors and heralds of God's plan, bridging the divine and mortal realms with transformative messages.

Symbolically, Archangels are depicted with military or heraldic attire—Michael often with sword and armor, Gabriel with a trumpet or lily symbolizing proclamation and purity. Their presence evokes both strength and divine revelation.

Through the archangels, believers perceive the intersection of heavenly power and historical destiny—the unfolding of God's redemptive work communicated and defended by these mighty celestial beings.**Angels: The Guardians and Ministers to Humankind**The final and most familiar order comprises the angels closest to humanity. Unlike the other orders' more transcendent roles, these angels serve as personal guardians, messengers, and ministers directly engaged with individual lives and earthly affairs.

The Bible provides numerous accounts of these angelic appearances—guiding, protecting, and delivering God's words (Genesis 18, Psalm 91:11–12, Matthew 18:10). They possess wings imbued with a gentle radiance, reflecting their role as comforting, vigilant protectors.

These angels cloak themselves in light abounding with love and mercy. Their wings symbolize swiftness and the ability to cross the boundaries between heaven and earth. They move quietly but powerfully, unseen escorts on the journey of faith.

Theologically, these angels illustrate God's intimate care for each person. Their presence affirms that no life is outside divine concern, that God employs celestial helpers to attend our path, shield from harm, and nurture spiritual growth.

Throughout history, millions have felt inspired by the notion of guardian angels, fostering trust in God's providence and the unseen yet palpable companionship of divine care.*****Synthesis and Reflection on the Angelic Hierarchy**The Nine Orders of Angels illustrate a divine cosmos alive with purpose, beauty, and order. From the blazing Seraphim at God's throne to the humble guardian angels alongside humanity, this intricate hierarchy conveys profound theological insights: the transcendence and immanence of God, the ordered nature of creation, and the boundless love extending from the Creator to every creature.

Each order shines with its distinctive light—whether the ardent fire of the Seraphim, the all-seeing gaze of the Thrones, or the protective embrace of guardian angels. Their wings, eyes, faces, and roles offer symbolic language that transcends human categories, inviting the faithful into a vision of reality where the spiritual and material blend.

Historically, the teachings of Pseudo-Dionysius, in his work *The Celestial Hierarchy*, provided a structured and poetic framework that shaped not only theological reflection but also devotional imagery and liturgical worship throughout Christian history. His vision blends biblical fragments into a coherent symphony of celestial beings, revealing a cosmos governed by order, love, and divine majesty.

Today, this hierarchy continues to inspire wonder, reverence, and hope. It reminds believers that behind the visible world lies an unseen host, all working mysteriously yet faithfully toward the fulfillment of God's plan. Whether contemplating the burning Seraphim's perpetual praise or feeling the quiet vigilance of one's personal guardian angel, the Nine Orders invite humanity to participate in the eternal dance of worship, service, and divine love.

In recognizing the celestial choir's ordered beauty, believers encounter a profound truth: that all creation is interconnected under God's sovereign reign, uplifted by angels who illuminate justice, embody love, and guard the way toward eternity. This celestial hierarchy, forged from scripture and tradition, remains a beacon guiding the soul's ascent toward divine communion—a sacred ladder of light extended from earth to heaven.

Seraphim: Flames of Devotion

In the vast and majestic realm of celestial beings, the Seraphim stand apart, distinguished not only by their proximity to the divine presence but also by the burning intensity of their worship and being. Among the hierarchy of angels described in Scripture, the Seraphim are unique, imbued with a brilliance and fervor that bespeak a direct and intimate communion with God's holiness. To contemplate the Seraphim is to glimpse the very essence of divine love manifested as flame—unceasing, purifying, and overwhelming. This subchapter seeks to explore these exalted creatures through careful examination of biblical testimony, rich theological reflection, and evocative imagery that invites readers to enter into the awe-inspiring reality of their celestial ministry.

The term "Seraphim" itself is derived from the Hebrew root *saraph*, meaning "to burn" or "to set on fire," an etymology that immediately calls to mind imagery of divine fire and passionate zeal. They are often translated simply as "burning ones," referencing their blazing nature, but this phrase cannot capture fully the layers of meaning embedded in their description. To understand the Seraphim is to appreciate them as both literal and symbolic figures of divine holiness—flames that neither consume nor destroy but rather illuminate and sanctify.

Our primary scriptural source for the Seraphim comes from the prophet Isaiah's transformative vision recorded in Isaiah 6:1-7. In this passage, Isaiah recounts a moment of overwhelming divine revelation: "In the year that King Uzziah died, I saw the Lord sitting upon a throne, high and lifted up; and the train of his robe filled the temple. Above him stood the seraphim. Each had six wings: with two he covered his face, and with two he covered his feet, and with two he flew." Here the Seraphim are portrayed not only as attendants but as guardians of the divine throne, their presence integral to the sanctity and majesty radiating from God's manifested glory.

The imagery Isaiah employs is rich with symbolic meaning. The six wings of each Seraph are not merely an ornamental detail but speak to layered spiritual significance. Two wings cover the face, an act suggestive of reverence and recognition of God's ineffable holiness—too brilliant to be gazed upon directly. This concealment is an exquisite gesture denoting humility before the divine majesty. Two wings cover the feet, a gesture often interpreted as modesty or perhaps protecting the very foundation or holiness on which God's throne stands, indicating respect even for the lowliest parts in the divine presence. The remaining two wings are used for flying, symbolizing their readiness to act at God's bidding, moving swiftly to carry out their divine functions.

Their positioning "above" the Lord highlights their exalted status: they are not mere servants at a distance but beings who dwell in immediate proximity to God's throne. This proximity signifies more than hierarchy—it speaks to an intimate relationship with the Divine essence itself. The Seraphim's continuous presence at the throne embodies their role as perpetual worshippers, guardians of sanctity, and agents of divine purification.

Isaiah's vision provides a glimpse of the Seraphim in a moment of liturgical grandeur. The Seraphim call to one another, "Holy, holy, holy is the LORD of hosts; the whole earth is full of his glory!" Their triple proclamation of God's holiness echoes the trisagion, a worshipful chant of unending reverence that penetrates the very fabric of creation. The repetition of "holy" thrice in a row intensifies the emphasis on God's complete and perfect sanctity, an attribute that sets Him utterly apart from all created beings and phenomena.

It is significant that the Seraphim's praise is not a private or isolated utterance but a loud, communal proclamation that fills the temple and extends implicitly throughout all creation. Their worship makes manifest the very glory of God, bursting forth in sound and presence, inspiring awe in all who perceive it. This unceasing liturgy reveals them as embodiments of perfect devotion, where worship is not a momentary act but an eternal vocation, reflecting the divine nature itself as life-giving praise.

The ritual act described next, wherein one seraph touches Isaiah's lips with a live coal taken from the altar, is one of profound spiritual cleansing and commissioning. The coal, described as having been "taken with tongs from the altar," symbolizes God's purifying fire—a transforming agent that removes unworthiness and guilt (Isaiah 6:6-7). The prophet's lips are "touched" or "purged" to remove his sin and guilt, enabling him to become a worthy messenger for God's word.

Here, the Seraphim's fiery nature is directly associated with purification. Their very being, as embodiments of burning holiness, serves as a consuming fire that sanctifies and readies the prophet for his divine mission. The image evokes a powerful spiritual metaphor: divine love and judgment are not separate forces but unified in the purifying flame of sacred fire, which both burns away impurity and ignites true dedication.

This dual function of the Seraphim—as agents of worship and instruments of purification—articulates their symbolic role in the broader Christian understanding of sanctity and spiritual transformation. They are not merely brilliant creatures of light and sound but living symbols of the process by which God's love refines human hearts. They beckon humanity toward a higher state of holiness, inviting us to recognize that worship itself is a fire that purifies and strengthens the soul.

The Seraphim's relation to fire is multi-dimensional, combining literal imagery with profound spiritual symbolism. Fire in Scripture often denotes the presence of God's glory and power (Exodus 3:2; Acts 2:3), the means of judgment (Hebrews 12:29), and a metaphor for passionate love (Song of Solomon 8:6). In the Seraphim, these elements converge. Their wings blaze with spiritual fire, signaling both their fierce zeal for God and their role in transmitting divine holiness to creation without destroying it.

This burning metaphor reaches beyond physical description into the realm of affective spirituality. The Seraphim stand as the living embodiment of perfect love's energy—unceasing, consuming, and illuminating—calling believers to respond with a kindred fervor. The spiritual passion of the Seraphim is a reminder that worship is not static reverence but an active, fiery engagement with the divine.

Some theologians have argued that the Seraphim represent the highest expression of love and adoration in the heavenly hierarchy precisely because of this symbolic use of fire. They suggest that fire captures the essence of divine love's sanctifying power and consuming presence better than any other natural image. Just as fire refines precious metals, so love purifies the soul; just as fire radiates light, so divine love makes all truth known; and just as fire can warm the cold, so the passion of God's presence revives the weary spirit.

In many classical Christian traditions, the Seraphim have become emblematic of the mystic's encounter with God's holiness—a fiery experience both terrifying and transformative. The prophet Isaiah's encounter parallels the journey of spiritual purification common to mystics, wherein one's own defilement is consumed by holy fire, making possible a closer union with God. This theme resonates throughout Christian theology, inviting believers to see themselves not only as spectators but as participants in this ongoing process of sanctification.

Beyond Isaiah's vision, the literature of Christian tradition has richly expanded upon the Seraphim's characteristics. For instance, in the writings of Pseudo-Dionysius the Areopagite, the Seraphim are described as the "Fiery Ones," the closest celestial beings to God's throne, ablaze with love and light. Dionysius's hierarchy elevates them as those who "surround the throne of God in eternal praise and divine contemplation," illuminating the infinite nature of divine love.

In later Christian art and iconography, the Seraphim are often depicted as six-winged beings with flaming bodies or surrounded by radiant light, reinforcing their identity as living icons of divine holiness. Their multiple wings are not only an indication of their power and swiftness but also emphasize their inability to face God's fullness directly, reflecting a profound humility amid their closeness to the divine.

These artistic and theological portrayals underscore an important paradox: the Seraphim are the most welcomed yet simultaneously the most reverent and restrained of all heavenly beings. They are enveloped in fire's brilliance, yet they veil their faces and feet, balancing intimacy with awe, love with fear, presence with humility.

This balance teaches a vital spiritual lesson: to approach God requires both an ardent love that burns up spiritual lethargy and a profound humility before the overwhelming holiness of the divine. The Seraphim, in this sense, become models of authentic worship—exalting God's holiness while bowing deeply in awareness of their own creatureliness.

Examining the Seraphim's symbolic function exposes their broader theological significance as well. They serve as embodiments of spiritual purification—a flame that consumes sin but does not consume the sinner, a purifying fire that refines rather than destroys. This aligns with biblical themes of God's judgment as redemptive rather than merely punitive.

Furthermore, the presence of Seraphim points to the dynamic nature of divine love, which is never passive but always active, a consuming force that invites and transforms. Their constant proclamation of God's holiness reminds us that holiness is not static or distant but vibrantly alive and continually calling for participation.

The Seraphim's ministry also speaks to the eschatological hope rooted in God's ultimate restoration. Their perpetual worship foreshadows the eternal praise that Christians believe will fill heaven in the fullness of God's presence. In this way, they symbolize the destiny toward which humanity is drawn: the unfolding of a life wholly saturated with divine love, passion, and holiness.

Finally, the Seraphim inspire a contemplative spirituality that aspires not only to worship God with fervor but also to be transformed by that worship. Their fiery devotion challenges believers to examine the depth and authenticity of their own praise—whether it is a flickering candle or a consuming fire. They call forth a response that is whole-hearted and holy, marked by both reverence and zeal.

In summary, the Seraphim are celestial beings whose very essence is defined by fire—fire that sanctifies, illuminates, and glorifies. Their six-winged form guards the ineffable holiness of God's throne, while their voices lift an eternal hymn of praise that fills all creation. Through the prophet Isaiah's vision, we gain insight into their role as agents of purification and communion, inviting all who read these words to enter into the brilliance of divine love itself.

As flames of devotion, the Seraphim command our imagination and our hearts. They are both an awe-inspiring mystery and a sustaining presence, offering profound lessons about the nature of holiness, worship, and the transforming power of God's love. In contemplating these fiery creatures, we catch a glimpse of the celestial chorus forever engaged in the dance of praise, reminding us that the ultimate heart of all worship is the burning love of God revealed through the unending song of the burning ones.

Cherubim: Guardians of Divine Mystery

Within the vast tapestry of angelic beings described in Scripture, the cherubim stand as some of the most enigmatic and awe-inspiring figures. Their depiction oscillates between the awe-inspiring and the inscrutable, presenting a celestial presence that defies simple categorization. Unlike the more familiar angels who serve as messengers or warriors, cherubim embody a complex duality, serving both as vigilant guardians of divine sanctuaries and as conveyors of sacred knowledge. Their profound significance is woven through biblical narrative, prophetic vision, and theological reflection, inviting deeper contemplation of their symbolic and literal roles within the heavenly hierarchy.

The earliest biblical appearances of cherubim hint at their protective function within the divine realm. In Genesis, cherubim first appear at the gates of Eden, stationed to prevent humanity's re-entry into the garden after Adam and Eve's expulsion. "He drove out the man; and at the east of the garden of Eden he placed the cherubim, and a flaming sword that turned every way, to guard the way to the tree of life" (Genesis 3:24). This passage sets the tone for the cherubim's association with sacred boundaries, marking the threshold between the divine and the mortal, the holy and the profane. They stand as living sentinels, embodying not only the power to bar access but also the solemnity of divine judgment and the mystery of lost paradise.

Yet the cherubim's identity extends far beyond the gatekeepers of Eden. They are ubiquitously present in the intricate design of the tabernacle and the temple, symbolizing God's immanence and transcendence. Instructions for the tabernacle in Exodus provide detailed descriptions for cherubic figures fashioned upon the mercy seat of the Ark of the Covenant. "You shall make two cherubim of gold; make them of hammered work at the two ends of the mercy seat" (Exodus 25:18). These cherubim face each other, their wings overshadowing the mercy seat, so that God's presence hovers between them. Here, they appear as bearers of divine presence, a reminder that God's glory is both protected and manifested within the most sacred locus of worship.

Scriptural accounts emphasize the remarkable and often bewildering physical forms attributed to the cherubim. In particular, the visions of the prophet Ezekiel reveal a creature whose appearance challenges human imagination and invites profound theological reflection. Ezekiel's vision, recorded in the opening chapters of his prophetic book, offers the most intricate and vivid depiction of cherubim in the Old Testament. These beings are described with multiple faces: that of a man, a lion, an ox, and an eagle (Ezekiel 1:10). Each face symbolizes different dimensions of creation—the human intellect, the wild's regal power, the strength of domesticated beasts, and the soaring freedom of birds—suggesting the cherubim's comprehensive connection to all aspects of creation.

Alongside these faces, the cherubim possess four wings: two raised to cover their bodies and two stretched outward for swift movement (Ezekiel 1:6). Their feet are described as straight, like calves' hooves, shining with gleaming brightness. Their bodies and backs are covered with eyes, symbolizing omnipresent vigilance. This profusion of eyes epitomizes the idea of all-seeing guardianship, transcending human limitations and reflecting divine omniscience. The motion of the cherubim is synchronized with that of the divine spirit, moving effortlessly and swiftly in perfect unity without turning, as if guided by an intent and purpose beyond mortal comprehension.

The mystery and complexity of this vision have prompted extensive commentary throughout the centuries. The multiplicity of faces and watchers represents integration and harmony in divine creation, while their ability to move in any direction without turning underscores a readiness to act upon God's will instantaneously. Their many eyes convey the depth of divine insight, a constant and unblinking watchfulness over the sacred. This imagery challenges the reader to move beyond anthropomorphic conceptions of spiritual beings and embrace the transcendent reality of divine servants who operate within the realm of mystery and divine wisdom.

In the prophetic vision, cherubim also function as the bearers of God's throne or chariot, known as the "Merkabah." This vehicle for divine travel typifies God's sovereignty and majestic presence in the cosmos. As custodians of this sacred throne, cherubim occupy an unparalleled position within the celestial hierarchy, linking the divine transcendence to earthly experience. They serve as intermediaries through whom the holy's ineffable majesty becomes manifest in prophetic encounters and liturgical worship.

The protective role of cherubim can be seen as parallel to the safeguarding of sacred spaces and places of divine encounter in Scripture. They symbolize the boundary between God's inaccessibility and the invitation to communion that God extends to humanity. In temple worship, this delicate balance manifests in the cherubim's portrayal on the Ark of the Covenant's mercy seat, emphasizing that while God's holiness may be beyond reach, it is not withdrawn but present among His people. The wings arching protectively over the mercy seat visually articulate the paradox of divine accessibility and the sanctity that must not be violated.

Theological reflection regards cherubim's protective function not merely as physical guardianship but as manifestations of divine holiness—an expression of a sacred order established by God to maintain cosmic and spiritual harmony. They function as a barrier against impurity, disorder, and chaos, emblematic of a deeper spiritual principle: that divine holiness demands reverence and observance of boundaries as a prerequisite for relationship with God. Their presence recalls the sanctity of divine mysteries and the necessity of maintaining an attitude of humility and awe before the sacred.

But to understand cherubim solely as guardians would be to overlook their profound association with divine wisdom. Throughout biblical tradition, cherubim are closely linked to the revelation of esoteric knowledge and divine secrets, serving as channels through which God's mysterious purposes are disclosed. They epitomize the confluence of majesty and intellect, power and insight.

In passages beyond Ezekiel's vision, cherubim often appear as attendants to God's throne, bearing a symbol of illumination and understanding. Their many eyes are emblematic of vision not only in the literal sense but also of spiritual perception. In this way, cherubim personify an intellectual vigilance—watching over creation, absorbing divine mysteries, and transmitting sacred truth. Their complex forms, amalgamating various creatures and qualities, symbolize the integration of diverse wisdom traditions and the totality of knowledge under divinely ordained order.

This dual nature—as both guardians and sages—is reflected powerfully in the intersection of theology and artistic representation. Ancient Near Eastern iconography frequently depicts cherubim as composite creatures, combining human and animal elements into forms that convey both majesty and enigma. These forms articulate a language of symbols that convey truths transcending simple description. Egyptian, Assyrian, and Babylonian art, for example, show winged creatures with multiple faces or bodies suggesting omnipotence and protection, echoing but never quite overlapping with biblical cherubim imagery. The biblical text absorbs, transforms, and sanctifies these artistic conventions, adapting them to communicate its unique revelation of the divine.

In later Jewish and Christian art, cherubim continue to be represented as winged beings of striking complexity and beauty. They sometimes appear as youthful angels with multiple wings or faces, flanking thrones and altars. Medieval illuminated manuscripts abound with cherubic figures whose tender yet powerful features articulate the paradox of innocence endowed with overwhelming authority. Renaissance and Baroque painters, such as Raphael and Bernini, often depicted cherubim or putti as literal cherubic infants, softening their fearful biblical descriptions but maintaining their symbolic presence as divine attendants.

Yet behind this softened popular imagery remains the original biblical awe and mystery—a reminder that cherubim symbolize realities beyond human comprehension. Their rich symbolism invites believers and scholars alike to explore deeper mysteries of faith: the intimate relationship between God's holiness and knowledge, the nature of divine presence, and the spiritual realities that undergird the created order.

The enduring fascination with cherubim invites readers to enter a world where artistic imagination and theological insight merge. Their intricate and majestic forms challenge a simplistic understanding of angelic beings, urging contemplation of a divine order characterized by beauty, complexity, and sacred guardship. They hold a place not simply in divine service, but within the cosmic mystery of God's governance of creation and revelation to humanity.

Throughout biblical history, cherubim safeguard the places where heaven and earth meet—the garden, the tabernacle, the temple, and the throne itself—reminding us of the thin veil between the human and the divine. They invite us to recognize the sacred boundaries that protect holiness, while also pointing toward the wisdom and knowledge that flow from God's presence.

By contemplating the cherubim's multifaceted nature—their symbols of watchfulness, power, wisdom, and devotion—we gain richer insight into the spiritual dynamics of the divine-host hierarchy and the profound manner through which God reveals himself to the world. In this way, cherubim stand as eternal guardians not only of divine spaces but of divine mysteries, inviting awe, reverence, and deeper study within the unfolding narrative of Scripture and faith.

Hierarchy and Human Understanding

The celestial hierarchy, as revealed through biblical texts and theological reflection, serves not merely as a catalog of angelic ranks but as a profound structure through which human beings can begin to apprehend the divine order underlying all creation. In contemplating the ordered nature of the heavenly host, believers are invited to step beyond the realm of the merely visible and tangible, entering into a spiritual framework where mystery and revelation are in constant dialogue. This subchapter explores how the knowledge of angelic hierarchy enriches human understanding of spiritual realities, informing faith, worship, and the very posture with which humanity approaches the ineffable majesty of God.

At the heart of the biblical worldview is the conviction that God reigns supreme over all, sovereign and majestic beyond human comprehension. Within this divine sovereignty, angelic beings function not as independent agents but as servants and messengers who reflect divine will and purpose with precision and glory. Their ranks, as classified variously in scripture and tradition—seraphim, cherubim, thrones, dominions, virtues, powers, principalities, archangels, and angels—serve to delineate a cosmos ordered by divine wisdom. To perceive this hierarchy is to gain a glimpse into the harmony that pervades creation, where every being has its place, function, and relationship to the ultimate source of all being.

Humans, created in the image of God, are uniquely positioned to reflect on these realities. Although finite and limited, the human spirit is endowed with a hunger to understand and connect with the transcendent. The angelic hierarchy, while inevitably mysterious, becomes a bridge between the seen and unseen worlds, inviting humans to contemplate the vastness of divine governance and the interplay of spiritual forces beyond mortal sight. It opens a window onto the cosmic theatre in which good and evil engage, where angels execute divine justice, deliver mercy, and participate in the unfolding drama of salvation history.

The theological significance of angelic ranks extends beyond curiosity or academic classification. It shapes worship and devotion by orienting believers' hearts towards the grandeur of God's presence and the perfection of His governance. Liturgical traditions, both ancient and modern, often invoke the choirs of angels as participants in heavenly praise, reminding worshippers that their earthly praise is but a reflection of an eternal chorus that surrounds the throne. The vision of Isaiah, where seraphim cry "Holy, holy, holy," echoes down through the ages, encouraging humanity's participation in the sanctification of God's name and the acknowledgment of His absolute holiness.

Yet, the presentation of this celestial order is not intended to reduce the mystery of God to a mere intellectual framework. Rather, it acknowledges the limits of human language and comprehension when approaching holy things. The hierarchy is an invitation to reverence, to a sense of awe before realities that surpass human grasp. There is a delicate balance between revealing the structure of the heavenly host and preserving the ineffability of divine majesty. To attempt to capture the fullness of angelic being or the totality of their functions is to encounter the boundaries of human understanding and to be drawn forward into deeper wonder and worship.

This tension between mystery and revelation is essential to the spiritual formation of believers. As the Apostle Paul writes, "Now we see through a glass, darkly; but then face to face" (1 Corinthians 13:12). The knowledge of angelic hierarchies and their spiritual functions is a partial revelation, a foreshadowing of a more complete understanding that will come only in the fullness of God's kingdom. In this life, humans are called to live in humble recognition of what has been made known, embracing both the clarity God allows and the profound obscurity that preserves divine transcendence.

Through this posture, the study of angelic orders moves beyond theological abstraction into the realm of lived faith. It calls believers to participate in the readiness and vigilance exemplified by angels, who stand continually before God, executing His will and ministering to humanity. The call to holiness, to spiritual attentiveness, resonates in the knowledge that the heavenly host is arrayed in perfect obedience and praise. For humans, this becomes a model and a motivation for aligning their own lives under God's sovereign rule.

Moreover, the interplay among various angelic ranks modeled in scripture speaks to a divine economy marked by cooperation and order. Thrones and dominions govern authority; virtues and powers uphold divine justice; principalities and archangels oversee nations and peoples; angels engage intimately with individuals. This multilayered coordination reflects a divine plan that marries unity with diversity, authority with service, majesty with compassion. The human community, reflecting this pattern, gains insight into a vision of social and spiritual harmony that transcends worldly chaos and division.

In reflecting upon the celestial hierarchy, we are reminded that every angelic function is ultimately rooted in God's desire for relationship with humanity. Angels are messengers of hope, carriers of divine guidance, and warriors against the forces of darkness. Their presence imbues biblical narratives with a sense of movement and dynamism, illustrating that the unseen realms are actively engaged in the history and destiny of the human race. Recognizing this involvement invites believers into a greater awareness of the spiritual realities that underpin daily life, encouraging a faith that sees beyond material circumstances into the eternal purposes of God.

The beauty and poetry found in the descriptions of angels—from their flaming seraphic wings to the cherubic guardianship of sacred spaces— serve to elevate the human imagination and inspire worship that transcends mere ritual. These images function as symbolic expressions of divine qualities such as purity, power, wisdom, and mercy. They draw the believer into a participatory experience of the sacred realm, prompting contemplation of the ineffable glory that angels themselves reflect and magnify.

Yet, while the hierarchy captivates the imagination and enriches theological insight, it neither diminishes nor replaces the centrality of God. Angels, despite their grandeur and might, remain created beings who praise, serve, and submit to the One True God. This truth guards against any misplaced exaltation or spiritual confusion. The hierarchy points always beyond itself to the source and goal of all things: the triune God whose wisdom ordains the order of heaven and earth.

In this light, the study of celestial choirs and hierarchies becomes a deeply spiritual endeavor. It encourages an attitude of reverent inquiry—

one that neither shrinks from divine mystery nor arrogantly claims full understanding. It invites believers to recognize that the angelic world, in all its splendor and order, is a witness to the ongoing unfolding of God's redemptive work and the eventual fulfillment of all things under Christ's sovereign reign.

Ultimately, the human engagement with angelic hierarchy is an invitation to spiritual transformation. As one contemplates the ranks and roles of angels, the heart is drawn toward greater holiness, attentive worship, and a renewed commitment to live under the governance of God's perfect will. The hierarchy teaches lessons in obedience, service, and community that find their highest expression in the life of faith.

In the quietude of reflection upon the celestial host, one may glimpse the horizon of eternity where the worship of angels and saints converges in an unending symphony of praise. It is a call to hope, to endurance, and to joy in the knowledge that human lives are part of a grander narrative— one authored by God and enacted in the harmony of heaven's ordered choirs. The study of angelic hierarchy thus becomes a doorway into a richer understanding of the spiritual cosmos, a cosmos in which humanity's destiny is forever entwined with the divine order.

Through this lens, the images and teachings of the heavenly host are not distant or detached but intimately connected to the spiritual pilgrimage of believers. The hierarchy reveals the vastness of God's plan and the tender care with which this plan is administered. It affirms that every act of worship, every pursuit of holiness, participates in a reality far greater than ourselves—a reality animated and sustained by the ceaseless service and praise of angels around the throne.

In the final contemplation, the human grasp of angelic hierarchy becomes a mirror reflecting our deepest yearning: to know God, to honor God, and to dwell within the divine harmony that angels so faithfully embody. It is an invitation to lift the eyes from the temporary shadows of earthly life toward the radiant light of heavenly order and eternal love. In this way, the study of celestial choirs and their ranks enriches both the mind and the soul, drawing believers closer to the heart of God and preparing them to share in the eternal chorus of praise that fills the courts of heaven.

Guardians and Guides: Angels' Roles in Human Destiny

Protective Beings on Life's Journey

Throughout the vast and intricate tapestry of scripture, angels emerge not merely as distant celestial beings but as intimate guardians closely intertwined with human existence. These protective beings serve as life's steadfast companions, guiding, sheltering, and comforting individuals and communities alike through their varied trials and journeys. This subchapter delves deeply into the biblical portrayals and traditional understandings of angels as protectors, exploring their profound role as divine guardians who stand watch over humanity.

From the earliest pages of the Old Testament to the inspiring revelations of the New, angels are depicted repeatedly in roles that emphasize protection and guidance. Their watchful presence serves as a powerful reminder of God's ongoing care and concern for His creation. In these scriptural accounts, angels do not act merely as messengers delivering divine decrees but as compassionate sentinels actively involved in the everyday realities of people's lives—offering safety amid danger, solace in times of distress, and wisdom when direction is needed.

One of the most foundational biblical portrayals of angelic guardianship appears in the story of Jacob's dream at Bethel (Genesis 28:10-22). As Jacob flees from his family home, uncertain and vulnerable, he dreams of a ladder stretching from earth to heaven, with angels ascending and descending upon it. This vision not only symbolizes a connection between God and humanity but also reflects the constant presence of angelic beings who traverse the space between the divine and mortal realms. Though the text centers on Jacob's spiritual encounter, the angels represented here implicitly embody the protective watchfulness that God extends to His chosen servants. Their ascent and descent suggest vigilance—a continual guarding over Jacob as he journeys through uncertainty toward his destined future.

In another powerful account, the narrative of the protecting angel who delivers Lot from Sodom's destruction (Genesis 19) highlights the angels' role in not only forewarning but also physically escorting and guarding the righteous in times of imminent peril. When divine judgment descends upon the cities of the plain, angels intervene by warning Lot and his family and guiding them safely away from destruction. Their intervention underscores a fundamental aspect of angelic guardianship: a merciful presence that offers both warning and a path to salvation. The tender urgency with which these angels lead Lot's family away, instructing them to flee without looking back, conveys an intimacy and care emblematic of the protective angel's role throughout scripture.

Angelic protection becomes even more vivid in the story of the Israelites' exodus from Egypt. As the people of Israel embark on their harrowing journey through the wilderness, an "angel of God" moves before them as a pillar of cloud by day and a pillar of fire by night, providing guidance and protection against hostile forces (Exodus 14:19-20). This divine escort fashions a direct link between angelic agency and the safeguarding of God's people. The angel's presence acts as a tangible symbol of divine protection—both literal and spiritual—guiding Israel through the wilderness toward the promised land. Moreover, traditions among Jewish and Christian interpreters often identify this angel as a manifestation of God's own presence, underscoring the unique and revered status accorded to these celestial guardians.

The Psalms, rich in poetic reverence and spiritual reflection, offer profound insights into the protective qualities of angels. Psalm 91:11-12 declares: "For he will command his angels concerning you to guard you in all your ways; on their hands they will bear you up, lest you strike your foot against a stone." This passage affirms that angelic guardianship is not an abstract concept but an active, personal reality. It reassures believers that angels are commissioned by God to protect every individual through life's hazards and uncertainties. The vivid imagery of angels lifting and bearing up those under their care reflects the compassionate tenderness attributed to these heavenly protectors, depicting them as both strong defenders and caring attendants.

The compassionate and tender qualities of angelic guardians are further illustrated in the story of the prophet Elijah's flight into the desert (1 Kings 19:1-18). After a moment of despair and solitude, Elijah is ministered to by an angel who provides him with food and water, encouraging him to endure. This angelic care is not only physical but spiritual, renewing Elijah's strength and courage in the face of overwhelming challenges. The narrative presents the angel not merely as a distant warrior figure but as a source of mercy, hope, and intimate encouragement—a portrayal that offers profound comfort to readers facing their own trials.

Similarly, New Testament passages reinforce the motif of angels as divine protectors and helpers. When the apostle Paul was shipwrecked on the island of Malta (Acts 27-28), an angel appeared to him during the storm, reassuring him that no lives would be lost. This reassurance was fulfilled as Paul and all aboard survived the ordeal, emphasizing the angel's role as a guardian of life amid mortal danger. Here, the angel's presence manifests both promise and power; it bridges the divine will and the vulnerability of human life, echoing themes found throughout earlier scripture.

Perhaps one of the most evocative images of angelic guardianship appears in the story of Jesus' infancy. The angel Gabriel's annunciation to Mary (Luke 1:26-38) is often the focus for its message of divine revelation, but it also carries an undertone of protection. By announcing the miraculous birth and providing guidance, Gabriel acts as a divine guardian, preparing Mary for the immense spiritual responsibility ahead. Furthermore, in Matthew 2:13-15, an angel warns Joseph in a dream to flee to Egypt with Mary and Jesus, protecting the Holy Family from Herod's murderous intent. Here, the angel's intervention directly preserves the life of the Messiah, underscoring the critical role these celestial beings play in safeguarding the unfolding divine plan.

Beyond these scriptural examples, the tradition and devotional life of Christian communities have revered angels as close protectors who do not abandon humanity amid life's struggles. The concept of a "guardian angel" who watches over each person individually gained significant prominence in the early centuries of the Church and continues to inspire believers today. This personal angelic companion provides reassurance that no one embarks on life's journey alone—that behind every step are protective beings who attend, shield, and intercede.

The tender and compassionate nature of these guardian angels is often emphasized in spiritual writings and devotional prayers. They are portrayed as ministers of mercy, bringing comfort in times of sorrow, courage in moments of fear, and light in the midst of darkness. Their presence is likened to a gentle hand resting upon the shoulder or a quiet whisper of reassurance when one feels most vulnerable. Such imagery invites believers to cultivate a personal awareness of angelic guardianship—not as mere myth, but as a living spiritual reality that accompanies, supports, and uplifts throughout life's journey.

Communities as well as individuals are also depicted as receiving angelic protection in scripture. In the book of Daniel, the angel Michael appears as the great protector of Israel (Daniel 12:1). His role as a celestial warrior defending God's people reflects a corporate guardianship that embraces the collective well-being of the covenant community. Michael's appearing during times of national crisis provides a model for understanding angelic protection not only at a personal level but also within the wider context of community and nation. The tradition of

Michael as the "chief prince" and defender continues to inspire believers who recognize the need for spiritual protection against forces that threaten communal faith and identity.

The compassionate role of angels as protectors extends beyond physical salvation to include spiritual guidance and encouragement. Angels intervene not only to preserve life but also to keep the soul on the right path. This is evident in instances where angels minister to prophets and apostles, reinforcing faith and inspiring perseverance. For example, at the resurrection, an angel's presence confirms the victory over death and assures the disciples of the hope that lies ahead (Matthew 28:2-7). Such moments highlight the angelic role as bearers of hope and mercy, reassuring humanity of God's unceasing care and the ultimate triumph of divine justice.

Spiritually, the belief in angels as protective beings offers believers comfort amid life's uncertainties and trials. The presence of guardian angels embodies a divine promise that no circumstance is so perilous that God's care does not reach there first. This assurance revitalizes faith, fostering a profound sense of security rooted not solely in human strength but in heavenly assistance. In this way, angelic guardianship serves as a tangible expression of God's mercy and love, manifesting through invisible but powerful agents who accompany each believer's pilgrimage.

Modern reflections on angelic guardianship continue to resonate deeply within contemporary faith life. Many Christians find solace in the conviction that they are watched over and accompanied by protective angels, particularly in moments of crisis, illness, or grief. The invocation of guardian angels in prayer reflects a vibrant and enduring tradition acknowledging the intimate relationship between human vulnerability and divine care mediated by these celestial beings.

Moreover, the language of angelic protection can be a profound source of inspiration for ethical living. Knowing that compassionate, protective beings accompany every step can heighten a consciousness of moral responsibility and the sacredness of life's journey. This awareness encourages believers to move forward with courage and hope, embracing life's challenges with the confidence born of divine companionship.

In pastoral care, the image of angels as protective companions offers meaningful comfort to those struggling with fear and loneliness. Teaching about angelic guardianship can help individuals see themselves as part of a larger spiritual narrative—one where divine love is continuously at work through watchful protectors. Such understanding fosters resilience and nurtures a hopeful outlook, reinforcing the belief that God's mercy is alive and active in the lives of His people through the ministry of angels.

It is also noteworthy that in various Christian traditions, feast days and devotions specifically honor angels in their protective role. The Feast of the Guardian Angels invites the faithful to reflect on the gift of angelic presence, encouraging a deeper awareness and appreciation. These liturgical celebrations serve as powerful reminders of the ongoing relevance and importance of angelic guardianship within the life of the Church.

In sum, the biblical and traditional portrayals of angels as protective beings form an essential strand within the broader understanding of their roles in human destiny. Far from distant or impersonal entities, angels reveal themselves as tender, compassionate sentinels—divine companions who offer safety, guidance, and hope amid the challenges of life. Their watchful presence affirms God's faithful care, providing comfort and strength to those navigating the uncertainties of the earthly pilgrimage.

As believers encounter life's joys and sorrows, successes and failures, the knowledge that protective angels walk alongside them imparts a profound sense of assurance. These celestial messengers embody the tangible expression of God's love, serving as beacons of hope and mercy. Their compassionate guardianship continues to inspire faith, fortify courage, and deepen trust in the divine plan. Thus, the role of angels as protective beings remains a vital and living reality, one that invites continual reflection and a heartfelt embrace within the journey of Christian life.

Angelic Mediation: Bridging Heaven and Earth

The notion of mediation is foundational to understanding the relationship between the divine and humanity in biblical theology. Throughout Scripture, God's transcendence and holiness establish a vast gulf between the Creator and created beings. Yet, in His sovereign grace, God bridges this divide by appointing messengers—angels—who serve as intermediaries, facilitating communication, guidance, and intervention in human history. This subchapter delves into the theological theme of angelic mediation as a vital mechanism in the divine-human encounter, exploring how angels embody God's presence, execute His will, and enable humanity to participate more intimately in the unfolding of His redemptive plan.

The prophetic voices of the Old Testament frequently reveal angels as divine envoys, sent forth to deliver God's word or direction to individuals or nations. For example, in the book of Genesis, angels engage with key patriarchs at decisive junctures. The angelic visitation to Abraham in Genesis 18 highlights this mediation vividly. Three visitors, understood to be angelic beings with divine authority, come to announce the forthcoming birth of Isaac and to intercede for the fate of Sodom and Gomorrah. Their arrival signals not merely the transmission of a message but also an embodiment of God's active presence among His servants. The angels carry out specific tasks—communication, intercession, judgment—thus functioning as mediators who knit together divine intention and human response. This narrative sets a pattern that reverberates throughout biblical history, where angels serve as conduits of God's will.

Theologically, angelic mediation occupies a unique place that differs both from the direct communication between God and prophets and from the sacramental or priestly mediation present in Israel's cultic system. Angels do not merely announce or relay messages; they often engage with human agents in ways that affect destiny on both personal and communal levels. Their interventions are not passive transmissions but active participations in God's plan. This dynamic quality is evident in the story of Jacob's dream at Bethel (Genesis 28), where he envisions a ladder stretching from earth to heaven with angels ascending and descending. This image captures the continuous movement and interaction between heaven and earth, with angels serving as the vehicles of this celestial traffic. The vision encapsulates the essential role of angels as bridges or mediators, linking the human experience with divine reality.

Moreover, angels function as divine agents who facilitate worship and covenantal fidelity. In Exodus 23:20-23, God promises to send an angel ahead of the Israelites to guard them, instruct them in ways, and bring them to the place He has prepared. The angel is depicted as a mediator who guides the people while maintaining God's ultimate authority. This passage emphasizes both protection and instruction—aspects intrinsic to mediation. The angel is not an autonomous figure but one who acts on God's behalf, ensuring that the human community remains aligned with divine purposes. This concept is echoed in Psalm 103:20-21, which extols the angels as ministers who execute God's commands to serve those who will inherit salvation, affirming their role in facilitating human communion with God's saving work.

In the prophetic tradition, angelic mediation becomes particularly significant when human destinies are shaped. The book of Daniel offers profound examples where angels communicate visions, explain mysteries, and enact divine decrees that determine the course of empires and individuals. Gabriel's interpretation to Daniel (Daniel 8:16-19; 9:21-23) not only discloses future events but also illuminates God's sovereign governance through angelic agency. Gabriel's role as a mediator combines revelation with instruction, enabling Daniel's understanding of God's plan and preparing him to respond appropriately. This mediation is deeply spiritual and existential, underscoring how angels operate within the divine economy to weave human history into the tapestry of God's unfolding will.

In the New Testament, the theme of angelic mediation continues with pronounced theological depth. Angels announce the incarnation of Christ, marking the epochal intersection of heaven and earth in the person of Jesus. The angel Gabriel's annunciation to Mary (Luke 1:26-38) embodies the mediation of divine grace and revelation. Gabriel conveys God's message yet also evokes Mary's response of faithful assent. This interaction reveals angels as messengers who not only speak but also facilitate human cooperation with divine initiative. The angelic message inaugurates a pivotal moment when the divine plan of salvation enters redemptive history in a tangible human form.

Following the incarnation, angels appear repeatedly to minister to Jesus, highlighting their ongoing role as divine intermediaries supporting the fulfillment of God's purpose. During Jesus' temptation in the wilderness (Matthew 4:11), angels come to minister to Him after His period of trial. This ministry signifies angelic participation in cosmic spiritual warfare and affirms their function as caretakers in the realm of human destiny. Angels also appear at critical points such as the resurrection, announcing the defeat of death and the promise of new life (Matthew 28:2-7). Here angels mediate the truth of the resurrection, bearing witness to the divine victory and inviting human belief. Their role is both revelatory and invitational, bridging the transcendent reality of resurrection with the lived experience of the early Christian community.

A significant theological dimension of angelic mediation is their function as protectors or guardians, a theme intimately linked with divine providence. The concept of guardian angels emerges from biblical texts suggesting that specific angels are assigned to watch over individuals or groups. In Psalm 91:11-12, the psalmist declares that God commands His angels to guard the faithful in all their ways, lifting them up lest they stumble. This custodial role implies a close and ongoing interaction between angels and humans, making angels not only messengers but also protectors within the divine economy. The Epistle to the Hebrews (Hebrews 1:14) describes angels as "ministering spirits sent to serve those who will inherit salvation," emphasizing their ministerial function as facilitators of human participation in salvation history. Here, angelic mediation contributes not only to communication but also to preservation and guidance, ensuring that the divine plan proceeds unimpeded.

Angelic mediation also intersects with the concept of spiritual warfare, wherein angels operate as agents executing God's judgments or delivering protections in the cosmic struggle between good and evil. This battleground dimension is evident in Daniel's vision of a heavenly being fighting the "prince of Persia" (Daniel 10) and the apocalyptic depiction of Michael the archangel contending with Satan in Revelation 12. These narratives portray angels as divine warriors whose mediation involves both delivering God's decrees and defending the faithful. Their intervention is thus both communicative and martial, shaping human destiny by restraining evil and advancing God's kingdom.

From a symbolic standpoint, angels illustrate the invisible realities of divine governance. They personify the divine will extended into the created order, embodying the principle that God is continually involved in creation's affairs. Their mediation signifies that human history is not random but orchestrated by a sovereign hand. Angels function as living signs of God's intimate presence, threading human stories into the broader narrative of salvation. Their appearance at key moments—birth, covenant, trial, death, resurrection—reveals their role in affirming the sacred significance of human experience.

Furthermore, angelic mediation deepens the understanding of Christian prayer and worship as interactive experiences between heaven and earth. Angels are often portrayed in Scripture as participating in worship alongside the faithful (Isaiah 6; Revelation 4-5), indicating their role in connecting the human and divine realms liturgically. This participation suggests that angels facilitate the ascent of prayer and praise to God while simultaneously bringing divine blessings down to people. In this sense, angels embody the dynamic interchange between humanity and the divine, making them essential players in spiritual communion.

The experiential dimension of angelic mediation should not be overlooked. Throughout Christian history, believers have sensed the presence of angels as protectors, guides, and comforters. This anticipates the biblical testimony by acknowledging the ongoing, living reality of angelic ministry. The theological reflection on this reality invites believers to recognize angels as God's instruments for directing, safeguarding, and sustaining the journey of faith. Such recognition nurtures a spirituality that is attuned to the divine interplay manifest in angelic mediation.

In summary, the biblical portrayal of angels as mediators captures a multifaceted role whereby these celestial beings convey God's will, safeguard the faithful, declare divine truth, and participate in the cosmic drama of salvation. Their mediation is integral to human destiny, functioning as connective threads that weave individual lives and communal histories into the grand design of God's plan. This theme enriches the biblical understanding of angels not merely as passive messengers but as active, dynamic agents who embody and advance the divine purpose across the temporal and spiritual realms.

By exploring scriptural illustrations—from the patriarchal narratives, prophetic revelations, and covenantal promises of the Old Testament to the incarnation, ministry, and resurrection experiences portrayed in the New Testament—we gain insight into how angels facilitate a profound communion between heaven and earth. They stand as living testimonies of God's nearness and concern, bridging the infinite Godhead with finite humanity and ensuring that human stories do not unfold in isolation but within the embrace of divine providence.

Ultimately, angelic mediation reveals the profound mystery of God's care and engagement in human affairs, inviting believers to trust in a reality where the unseen agents of heaven actively support and guide God's people. The presence of angels assures that the divine narrative continually intersects with human destiny, that God's plans are faithfully communicated and realized, and that the pathway between heaven and earth remains open through these celestial messengers, forever bridging the realms of the divine and the human.

Accounts of Guidance and Intervention

Throughout the sweeping tapestry of biblical history, angels emerge not merely as distant celestial beings but as intimate agents of divine will—guides and guardians whose appearances punctuate moments of human need, revelation, and transformation. These accounts, scattered across Scripture and echoed in the annals of sacred tradition, reveal a panorama of angelic involvement that transcends the spectacular and enters the realm of the profoundly personal. From the hush of a solitary vision to the thunderous interruption of war, angels have stood as divine heralds, protectors, and instructors—vehicles of God's guidance and intervention in the lives of individuals and communities alike. By immersing ourselves in these narratives, we encounter not only the extraordinary manifestations of heavenly aid but also the subtle, quiet ministrations that shape destinies in ways often unseen yet profoundly felt.

Consider the ancient patriarch Abraham, whose life is marked repeatedly by angelic encounters that signal pivotal turning points in God's unfolding covenant with humanity. In Genesis 18, the appearance of three visitors at the oaks of Mamre carries the weight of imminent divine judgment yet also showcases the angelic role as bearers of both warning and promise. These messengers, who take on the guise of men, bring news of Sarah's forthcoming child, illuminating the miraculous possibility resting beyond the horizon of human expectation. Here, the angelic intervention is not mere spectacle but a tender, hopeful guidance—a celestial encouragement toward faithfulness amidst impossible odds.

This pattern of angelic accompaniment continues with Abraham's servant, whose assignment to find a wife for Isaac is sanctified by an unseen but divinely orchestrated guidance. In Genesis 24, the servant prays for a sign, and an angelic hand seems to steer events, for Rebekah's arrival and kindness align precisely with the servant's request. Though angels do not always appear as radiant figures, their influence is discernible in the providential unfoldings that shape human lives, subtly compelling decision and drawing hearts toward God's intended design.

Turning from the patriarchal narratives to more dramatic interventions, the story of Lot's deliverance from the destruction of Sodom and Gomorrah vividly portrays angelic urgency and protection in the face of impending doom. In Genesis 19, two angels physically escort Lot and his family from danger, their presence a barrier against evil's overwhelming tide. The urgency with which they act, their insistence on haste, and their command that none look back—themes laden with theological symbolism—exemplify the proactive and protective nature of angelic ministry. These moments resonate deeply: angels are not passive watchers but active participants, intervening decisively to preserve the righteous and enact divine justice.

Beyond patriarchal contexts, angels resurface in the life of Hagar, the Egyptian maidservant, whose plight in the wilderness underscores the angel's role as comforter and revealer of hope in desolation. In Genesis 16, the angel's encounter with Hagar transforms her despair into a witness of God's care, announcing the birth of Ishmael and affirming her future. This intimate, compassionate encounter illuminates the angelic ministry as one that reaches into the depths of personal anguish, offering reassurance and a renewed sense of purpose. Here, the dramatic and the tender converge, showcasing angels as both heralds of destiny and bearers of solace.

The narrative arcs of the Exodus further exemplify angelic involvement in the communal destiny of Israel. As the Israelites flee slavery under Moses' leadership, angelic guidance assumes a protective, directing role. In Exodus 23:20-23, God promises to send an angel before the people to guard their way, ensuring their safe passage to the Promised Land. This protective angel functions as a battleground force, a guidepost, and a mediator between God's intention and human obedience. During this national deliverance, angels serve as tangible symbols of divine presence, rallying Israel's hope and reassuring them of God's unwavering commitment.

One of the most striking accounts of angelic intervention in the Old Testament is found in Psalm 91, often linked to the imagery of God's protecting angel. The psalmist declares that angels "will bear you up in their hands, lest you strike your foot against a stone" (Psalm 91:12, ESV), evoking a powerful image of guardian angels who shield the faithful from harm. This poetic articulation not only amplifies the idea of angelic protection but also spiritually anchors the believer in the confidence that God's messengers are ever vigilant, working unseen to uphold human lives against danger.

This motif of angelic guardianship extends into the story of Daniel, whose personal faithfulness places him directly under supernatural threat and protection. In the lion's den narrative (Daniel 6), while the biblical text does not explicitly state angels' involvement, later Jewish and Christian traditions affirm that an angel shut the mouths of the lions, preserving Daniel's life. Furthermore, in Daniel's visionary experiences, angels serve as interpreters and guides, elucidating difficult prophecies and revealing God's plan. The angelic presence here is both protective and revelatory—a dual role that characterizes much of their ministry throughout Scripture.

The New Testament continues and enriches these themes of angelic guidance and intervention, often focusing on individuals at moments of theological and personal significance. The story of Mary's annunciation by the archangel Gabriel (Luke 1:26-38) stands as a cornerstone of angelic communication—an awe-inspiring, transformative encounter that announces God's redemptive plans for humanity. Gabriel's greeting to Mary is laden with divine favor and purpose, as well as an invitation to faith and obedience despite uncertainty and risk. The angel's role is both revelatory and empowering, preparing Mary to become the mother of the Savior while enveloping the scene in profound mystery and grace.

Similarly, the angelic ministry extends to Joseph, Mary's betrothed, through a series of dream visitations. These nocturnal angelic instructions guide Joseph to embrace his role in God's plan, providing both reassurance and warning. Whether directing him to accept Mary as his wife or commanding flight to Egypt to protect the child Jesus from Herod's murderous intent (Matthew 1:20-21; 2:13-15), the angels' interventions are precise and life-altering. Here, angels assist not only in individual destiny but also in the wider salvific narrative, their intervention critical for the survival and fulfillment of God's covenant promises.

The shepherds' experience outside Bethlehem (Luke 2:8-14) offers another vivid example of angelic intervention. In the stillness of the night, angels proclaim the birth of Christ with a message of joy and peace. This announcement is both public and intimate, bringing heavenly light into a humble, earthly setting. The multitude of angels appearing in this scene underscores the glory and magnitude of God's act of salvation, while their song of praise invites all who hear to witness the unfolding of divine love. The shepherds' encounter is transformative, illustrating how angelic messages can spark faith and adoration across ordinary lives.

On the road to Emmaus (Luke 24:13-35), angels appear as witnesses to the resurrected Christ, comforting the disciples and confirming the reality of the resurrection—though not directly interacting, their presence undergirds the disciples' experiences with the risen Lord, reinforcing angelic participation in God's redemptive work. Likewise, during Jesus' own 40 days of temptation, angels minister to him after his victory over Satan (Matthew 4:11), an act revealing the dual role of angels as both protectors and supporters in spiritual warfare and mission.

Beyond the sacred texts, early Christian history provides numerous testimonies of angelic intervention that parallel biblical accounts. The Church Fathers recount stories of angels guiding believers through trials, persecutions, and moments of profound decision. One such example is the account of Saint Monica, who wrote of angels encouraging her and her son Augustine in their conversion journeys. These historical testimonies, woven into the Christian tradition, attest to a continuity of angelic guidance that transcends the biblical era and enters the lived experience of faith communities.

Medieval hagiographies are replete with narratives of saints aided by angels—whether offering direction in solitude, protection from harm during pilgrimages, or spiritual consolation in moments of doubt. The legend of Saint Michael's intervention during the Battle of Montgisard in 1177, where the archangel is said to have appeared to aid the Crusader forces, exemplifies angels acting directly in the fate of nations. Though often recorded with dramatic flourish, such stories resonate with the biblical pattern of angelic involvement in human affairs, reinforcing the conviction that divine messengers continue to engage actively in the defense and guidance of the faithful.

Yet, not all angelic interventions are heralded by light and triumph. The Bible also reveals angelic encounters marked by solemnity and warning. The prophet Isaiah's vision of seraphim (Isaiah 6), fiery beings who call God's holiness to the attention of the prophet, underscores the role of angels as agents of divine purification and renewal. Similarly, the angelic proclamations to John in the book of Revelation combine messages of judgment with hope, signifying the cosmic scope of angelic ministry—extending beyond individual lives to the fate of entire creation.

This duality of angelic function—comfort and warning, salvation and judgment—enriches our understanding of their involvement in human destiny. The angels' presence is not always a balm for ease, but rather an invitation to alignment with divine purpose, often involving challenge and transformation. Their interventions call forth human response, faith, and obedience, underscoring the dynamic interaction between heaven and earth.

Intriguingly, some biblical accounts suggest that angelic guidance continues subtly in ways that transcend dramatic appearances. The notion of guardian angels, referenced in passages such as Matthew 18:10, where Jesus speaks of angels who "always behold the face of my Father," points toward a perpetual, intimate guardianship entrusted to these celestial beings. This idea invites the believer to embrace a consciousness open to angelic assistance, recognizing that guidance and protection may come not only through extraordinary visions but also through quiet promptings and circumstances orchestrated beyond human perception.

Thus, the stories collected in this subchapter serve as both a testament and an invitation—testaments to the multifaceted ways angels have intervened in human history and invitations to consider their ongoing presence in our own lives. Whether through thunderous rescue, whispered counsel, or faithful companionship, angels bridge the divine and human, enabling the fulfillment of God's purposes amid the complexities of human freedom and frailty.

In this blend of narrative and testimony, readers are encouraged to dwell in these mysteries with awe and openness. The biblical and historical accounts of guidance and intervention reveal that angels' involvement in human destiny is neither anecdotal nor merely symbolic—it is a profound, living reality rooted in God's continuous engagement with the world. To entertain this possibility is to acknowledge a universe alive with meaning and care, where the unseen hand of the divine is steadily at work, guiding, guarding, and inspiring the journey of faith.

As we reflect on these moments of angelic presence, it becomes clear that such encounters, dramatic or subtle, are invitations to trust in a God who does not leave humanity to wander alone. The angels stand as celestial reminders that human destiny is not solely forged by mortal endeavor but is also shaped by the gracious interventions of heavenly messengers, tirelessly interceding to bring God's love, justice, and mercy into the unfolding story of our lives.

Gary E. Risenhoover

Battlefields of Light: Angels in Spiritual Warfare

The Cosmic Conflict Landscape

In the vast expanse of biblical revelation, the unseen realms ripple with conflict—a collision of light and darkness, order and chaos, good and evil. From the earliest pages of Scripture to its apocalyptic crescendo, the Bible unveils a cosmic landscape where spiritual forces engage in battles beyond human sight, yet deeply entwined with human destiny. This grand theater of celestial warfare is not the stuff of myth but a profound reality embedded in divine revelation. It is here, amid roaring thunder and radiant glory, that angels emerge not as mere messengers or benign watchers but as valiant warriors summoned to wield God's justice against encroaching darkness.

To understand the role of angels in spiritual warfare, one must first step onto this cosmic battleground—a realm simultaneously majestic and terrifying, blazing with heavenly fire and shadowed by the brooding presence of rebellion. It is a realm described with vivid and thunderous imagery: glowing swords cleaving through shadows, celestial trumpets sounding summons to righteous war, thunderous hosts arrayed with armor shining like the sun, and swirling ranks moving like a storm through the ether. The biblical cosmology that frames this epic conflict weaves together visions of divine sovereignty, the perils of fallen rebellion, and the indomitable purpose of angels as agents of God's justice.

The book of Revelation provides one of the most sweeping depictions of this cosmic struggle. Early in the narrative, amid flashes of lightning and peals of thunder, a war erupts in heaven—Michael and his angels battle the dragon and his cohorts, casting them down from heaven's heights (Revelation 12:7-9). The imagery is both dramatic and symbolic. Michael, the archangel, is not merely a figurehead but a mighty cosmic warrior, wielding authority directly from God, leading a host that embodies celestial power and divine judgment. The adversary is portrayed as the ancient serpent, the embodiment of evil and deception, now arrayed as a fearsome dragon. This battle is more than mythic storytelling; it encapsulates the perennial conflict between God's order and satanic chaos.

This vision is enriched by connections to the Old Testament, which grounds the cosmic conflict in thundering proclamations and judicial decrees. The prophet Daniel, for example, describes angelic entities contesting not only spiritual but political authority, depicting an unseen battle for dominion over nations (Daniel 10:12-13). Here, angels are not passive observers but active combatants engaged in a heavenly diplomacy that reflects earthly struggles for power and righteousness. These angelic warriors serve as God's emissaries, executing judgment, protection, and warfare in accordance with divine will.

Throughout Scripture, the sword emerges as a potent symbol of divine authority and spiritual power wielded by angels. The flaming sword wielded by the cherubim to guard Eden (Genesis 3:24) signifies both judgment and protection, blocking the ways of transgression with fiery justice. In the New Testament, the "sword of the Spirit" described by Paul (Ephesians 6:17) further illustrates the weaponry entrusted to God's servants—a metaphor not only for the Word of God but also for the piercing, decisive force angels embody in spiritual confrontation. It is a weapon that is both destructive against evil and redemptive in the hands of divine agents.

The sound of trumpets reverberates throughout biblical accounts of spiritual warfare, evoking the call to arms and the heralding of divine action. In the book of Joshua, the blasts of trumpets bring down the formidable walls of Jericho, signifying God's triumph through supernatural means (Joshua 6). In Revelation, seven angels with seven trumpets announce successive judgments upon the earth, each blast unleashing further chaos upon the forces of darkness. The trumpet's voice is a celestial alarm, a call to awakening and a signal that the divine combat is underway, stirring both heaven and earth into cosmic engagement.

The heavens themselves provide the arena for these battles. Biblical cosmology depicts the cosmos not as a sterile void but as a layered reality filled with living powers and realms of influence. The "third heaven" where God's throne resides (2 Corinthians 12:2) contrasts with lower "heavens" or spiritual realms inhabited by different angelic and demonic beings. Within these celestial spheres, battles are waged, and strategic victories won, each echoing far into the physical world. In this worldview, earthly events reflect and are shaped by spiritual realities, revealing a divine battlefield where angels and demons contest the fate of nations and souls.

Angels in this cosmic conflict carry out multifaceted roles that extend beyond mere warfare to the orchestration of divine purposes. They serve as messengers with urgent news of judgment or salvation. They act as protectors of God's people, shielding and guiding (Psalm 91:11-12). They also function as executors of divine justice, responding to rebellion with swift and often terrifying power. This dual nature—as messengers and as warriors—imbues angels with a critical ambassadorship between the heavenly and earthly realms, making them indispensable to the unfolding drama of spiritual warfare.

The theological import of these images challenges readers to recognize the seriousness and reality of spiritual warfare. The biblical writers do not merely describe angels as mythic characters or distant specters. Rather, they portray a dynamic conflict that is ongoing and vital to the divine plan. Angels are depicted as the tangible, visible agents of a spiritual struggle that shapes human history. Their presence is not incidental but essential to the establishment of justice and the eventual defeat of evil. In this view, the cosmic conflict stands as an eternal struggle, with angels as the frontline warriors who implement God's will, protect the faithful, and confront the dark powers that seek to thwart divine order.

The psalmists frequently invoke the protective power of God's angels in the face of enemies, reflecting an intimate awareness of this invisible warfare. Psalm 34 declares, "The angel of the LORD encamps around those who fear him, and delivers them" (Psalm 34:7). Such verses resonate with thunderous assurance—a spiritual fortress that surrounds the righteous, prepared to repel the assaults of malign forces. This protective role is inseparable from the angelic identity as warriors in the cosmic battle, a reassurance that the forces aligned with God's justice are actively engaged in defending His people.

Exploring angelic combat within biblical poetry and prophetic literature unearths motifs of thunder and fire that intensify the imagery of battle. In Isaiah, God's presence is accompanied by storm-like power—thunder, lightning, and the shaking of the earth—signaling divine judgment and combat readiness (Isaiah 29:6; 30:30). Angels, as God's emissaries, share in this expression of power, their intervention likened to the crackling of firebrands and the crash of thunderstorms, embodying the fierce energy of spiritual warfare. These sensory images draw the reader into the overwhelming intensity of the conflict, transcending the mundane and thrusting them into the realm of heavenly battle.

The apocalyptic literature further layers this cosmic drama with a rich tapestry of symbolism. The "great dragon," the "beast," and the "false prophet" stand opposed to Michael and his angelic legions, representing evil's persisted will to usurp God's authority and corrupt creation (Revelation 13, 19). The climactic battles that conclude this literature depict angelic forces wielding justice with sharp, double-edged swords, voices like rushing waters, and eyes aflame with fiery judgment (Revelation 19:11-16). These grand, almost cinematic portrayals of battle underscore the cosmic scale and spiritual significance of the warfare in which angels are principal combatants.

Underpinning the dramatic imagery is a firm theological framework emphasizing God's sovereign control over the conflict. Angels fight not for independent agendas but as executors of the divine will. Their victories are not merely tactical wins but expressions of God's ultimate purpose—to restore creation, defeat evil, and establish a new heaven and earth (Revelation 21). This sovereignty underscores the hope embedded in the cosmic conflict: despite the ferocity of the battles, the outcome is assured in God's eternal justice and reign.

This theological clarity prevents misreads that might elevate angels to autonomous warrior figures operating apart from God's authority—an important distinction for sound doctrine. Rather, biblical angelic warfare portrays a harmony of divine command and celestial obedience, where angels respond in fulfillment of God's holy purposes. Every sword stroke and trumpet blast calls attention to God's power and righteousness, with angels as faithful instruments of His justice.

The cosmic conflict landscape also invites reflection on the present spiritual realities facing believers. The biblical witness challenges Christians to recognize that the warfare depicted is not confined to distant heavens or end times but intersects with their spiritual experience. Ephesians 6 urges believers to don the "full armor of God" to stand firm against "the powers of this dark world" and "spiritual forces of evil in the heavenly realms" (Ephesians 6:12). Within this exhortation lies an acknowledgment of an ongoing cosmic conflict in which angels participate as protectors and warriors alongside the faithful.

This ongoing nature of the conflict highlights the vital role of angels in the daily spiritual battles confronting the church. Angels act as divine reinforcements, messengers of encouragement, and enforcers of spiritual boundaries against malevolent forces. Their participation affirms that the unseen world is dynamic, contested, and infused with divine intervention, underscoring the reality that believers are not left to fight against darkness alone.

In summary, the biblical cosmology of spiritual warfare reveals a cosmic conflict of majestic proportions, dazzling with thunderous intensity and celestial power. It unfolds in the layered heavens, where angels clad in shimmering armor wield glowing swords and sound the blasts of mighty trumpets. These angelic legions are not abstract symbols but living agents of God's justice, dynamically engaged in the ancient struggle against evil's forces. The biblical imagery of war—fiery swords, storm-tossed skies, thunderous voices—immerses readers in a drama of supernatural struggle whose implications ripple into every dimension of creation and human history.

As the stage is thus set, we come to perceive the battlefield where spiritual realities collide, strategize, and strive. It is here that angels find their highest calling—not only as messengers of God's word but as glorious warriors for light. The cosmic conflict landscape is therefore the grand backdrop against which the ministry and mission of angels are most fully realized, a testament to their pivotal role in the divine plan, eternally engaged in the war for the ages.

With these foundations, the ensuing chapters will explore the distinct functions and appearances of angels in spiritual warfare, how their intervention shapes biblical events, and what their ongoing presence means for Christian faith and practice. This cosmic battleground beckons readers to look beyond the veil, to listen for the thunder of celestial armies, and to behold the splendor and terror of angels in the thick of the divine conflict.

Michael the Archangel: Warrior and Protector

Michael the Archangel stands as a towering figure within the biblical narrative, emblematic not only of celestial strength but of divine justice and protection. His presence within Scripture marks him distinctly as the archetype of the warrior angel—one who engages in the unseen battles that shape the spiritual realms and by extension, human destiny. This subchapter delves deeply into Michael's scriptural roles, his vivid portrayal as a luminous warrior and guardian, and the rich theological symbolism that has evolved around him. Through this focused study, readers will gain insight into Michael's unique position as both a celestial commander and a personal protector, inspiring steadfast faith and courage in the face of spiritual adversity.### Scriptural Foundations of Michael's Warrior Role Michael first emerges from the biblical milieu as more than a mere messenger; he is a principled combatant in divine warfare. The earliest explicit mention of Michael appears in the book of Daniel, a text replete with apocalyptic imagery and celestial conflict. In Daniel 10:13, Michael is described as "one of the chief princes" who comes to aid an angel struggling against the "prince of the kingdom of Persia." This passage situates Michael as a high-ranking celestial being entrusted by God to intervene in spiritual battles that influence earthly empires and histories. Here, Michael is not simply involved in isolated skirmishes but participates in cosmic conflicts that have direct consequences on the unfolding of God's sovereign plan.

Further, Daniel 12:1 elevates Michael's role with clarity: "At that time shall arise Michael, the great prince who has charge of your people. And there shall be a time of trouble, such as never has been since there was a nation till that time. But at that time your people shall be delivered, everyone whose name shall be found written in the book." This passage presents Michael as the divine protector and deliverer of Israel in its most desperate hour — a spiritual champion who stands as a bulwark against destruction. His status as "the great prince" highlights an authoritative leadership among angelic powers, emphasizing the personal dimension of his guardianship over God's chosen people.

The New Testament further reveals Michael's warrior role with even greater drama and cosmic scope. Revelation 12:7 provides one of the most vivid depictions: "Now war arose in heaven, Michael and his angels fighting against the dragon. And the dragon and his angels fought back, but he was defeated, and there was no longer any place for them in heaven." Here, Michael transitions from being a protector of Israel to the champion of heavenly order, standing against Satan, the dragon, who embodies rebellion and evil. This celestial conflict is portrayed as a decisive, world-altering battle—Michael's victory represents the triumph of divine righteousness over the forces of darkness. The imagery of this cosmic war enshrines Michael as the victorious commander whose power echoes through the spiritual and temporal worlds.### Michael as a Fierce, Luminous ProtectorThe scriptural narrative attributes to Michael not only leadership but also an almost palpable intensity and power. He is a figure of blazing holiness, a warrior whose very presence reflects the luminescence of God's glory. Though the Bible contains no physical descriptions loaded with detail about his appearance, the context in which Michael acts strongly implies a radiant, awe-inspiring force. His fighting is not merely physical but spiritual, employing explosive celestial power that shatters demonic strongholds and protective spiritual barriers.

The imagery surrounding Michael often contrasts darkness and light, evil and purity, chaos and order. He is depicted as a being of light battling the darkness of Satan and his minions. This symbolism carries profound theological weight. Michael's luminance represents the presence of divine truth and justice piercing through the shadowy realms of deceit and destruction. His role is not only martial but redemptive: by confronting evil, he restores and upholds the divine order.

In Jewish and Christian traditions, Michael's protector role extends beyond the battlefield to the personal sphere. He is often invoked as a guardian of the faithful, a celestial shield who defends individuals and communities from spiritual harm. This protective aspect complements his warrior identity, emphasizing both offense and defense in his mission. The vivid metaphor of Michael wielding explosive celestial power evokes a sense of uncontainable divine energy directed against evil—an energy entrusted to him to safeguard creation.### Leadership in Spiritual Battles: Command and Strategy Michael's role as a leader among angels reflects a hierarchy and order within the heavenly realm. His title as "archangel" means "chief angel," indicating his position at the apex of angelic hosts. This transcends mere strength; it includes wisdom, strategy, and authority. Scriptural and theological traditions portray Michael not only as a frontline warrior but as a commander who orchestrates the forces of light against demonic rebellion and spiritual chaos.

This leadership role is particularly evident in the Revelation passage, where Michael and his angels conduct a coordinated celestial assault against Satan. He commands a legion of angels, suggesting a military structure in the heavenly host. The cooperation between Michael and his forces exemplifies divine order and unity. It also assures believers that spiritual warfare is not a chaotic contest but a well-organized campaign under God's sovereign control.

Beyond Revelation, some apocryphal and extracanonical texts expand on Michael's leadership, depicting him as a judge and advocate for the faithful. While these elaborations go beyond the canonical Bible, they enrich the theological understanding of Michael's protective and governing functions in tandem with his warrior role. Whether in heavenly battle or divine judgment, Michael represents transcendental justice and strength. ### Theological Reflections on Michael's Symbolic Significance Michael's portrayal as a warrior and protector resonates deeply within Christian theology, serving multiple symbolic functions. First, he embodies the principle that God's justice is active and militant against evil. Far from a passive or indifferent deity, God is depicted as one who actively deploys his agents to combat the spiritual adversary. Michael, therefore, becomes the visible (though spiritual) manifestation of divine resolve, a symbol of God's uncompromising stance against sin and rebellion.

Second, Michael inspires courage and hope among believers. The biblical accounts of his victories reassure the faithful that evil, though persistent and potent, is ultimately subordinate to God's power. Michael's triumphs encourage Christians to remain steadfast in their faith, even when facing persecution or spiritual attacks. His image as a warrior protector invites believers to align themselves not with fear but with trust in divine deliverance.

Third, Michael's dual role as both cosmic commander and personal guardian emphasizes the intimate connection between the universal and the individual in Christian spirituality. He is not only battling Satan on the grand scale but also intervening on behalf of individuals and congregations. This duality reinforces the belief that no believer is isolated from the larger cosmic struggle but is enveloped within the protective arms of God's heavenly host.

Finally, Michael is a figure of eschatological significance. The battles in Daniel and Revelation point toward the ultimate confrontation between good and evil at the end of time. Michael's leadership in these conflicts signals the certainty of God's final victory and the establishment of an eternal kingdom of peace and righteousness. Thus, Michael's warrior role is intertwined with hope for the future and the fulfillment of God's redemptive plan.### Vivid Narrative: Imagining Michael in Action To appreciate fully the force and majesty of Michael the Archangel, one may imagine the scenes described in Scripture with vivid imagery and dramatic intensity.

Picture the heavens as a vast, transcendent battlefield where Michael, radiant like the sun yet clad in armor forged of purity itself, marshals legions of angels. Their swords gleam with an ethereal light, their voices echoing with battle hymns that shake the demonic legions arrayed against them. The dragon—Satan—and his fallen angels retaliate with fiery rage, but Michael moves with swiftness and precision, unleashing bursts of divine energy that ripple like lightning through the darkness.

In another scene, envision Michael standing firm beside Israel during their darkest hour as foretold in Daniel. The archangel's presence is a shield around the faithful, a beacon of hope amid the encroaching chaos. His calm yet relentless defense shapes the tide of battle, ensuring that those whose names are inscribed in the book of life are preserved.

Such imagery, though poetic, captures the essence of Michael's character as both awe-inspiring celestial warrior and tender protector of God's people—a figure whose power is tempered by purpose and whose might serves love.### Michael's Role in Christian Spiritual Practice and Devotion Throughout centuries of Christian history, Michael's image as warrior and protector has influenced liturgy, prayer, and popular devotion. He is invoked in prayers for protection against evil and spiritual assault, particularly during times of trial or persecution. The traditional "Prayer to St. Michael," written in the late 19th century by Pope Leo XIII, echoes many of the themes found in Scripture: a plea for Michael to defend against the devil's snares and to protect the Church and individual souls.

This devotional use of Michael encourages the faithful to participate spiritually in the ongoing battle against evil. It also nurtures a sense of communion between believers and the heavenly realm, where Michael and the angels work ceaselessly on humanity's behalf. His symbolic role thus bridges biblical narrative and lived faith, reinforcing the practical hope and reassurance embedded in Christian spirituality.### Conclusion: Michael as the Embodiment of Divine Strength and Protection Michael the Archangel emerges from biblical texts not merely as an angelic being but as the embodiment of divine strength, justice, and protection. His scriptural appearances make it unmistakably clear that he is the preeminent warrior of God's heavenly host, commanding forces to uphold the divine order and to guard the faithful from evil's attacks. The luminous imagery that surrounds him speaks to his transcendent power and holiness, while his leadership role highlights the organization and sovereignty operative within the spiritual realm.

Theologically, Michael stands as a potent symbol of God's active engagement in spiritual warfare, a source of courage and faith for believers confronting both visible and invisible adversities. His story is not only an ancient tale of cosmic conflict but a living inspiration for contemporary

Christians, reminding all that the battle between light and darkness, good and evil, is waged with certainty of ultimate victory.

In every role Michael plays—as warrior, leader, protector—he summons the faithful to stand firm, to trust in God's power, and to embrace the hope that evil will be overcome and that God's kingdom will endure forever. In this way, Michael the Archangel serves as a luminous sentinel, forever guarding the boundaries between heaven and earth, and forever proclaiming the triumph of light.

Angelic Forces Against Darkness

In the vast expanse of biblical narrative, the unseen struggle between light and darkness emerges as a profound and persistent motif. The spiritual realm, though invisible to the human eye, unfolds as a battleground where celestial beings—angels—stand as steadfast warriors against the encroaching forces of evil. This subchapter delves deeply into the manifold roles of angelic agents in spiritual warfare, specifically focusing on their confrontation with demonic adversaries. Through scriptural exposition and traditional interpretations, it unravels how these angelic forces safeguard divine order and cosmic harmony, symbolizing the eternal conflict between good and evil. The narrative tone will evoke the majestic and often fearsome grandeur of these celestial battles while inviting reflective contemplation on their spiritual and psychological resonance for humanity.

The biblical witness to angelic combat reveals a celestial theatre where angels act not merely as messengers or servants but as powerful agents of God's justice and protection. One of the most vivid and archetypal depictions of angelic conflict appears in the apocalyptic visions of the Book of Revelation, where Michael the archangel leads the heavenly hosts against the dragon and his minions. This cosmic clash describes an inevitable, divinely ordained confrontation: "Michael and his angels fought against the dragon; and the dragon and his angels fought back"

(Revelation 12:7). This passage encapsulates the essence of spiritual warfare—not as a metaphor confined to human experience but as a real, dynamic engagement within the unseen realm.

Michael, whose name means "Who is like God?", occupies a premier place among these divine warriors. Traditionally, he is presented as the protector of Israel and the defender of God's people against spiritual wickedness. His role as commander of the angelic army emphasizes the martial aspect of angelology, where celestial beings are envisioned as disciplined and formidable forces marshaled to execute God's sovereign will. The battle between Michael and the dragon thus symbolizes the grand cosmic principle: the unyielding opposition of divine righteousness against the forces that seek to undermine it.

Beyond Revelation, the Old Testament offers glimpses into angelic participation in divine warfare. The narrative of Joshua's encounter with the "commander of the army of the Lord" (Joshua 5:13-15) provides a striking example. This mysterious figure, often interpreted as a theophany or an angelic commander, indicates the presence of a celestial warrior guiding and empowering Israel's conquest over the land. The presence of this angel in a military context conveys the theological conviction that earthly victories are ultimately grounded in spiritual authority and angelic support.

Similarly, the account of the angelic destruction of the camp of the Assyrians in 2 Kings 19:35 underscores the immanent power of angelic agents to intervene dramatically in human history. In a single night, an angel of the Lord struck down 185,000 Assyrian soldiers, turning a siege into a stunning divine deliverance for Jerusalem. This event vividly demonstrates the angels' role not only as symbolic figures but as active participants in judgment and salvation, wielding power that transcends mortal capabilities.

Traditional Jewish and Christian writings expand on these themes, developing a hierarchy of angelic beings engaged in spiritual warfare. The figure of Gabriel, for instance, appears predominantly as a messenger, but some apocryphal and pseudepigraphal texts attribute martial activities to him as well, suggesting a dual function as guardian and herald. Similarly, the seraphim and cherubim, whose names and imagery evoke fiery and protective qualities, embody angelic zeal in purifying and safeguarding the divine presence against corruption and evil.

The confrontation between angels and demons thus encapsulates a complex theological vision: the maintenance of divine order requires a persistent struggle. Angels function as upholders of cosmic harmony, battling the encroachment of chaos personified by demonic entities. This battle is not merely physical but spiritual, involving authority, truth, and moral governance. The angelic struggle against darkness ensures the ongoing realization of God's kingdom, reflecting the biblical theme that cosmic discord ultimately succumbs to divine sovereignty.

Poetically, the imagery of these battles draws on awe-inspiring metaphors to convey their intensity and significance. The "war in heaven" of Revelation evokes thunderous clashes, flashing swords, and celestial hosts arrayed like stars in the night sky—much like the vivid portrayals of mythic combat found in ancient Near Eastern literature, yet distinctively oriented toward a monotheistic God's triumph. The wings of the angels beat like winds, their voices sound as thunder, and their garments gleam like burnished gold. These images serve to intensify the dramatic tension, blending fear and hope, dread and the assurance of victory.

Within this cosmic struggle, the psychological dimensions reflect humanity's own inner battles. Just as angels contend with malevolent forces in the spiritual realm, individuals wrestle with temptation, doubt, and moral conflict. The angelic battles externalize the invisible war raging within the human soul—the tension between impulses toward goodness and the lure of sin. Angels, therefore, occupy a dual symbolic role: they are both literal participants in spiritual warfare and archetypes of divine assistance in human spiritual struggle.

The spiritual encounter with angelic forces — whether in moments of revelation, protection, or conflict — serves to remind believers of the ever-present reality of good and evil beyond visible reality. Angels inspire courage and faith, standing as celestial sentinels who intervene when human strength falters. Their struggle against darkness reassures the faithful that evil, no matter how threatening, is ultimately subordinate to the light of God's justice.

Scripture also suggests that angels exercise a prudential role in spiritual warfare, responding as instruments of God's will rather than autonomous forces. Their power and victory are contingent upon divine commission. As such, the angelic battles underscore God's sovereignty: while angels fight, God reigns over all circumstances. This theological nuance invites believers to trust in God's omnipotence amid the chaos of spiritual conflict.

In the Gospels, angels appear less frequently in overt battles but maintain their protective functions. They minister to Jesus during his temptation in the wilderness (Matthew 4:11) and announce his resurrection to the women at the tomb (Luke 24:4-7). Here, angelic agency is displayed through deliverance and proclamation rather than martial conquest, highlighting that ultimate victory over darkness is achieved through divine incarnation and sacrifice, reconciling the cosmic conflict through love and redemption.

Moreover, the epistles counsel believers to recognize the spiritual nature of their struggle, exhorting them to "put on the whole armor of God" (Ephesians 6:11) and reminding them of the reality of unseen forces of evil. Angels function in this context as emissaries of protection and encouragement, reinforcing the idea that spiritual warfare is both a cosmic and personal endeavor. Their presence attests to the fact that human endeavors to resist evil are supported by a greater heavenly infrastructure.

Beyond biblical texts, church tradition and the writings of the Church Fathers amplify the doctrine of angelic warfare. Early Christian thinkers like St. Augustine and St. Gregory the Great reflected on the role of angels in illuminating divine justice and punishing demonic rebellion. They portrayed angels as ancient enemies of Satan, waging war to guard the church and its members. Such interpretations emphasize the perennial nature of this conflict throughout salvation history.

Mystical literature and devotional writings likewise portray angels as protectors against supernatural evil forces. These sources often blend biblical narrative with imaginative elaboration, offering vivid accounts of angelic encounters that reinforce the believer's confidence in divine protection. The repetition of such themes in diverse contexts attests to the enduring spiritual significance of angelic combat.

While these celestial battles may seem remote from everyday life, their spiritual symbolism permeates Christian consciousness. Prayer traditions invoke angels as guardians who shield the faithful from harm. Liturgical imagery often depicts angels as victorious champions, solemn yet mighty custodians of heaven's peace. These devotional dimensions solidify the angelic presence as a living reality within the spiritual life of believers, linking cosmic struggle to personal sanctification.

Theologically, the ongoing struggle between angels and demons invites profound reflection on the nature of evil and the cosmic order. Angels, created as beings of light and purity, participate actively in resisting the corruption introduced by rebellion. This resistance aligns with their primary commitment: manifesting God's will and safeguarding the integrity of creation. Their battles are not mere conflict for conflict's sake but purposeful actions that restore balance and thwart the spread of chaos.

The imagery of light versus darkness underscores the metaphysical polarity that frames the angelic conflict. Light embodies knowledge, holiness, and divine presence—forces that overcome shadows of ignorance, sin, and despair. Angels, as "messengers of light," illuminate the path toward salvation and stand as bulwarks against the gloom of spiritual malevolence. Darkness, represented by demonic powers, seeks to fracture this illumination, to upset divine order and subvert human freedom.

In some biblical poetic passages, this struggle is dramatized as a cosmic dance. The psalms, for instance, praise God for shattering the heads of monsters and crushing the forces of evil. These metaphors, while symbolic, capture the intense emotional and spiritual reality of angelic warfare. The language of battle appeals to the human longing for justice and the triumph of good in the face of seemingly insurmountable threats.

On a psychological level, angelic warfare invites believers to consider their own spiritual vigilance. Just as angels stand watch over the cosmos, so too are individuals called to guard their hearts and minds against evil influences. The angelic example of courage, obedience, and faithfulness serves as an enduring model for confronting moral darkness and pursuing righteousness.

The notion of angels battling darkness also resonates within the broader narrative of salvation history. The conflict between good and evil spans from creation, through the fall, to redemption and ultimate restoration. Angels, as active participants in this grand drama, reveal God's commitment to reclaiming creation from the grip of sin and death. Their victories foreshadow the final triumph depicted in Revelation, when evil is cast into the lake of fire and the cosmos is renewed.

This hope emboldens believers, encouraging persistence in prayer, worship, and righteous living. The angelic presence communicates that spiritual warfare is neither abstract nor hopeless; it is a vital engagement where victory already belongs to God, who commands and empowers these celestial forces.

Ultimately, the angelic forces against darkness invite a holistic understanding of life as a spiritual journey marked by both visible and invisible realities. As guardians, warriors, and messengers, angels embody the perseverance of divine love confronting the forces that seek to destroy it. Their battles remind humanity that the eternal struggle between light and darkness is waged not only in distant heavens but also within every human heart—a struggle calling us toward faith, courage, and transformation.

In this way, studying angelic warfare enriches our grasp of biblical theology, deepening our appreciation for the cosmic scope of redemption and the complexity of the spiritual realm. It challenges believers to recognize the presence of divine helpers amid adversity and to embrace their own role in resisting darkness with the strength that only God's power can supply.

Thus, the angelic forces against darkness stand as luminous sentinels in the ongoing battlefield of light, ever vigilant, fiercely committed, and unwavering in their mission to uphold the divine order and bring about the ultimate restoration of creation. Their story is a story of hope, justice, and the invincible potency of good—a story that continues to inspire and shape the spiritual journey of all who seek the light.

Symbols and Signs: The Imagery of Angels in Scripture

Decoding Angelic Symbolism

Angelic symbolism permeates the Bible with a richness and complexity that both fascinates and challenges readers. Far beyond simple depictions of supernatural messengers, angels emerge within Scripture as intricate symbols woven with layers of theological and spiritual meaning. Their various images—wings, light, fire, trumpets, among others—function not only as literal descriptors but also as powerful metaphors that speak to divine realities, human experience, and cosmic order. Exploring these symbols invites us into an interpretative act that goes beneath the surface narrative, uncovering theological depths and spiritual resonances that illuminate the nature of God, the spiritual realm, and humanity's place within that sacred tapestry.**Wings: Emblems of Divine Protection and Transcendence**One of the most iconic features associated with angels in biblical literature is their wings. The image of wings is endemic to angelic descriptions, evoking immediacy not only of motion or speed but also of spiritual elevation and divine protection. The metaphorical significance of wings in Scripture extends well beyond physical attributes; it enfolds profound theological meanings that resonate through multiple layers of biblical texts.

Wings first appear within the biblical context as symbols of shelter and refuge. The psalmist famously declares, "He will cover you with his feathers, and under his wings you will find refuge" (Psalm 91:4). Although this passage directly addresses God, the imagery of wings carries over to angels as well, emphasizing their role as guardians who shelter the faithful under divine authority. Wings, then, represent both movement and sanctuary—a paradoxical blend of speed to fulfill God's purposes and stillness to shield and protect.

Furthermore, the wings of angels symbolize the transcendence of heavenly beings over earthly limitations. Scripture frequently portrays angels moving swiftly between heaven and earth, bridging divine will and human reality. The wings thus signify their function as intermediaries capable of navigating realms with ease, embodying a spiritual mobility unavailable to mortal beings. This symbolic function gains particular poignancy when considered against ancient Near Eastern backgrounds, where winged figures often represented otherworldly power or divine presence. The biblical use of wings hence carries with it a language of spiritual authority and unfettered movement within the cosmic order.

In visions such as those found in Ezekiel 1 and Isaiah 6, angelic beings are described with multiple pairs of wings, conveying a multiplicity of functions—covering the face for reverence, covering the feet for humility, and flying for service. These functions reinforce the layers inherent in the wing imagery: wings are not merely appendages but theological symbols communicating humility before God, reverence in divine presence, and readiness to act. Such symbolic richness demands interpretative attentiveness to the interplay between heavenly mystery and spiritual responsibility.**Light: The Radiance of Divine Presence**Light is an indispensable symbol linked to angels across Scripture, embodying not only purity and holiness but also revelation and guidance. Angels are often described as radiant or shining beings, qualities that underscore their origin in the divine light of God and their role in transmitting his truth.

The biblical narrative frequently associates light with God's glory (Hebrew: kavod) and holiness, and in turn, angels reflect and channel this glory. For example, when the angel of the Lord appears to the shepherds in Luke 2:9, the "glory of the Lord shone around them," a phrase that intertwines angelic presence with the divine effulgence. This radiance conveys both the transcendence of angels and the illumination they bring to darkened human circumstances, whether foretelling salvation or delivering divine commands.

In apocalyptic literature, angelic beings often bathe in brilliant light, reinforcing their roles as bearers of eschatological revelation. The symbolic language here suggests that angels act as conduits of divine knowledge, piercing through human ignorance like light dispersing darkness. Light thus functions as a metaphor for spiritual truth and moral clarity, qualities inseparable from angelic ministry.

Theologically, light also signifies purity and sanctity. In Christian symbolism, light frequently contrasts with darkness—both literal and metaphorical—representing the cosmic struggle between good and evil. Angels, as agents of divine will, are therefore associated with the luminous realm of God's presence. Their shining aspect suggests a participation in the divine holiness that sets them apart from the corruption and sin of the world.

This symbolism gains further depth when analyzed alongside biblical themes of enlightenment and revelation. Just as God's Spirit leads believers from darkness into light, angels as bearers of light invite humanity toward higher knowledge and spiritual awakening. Thus, the use of light imagery in angelic depictions functions poetically and theologically, signaling both divine purity and the transformative power of heavenly messages.**Fire: The Dynamic Purity and Power of Angels**Fire appears as another powerful symbol imbued with diverse meanings when connected to angelic figures. Fire's biblical connotations oscillate between judgment and purification, destruction and illumination, rendering it a fitting metaphor for the complex ministry of angels.

Angels associated with fire are often depicted as agents of God's holiness and power, executing divine decrees that can be both nurturing and fearsome. For example, in Exodus 3, the angel of the Lord appears in a burning bush—fire that consumes but does not destroy. This paradoxical fire illustrates divine presence that purifies and reveals, characteristic of angelic encounters as well.

Fire's association with angels carries the dimension of purifying judgment. The vision of the seraphim in Isaiah 6 captures this aspect vividly: "One seraphim flew to me, with a live coal in his hand... He touched my mouth and said, 'Now that this has touched your lips, your guilt is taken away'" (Isaiah 6:6-7). Here, fire symbolizes sanctification and cleansing, an essential attribute of angels involved in the divine purification of prophets and the people.

This purifying aspect of fire complements its role in divine protection and wrath. Angels as fiery agents of God's judgment appear in instances of plagues, destruction of cities, and spiritual warfare, such as the destroying angel in 2 Samuel 24 or the angels who execute judgment in the book of Revelation. The fire is a symbol of God's consuming holiness, the energy of divine justice that burns away evil and secures cosmic order.

Moreover, fire symbolizes illumination and divine inspiration. Throughout biblical history, fire is an emblem of God's guiding presence—like the pillar of fire that led Israel by night in the wilderness (Exodus 13:21). Angels associated with fire thus embody the dynamic vitality of God's guidance, leading the faithful through darkness into salvation. As a symbol, fire conveys the intensity and immediacy of angelic action, reflecting divine zeal and purpose.**Trumpets: Heralds of Divine Revelation and Judgment**Trumpets or horns emerge throughout Scripture as a recurrent symbol tied closely to angelic activity, especially in the prophetic and apocalyptic traditions. The blowing of trumpets signals significant divine announcements, calls to attention, and the unfolding of God's redemptive plans. In the Old Testament, trumpets serve both liturgical and military functions, heralding occasions for celebration, war, or divine warning. Within prophetic literature, especially in the book of Revelation, angels blowing trumpets announce a sequence of eschatological judgments and heavenly proclamations. These trumpet blasts mark transitions in the divine timeline and summon creation's attention to God's unfolding purposes.

The symbolic power of trumpets lies in their auditory character—they are meant to be heard, noticed, and acted upon. As angelic instruments, trumpets represent the communication of divine will in ways that cannot be ignored or overlooked. They demand human and cosmic response, underscoring the urgency and gravity of God's messages.

This lends the angelic trumpets a function beyond mere sound; they become symbols of revelation and accountability. Where angels play trumpets, the eschatological drama unfolds, reminding believers of divine sovereignty and ultimate judgment. The trumpet thus symbolizes a pivotal intersection between heavenly activity and human destiny.

Moreover, trumpets function as metaphors for the clarity and power of divine communication. Where human words can fail or be misunderstood, the trumpet's clear tone cuts through confusion, embodying the unmistakability of God's authoritative voice. The angelic connotation assures that these messages come from the highest source, adding an aura of solemnity and authenticity.**Other Symbolic Dimensions: Eyes, Faces, and Movement**Beyond the more familiar symbols of wings, light, fire, and trumpets, biblical angels are frequently depicted with additional features laden with symbolic meaning, particularly in prophetic and apocalyptic literature.

The multiple eyes seen on the cherubim in Ezekiel's vision (Ezekiel 10:12) signify divine omniscience and vigilance. Eyes represent insight, awareness, and the all-seeing nature of God's heavenly attendants. This element conveys that angels serve as watchful guardians of the divine order, capable of perceiving spiritual realities beyond human sight.

Similarly, composite faces (man, lion, ox, eagle) appearing on angelic creatures reflect the fullness of creation and the integration of various symbolic traits—strength, wisdom, nobility, and swiftness. These images resonate with the four living creatures in Revelation 4 and echo wider biblical motifs that draw upon the created world to express spiritual truths. The multiplicity of faces intimates the complexity and universality of angelic ministry, reinforcing their role as representatives of divine order across all domains of life.

Movement, rhythm, and sound also figure prominently as symbols. The ceaseless motion of angels and their harmonious praise typify the perfect alignment of divine beings with God's will. Their roles as servants who execute God's commands are dramatized in the dynamic imagery of flight, sound, and dance. Such symbolism points readers toward the active, participatory nature of angels in the spiritual economy.**Symbolic Language as a Gateway to Deeper Spiritual Engagement**The use of symbolic language surrounding angels within Scripture invites readers into an interpretative exercise that transcends surface-level understanding. Biblical authors employ these images not simply as artistic flourishes but as coded language charged with theological and spiritual significance. Symbols act as bridges connecting human perception with divine realities that surpass ordinary comprehension.

Engaging with angelic symbolism demands a posture of attentiveness, humility, and openness. Each symbol—wings, light, fire, trumpets—contains multiple meanings that interplay and overlap, resisting reductive interpretations. This multilayered symbolism encourages readers to meditate on the mystery of the heavenly realm and its relation to human experience.

For instance, wings may simultaneously suggest protection, elevation, and ministry; light may convey purity, revelation, and judgment; fire could indicate destruction, purification, and guidance; trumpets may herald warning, celebration, and eschatological fulfillment. Rather than isolating one meaning, the biblical symbolic web compels a holistic approach, appreciating how symbols converge to convey rich theological truths.

This symbolic complexity also affirms the sacred nature of biblical texts, which communicate divine truth through metaphor and vision. The poetic resonance of angelic imagery opens portals to spiritual insight, inviting believers into contemplation of heavenly realities and prompting transformation in the earthly sphere.**The Interplay of Cultural Context and Biblical Symbolism**To fully appreciate the symbolism of angels, a consideration of the biblical cultural milieu is essential. The ancient Near Eastern context, with its pantheon of supernatural beings and symbolic motifs, informs but does not constrain the biblical portrayal. Rather, Scripture reinterprets and sanctifies prevailing symbols, infusing them with uniquely monotheistic and covenantal meaning.

For example, winged creatures were common in surrounding cultures as symbols of gods or divine messengers; the Bible adopts this imagery yet explicitly subordinates angelic beings under the one true God. Thus, wings indicate royal servitude rather than autonomous divinity. Similarly, light and fire, widely associated with deity in the ancient world, are here connected to God's holiness and righteousness, reinforcing scriptural themes of monotheism and ethical purity.

This contextual awareness allows readers to discern when biblical symbolism employs familiar motifs to convey new spiritual truths. The angelic images become not mere borrowings but transformative symbols bearing the stamp of revelation. The dynamic interplay between tradition and innovation enriches the symbolic language, inviting ongoing reflection and exploration.**Conclusion: Symbolism as a Portal to the Divine**In summary, the angelic symbolism encoded in biblical literature operates on multiple levels to convey profound spiritual realities. Wings, light, fire, trumpets, and other symbolic features articulate complex dimensions of angelic function and identity. They invite readers to enter into a deeper theological conversation that goes beyond literal description into realms of mystery, reverence, and revelation.

This symbolism serves as a bridge between human understanding and divine transcendence, inviting believers to encounter the heavenly realm with wonder and discernment. The layered metaphors surrounding angels act as an interpretative beacon, guiding readers toward richer knowledge of God's purposes, the structure of the spiritual world, and the hope of ultimate redemption.

Ultimately, understanding angelic symbolism enriches not only our comprehension of biblical texts but also deepens our spiritual imagination and faith. These sacred images resonate through time and culture, offering perpetual invitations to behold the unseen, listen to the divine, and participate in the unfolding story of salvation. Through such symbolic decoding, angels become for us celestial messengers not only in narrative but also in the vital language of spirit and truth.

Contrasting Terrifying and Comforting Visions

Throughout the tapestry of Scripture, angels emerge not as one-dimensional figures but as complex messengers imbued with both magnificent and tender qualities. Their appearances bring forth a spectrum of human responses, from shuddering fear and overwhelming awe to profound relief and comforting assurance. This duality, vivid and pervasive, is integral to understanding the biblical portrayal of angels—not merely as distant, supernatural agents, but as dynamic manifestations of divine presence and intent. To glimpse the essence of these celestial beings, one must navigate the tension between their terrifying majesty and their gentle reassurance, discerning how these seemingly contrasting visions coexist and enrich the believer's spiritual experience.

Encounters with angels frequently begin with an overwhelming sense of awe that borders on fear. In many biblical narratives, their arrival heralds moments of great significance, often signaling divine judgment, revelation, or intervention. In these moments, angels appear formidable, their presence commanding a reverence that is both natural and sacred.

The prophet Daniel recounts such an encounter, writing, "And behold, a hand touched me and set me trembling on my hands and knees. He said to me, 'O Daniel, man greatly beloved, understand the words that I speak to you'" (Daniel 10:10-11). Here, the angel's touch is not one of casual kindness but of overwhelming power—an experience intense enough to unsettle even a revered prophet.

This phenomenon of fear at the sight of angels is no mere literary device; rather, it reflects a profound spiritual reality. Angels in Scripture often bear a visage so extraordinary that it transcends human comprehension. In the book of Ezekiel, the prophet offers one of the most striking and bewildering visions of angelic beings—cherubim with human faces, animalistic forms, and wheels within wheels, their very description evoking mystery and the sublime (Ezekiel 1:5-28). This overwhelming complexity of form and movement inspires awe that borders on terror. Such images teach that angels are not simply messengers who deliver news or perform tasks; they are manifestations of the divine mystery itself, reminders of the infinite otherness of God and of the holy realm.

The book of Revelation amplifies this sense of celestial fear and awe. John's apocalyptic vision includes angels who pour out divine wrath, proclaim eternal decrees, and stand as guardians of sacred truths. When John beholds an angel with a rainbow encircling his head, his face like the sun, and legs like fiery pillars (Revelation 10:1), he falls prostrate, overcome with terror. In these heavenly scenes, angels function not only as agents of God's mercy but also as the executors of divine justice—figures whose gaze penetrates human sinfulness and heralds realities beyond human control.

But the biblical narrative refuses to allow angelic encounters to be consumed only by fear. Alongside these formidable visions, Scripture also abounds with encounters in which angels embody tenderness, offering comfort, protection, and hope. At the heart of many of these instances is an invitation to trust in God's providence, communicated through the angelic messenger's gentle presence and encouraging words. This is the other side of the angelic coin—the reassuring auxiliary sent not to intimidate but to console.

Consider the angelic appearance to Hagar in the wilderness (Genesis 16:7-14). Here, the angel does not strike terror but offers compassion to a distressed woman. By guiding her, promising the sustainability of her offspring, and encouraging her hopeful return, the angel serves as a tender witness to divine care amid human desolation. The same compassionate role is evident when angels minister to Elijah (1 Kings 19:5-7), providing food and drink not with celestial grandeur but with simple nurturing acts, enabling the prophet to continue his arduous journey.

Perhaps the most poignant examples of comforting angels are found surrounding the birth and resurrection narratives in the New Testament. In Luke's account, the shepherds' fear is quickly transformed into joy when the angel announces the birth of the Savior: "Do not be afraid. I bring you good news of great joy" (Luke 2:10). The initial fear inspired by the angel's appearance is immediately qualified by the message of hope, peace, and salvation—an embodiment of angelic tenderness. Similarly, after the resurrection, angels appear to women at the tomb not as figures of terror but as messengers of victory over death, announcing Christ's resurrection with words designed to comfort and inspire faith (Matthew 28:5-7).These contrasting depictions invite a richer, more nuanced contemplation of angelic presence. The oscillation between fear and comfort is not a contradiction but a dynamic interplay intrinsic to the experience of divine encounter. The awe and trembling in the presence of angels remind believers of the holiness and sovereignty of God, who is utterly other and sublime. At the same time, the comforting appearances affirm God's immanent love, mercy, and personal concern for humanity.

This dual theme is underscored by the angelic greetings frequently recorded in Scripture, where the phrase "Do not be afraid" appears as a deliberate response to fright. This formulaic reassurance speaks volumes about the effect angels often impose on human witnesses. Their glory and majesty, so far beyond ordinary experience, naturally evoke fear; yet this fear is immediately tempered by a gentle invitation to trust. The message is clear: these beings, powerful as they are, come as emissaries of peace, bridging the terrifying holiness of God and the intimate care extended to each person.

Theologically, this tension reflects broader biblical themes about God's nature and how humanity relates to the divine. God is both the "King of Glory" who demands reverence, and the "Good Shepherd" who tenderly cares for the flock. Angels, as divine messengers, mirror this dual aspect. They reveal that the divine encounter is not solely about dominance or fear but also about covenantal love and relational healing. Their terrifying glory functions to humble, to awaken awe, and to highlight the holiness that transcends human sinfulness. Their comforting presence ensures that this holiness is not distant or destructive but is filled with mercy and the desire for restoration.

This balance also sheds light on the transformative purpose of angelic encounters. Fear provoked by angels jolts the witness from complacency, compelling a heightened spiritual awareness. Comfort, on the other hand, offers strength and assurance to face life's trials or divine commands. Together, these responses shape a holistic spiritual perception—one that neither diminishes the mystery of God nor obscures God's approachable kindness.

Reflecting on this interplay invites believers and readers into a contemplative space that embraces complexity without seeking to resolve it simplistically. To dwell with the biblical angel is to recognize that sacred encounters are profound and multifaceted, engaging the whole person: mind and heart, awe and hope, trembling and trust. It encourages spiritual maturity, teaching that the divine rarely fits neat categories. Instead, divine communication often arrives in complex forms that challenge yet console, that terrify yet nurture.

This perspective also honors the deep emotional honesty within Scripture. The biblical accounts do not sanitize or idealize angelic appearances; fear is not glossed over but remembered as integral to the encounter. At the same time, hope and healing remain equally central. For modern readers, this openness invites a more authentic spiritual engagement—one that acknowledges moments of fear when facing the divine while welcoming the sustaining comfort God provides through angelic ministry.

Viewed through this lens, angels appear as bridges between heaven and earth, embodying the paradoxical nature of divine revelation. They reveal that God's presence is at once awe-inspiring and tenderly intimate. Their fearsome glory affirms God's transcendent majesty; their soothing presence reminds us of God's abiding mercy. This duality invites believers into a spirituality that does not recoil from mystery or fear but embraces them as entry points to deeper faith.

Indeed, the fear and trembling evoked by angels become a sacred threshold, a space of encounter where human pride is humbled and the soul's longing for God is awakened. The subsequent comfort they bring restores and strengthens, enabling the faithful to walk faithfully in response to God's call. Such is the profound dance of angelic presence: an invitation to encounter both the fearsome holiness and compassionate love that define the heart of biblical faith.

In this intricate balance of terrifying and comforting visions, the angel reveals the multi-dimensional reality of God's interaction with humanity. Beyond simple symbolism or folklore, their biblical portrayals call readers to a spiritual awareness that respects divine mystery without losing sight of divine intimacy. To see angels truly is to see this divine tension lived out—majestic and gentle, overwhelming and reassuring, a reflection of a

God whose ways surpass human understanding but whose heart remains with the humble and seeking soul.

As we meditate on these contrasting visions, we are drawn into a deeper appreciation of the angelic role in Scripture—not as static figures, but as dynamic agents of God's complex engagement with the world. Their appearances disrupt ordinary assumptions, shake hearts with reverence, and open ears to words of hope. Through the oscillation between fear and comfort, angels embody the paradox of divine holiness and grace—a paradox that invites ongoing reflection, wonder, and spiritual growth.

This understanding nurtures a richer spirituality grounded in the reality that encounters with the divine often encompass emotional complexity. The biblical witness to angels teaches that it is natural to respond with trembling at the sacred and yet to receive encouragement and peace. This dual response frees believers from simplistic ideals about what spiritual experiences "should" feel like, allowing space for the whole human response to mystery.

Ultimately, embracing the dual nature of angels as both terrifying and comforting messengers invites a fuller vision of spiritual life—one in which awe and tenderness coexist, shaping a faith that is realistic, hopeful, and deeply anchored in the biblical narrative. The angel's message, therefore, transcends the moment of encounter and becomes an enduring call to live in the tension of divine transcendence and immanence, fear and trust, judgment and mercy. Herein lies not only the mystery of the angelic but also a glimpse into the profound nature of God's love for humanity itself.

Metaphors of Light and Sound

Across the tapestry of biblical literature, angels are often imbued with the profound symbolism of light and sound, anchoring the spiritual and transcendent qualities of these celestial beings in sensory metaphors that resonate deeply with human experience. The language of light and sound in Scripture serves not merely as descriptive ornamentation but as a powerful theological tool, evoking the ineffable presence, purity, and divine activity associated with angels. Through the interplay of dazzling luminosity, radiant flashes, and celestial harmonies, the biblical text invites readers into an immersive encounter with the angelic realm—one that transcends ordinary perception and nurtures a vivid spiritual imagination.**The Radiance of Light: Angles as Beings of Luminous Splendor**Light, in its multifaceted symbolism, occupies a central place in biblical descriptions of angelic beings. From the Old Testament to the New, angels emerge not merely as messengers of God but as radiant manifestations of divine glory and holiness. This radiant imagery reflects the transcendent nature of their origin and mission, emphasizing their intimate connection with the divine light that reveals God's presence to humanity.

One of the earliest and most powerful expressions of angelic light appears in the prophetic visions where angels are described as beings of dazzling luminosity. For example, in Ezekiel's vision of the cherubim (Ezekiel 1), the creatures are accompanied by a "radiant glow" akin to burning coals and flashes of lightning. The cherubim's appearance is suffused with vivid brightness, highlighting their otherworldly essence and the overwhelming holiness that surrounds them. Light here symbolizes purity, divine power, and the ineffable nature of God's attendants—beings who act as intermediaries but also as manifestations of divine majesty.

The Psalms, too, weave light into their portrayal of angelic presence, often associating light with salvation, guidance, and protection. Psalm 104:4 refers to God's angels as "flames of fire," suggesting both the blazing brilliance and dynamic movement of these heavenly emissaries. The metaphor of fire as a form of light encapsulates divine energy that is purifying and consuming, yet benevolent and protective. This duality—of light as both illuminating and transforming—is key to understanding angelic function.

The New Testament expands and intensifies the motif of luminous angels, especially in the Gospels' narrations of angelic announcements and interventions. Luke's account of the angel Gabriel's appearance to Mary begins with a striking description of brightness: "And the angel came to her, and the glory of the Lord shone around her" (Luke 1:28). This "glory" or *doxa* signifies an overwhelming radiance that makes the divine presence tangible and visible through the angelic figure. The light is not merely ambient but emanates actively from the angel as a bearer of God's message, summoning awe and reverence.

The account of the angel who rolls away the stone from Jesus' tomb likewise employs brilliant light imagery: the angel is described as clothed in a dazzling white robe, his appearance like lightning (Matthew 28:3). Lightning here is a concentrated flash of divine illumination—brief, powerful, and startling—symbolizing the clash between the heavenly and earthly realms as well as the explosive power of resurrection and redemption. The use of light in this context suggests an unveiling of divine mystery, a revealing of the victorious power over death, mediated through the angel's radiant presence.

Throughout various biblical narratives, the consistent use of light as a metaphor for angels accomplishes several theological purposes. First, it emphasizes the angels' proximity to divine holiness and their role as vehicles for manifesting God's presence to humans. The brightness surrounding angels signals their participation in God's glory, setting them apart from earthly beings shaped by corruption and sin. Second, light metaphorically bridges the visible and invisible worlds, illustrating how angelic beings serve as luminous thresholds that connect the finite human experience with the infinite divine realm. Third, the imagery of light invites readers to perceive angels not only as messengers but as bearers of revelation—illuminators who bring clarity, hope, and vision out of darkness and uncertainty.**Flashes and Flames: Movement and Power in Angelic Light**Beyond steady radiance, the biblical text frequently associates angels with flashes of light and fiery manifestations, introducing the dynamics of movement, power, and divine judgement. These flashes—brief, intense bursts of illumination—speak to the agility and suddenness of angelic intervention, as well as to the theological motif of God's swift and decisive action through his messengers.

In prophetic literature, the angelic flash often parallels the divine presence as a consuming fire or "pillar of fire" that guides, protects, and enforces God's will. In Exodus 13:21, God leads the Israelites by a "pillar of cloud by day and a pillar of fire by night," a visible and potent symbol of divine guidance made manifest through a brilliant luminous phenomenon. While not explicitly described as angels, the pillars symbolize God's attentive care and presence, echoes of which resound in angelic representations as fiery forms—flashes that cut through darkness and uncertainty.

The Book of Revelation offers striking examples of angelic beings enveloped in flashing fire and lightning, framing the end-times drama with a vivid sensory experience of God's judgment and glory. Revelation 10:1 introduces an "angel coming down from heaven, wrapped in a cloud, with a rainbow above his head; his face was like the sun, and his legs like pillars of fire." The sun-like face and fiery legs conjure an image of overwhelming brilliance and unassailable power. The angel's flashing appearance communicates the righteousness and authority intrinsic to divine execution of judgment and revelation.

This divine luminosity is not static; it is crackling with energy and uncontainable force—signified by flashes and flickering flames. The metaphor of fire emphasizes angelic agents as purifiers who burn away sin and corruption, a theme consistent with of seraphim described in Isaiah 6:1–7, where these angelic beings are associated with burning coal and purification through their ministering with fire. The interplay of light and fire serves to reinforce the dual roles of angels as both protectors and agents of divine discipline.**Celestial Music: Sound as Angelic Revelation**While light primarily engages the visual senses, sound is the auditory gateway through which angelic presence often becomes perceptible in Scripture. The biblical text's use of sound metaphors—ranging from thunderous voice to celestial music—captures the powerful and mysterious communication between heaven and earth facilitated by angels.

The roar and thunder of angelic voices punctuate key moments of divine revelation, imbuing these instances with awe and fear. For example, in the Book of Revelation, voices sound like thunder as angels proclaim God's judgment and eternal sovereignty. Revelation 14:2 describes a "voice like the roar of many waters" surrounding an angel, an echo of God's own voice described in the Old Testament, suggesting that angels carry divine authority wrapped in overwhelming sonic majesty. This deep, reverberating sound symbolizes God's power made audible to human ears through his heavenly emissaries; it arrests attention and signals the gravity of the message conveyed.

Simultaneously, sound in the Bible often emerges in the form of angelic singing or praise, elevating the spiritual atmosphere with harmonious music that transcends ordinary experience. The prophetic literature of Isaiah includes seraphim who call to one another with voices proclaiming "Holy, holy, holy is the LORD Almighty" (Isaiah 6:3). This triple acclamation, repeated with a choir-like intensity, conveys both the holiness of God and the ecstatic joy of angelic beings who exist perpetually in worship. The sound metaphor here evokes the transcendental nature of angels—beings who surround the divine throne with praise, their voices resonant with sacred meaning and spiritual elevation.

Similarly, in Luke 2:13–14, the angelic chorus announcing Jesus' birth brings a "multitude of the heavenly host" praising God with the words "Glory to God in the highest, and on earth peace, goodwill toward men." The imagery of heavenly music rings with jubilant proclamation and joyful revelation. This auditory vision invites readers to imagine the sonic landscape of heaven, a perfect harmony heralding divine intervention in human history. The angelic voices, heard as music, function not merely as a background element but as an active participant in the narrative, culminating in the announcement of the Messiah's arrival.**The Synergy of Light and Sound: A Multisensory Encounter with the Divine**Biblical descriptions of angels frequently combine the metaphors of light and sound, creating a rich multisensory experience that accentuates the supernatural and awe-inspiring qualities of these heavenly beings. This blending of sensory imagery serves to heighten the spiritual impact of angelic appearances and to communicate their transcendent nature in a manner accessible to human perception.

For instance, the angelic revelation to the shepherds in the Christmas narrative interweaves radiant light with powerful sound. Luke 2:9–13 recounts how the glory of the Lord suddenly surrounds the shepherds, and "an angel of the Lord appeared to them, and the glory of the Lord shone around them, and they were terrified." At once, a multitude of heavenly hosts appears singing praises, filling the night air with a celestial chorus. Here, the visual brightness of divine glory melds seamlessly with the auditory splendor of angelic song, creating an immersive encounter that overwhelms ordinary senses and invites a deeper spiritual reverence.

This convergence reflects a biblical worldview where sensory experiences—sight, sound, and sometimes even smell and touch— become conduits of sacred reality. The metaphors of light and sound coalesce to form a dynamic portrayal of the angelic sphere, emphasizing that encounters with angels are not merely intellectual or abstract but fundamentally affect the whole person, appealing to both imagination and emotion.

Furthermore, the interplay between light and sound in angelic imagery symbolizes divine communication's multifaceted nature. Light often denotes revelation and illumination—the unveiling of God's will and truth—while sound represents proclamation and response, the act of declaring and affirming that truth in song, speech, or thunderous command. Together, they portray angels as mediators who embody both the reception and transmission of God's presence and purpose.**Poetic Narratives and the Evocation of Spiritual Imagination**Beyond direct scriptural accounts, the biblical corpus and subsequent Christian poetic reflections amplify and elaborate the metaphors of light and sound, fostering a spiritual imagination that allows readers to 'hear' and 'see' the angelic realm as vivid realities rather than abstract concepts.

In the Psalms and prophetic poetry, metaphorical language invites readers to visualize angels as blazing flames or dazzling light that pierce the darkness, as well as to hear their thunderous voices or haunting melodies that echo God's eternal reign. This poetic narration transcends the literal, inviting a meditative and holistic engagement with biblical texts where sensory imagery evokes wonder, reverence, and heartfelt awe.

For example, Psalm 29 offers a striking poetic portrayal of divine majesty where the "voice of the LORD" is described in terms of thunder, lightning, and tempest, framing an auditory and visual symbolism that resonates with how angels mediate God's presence through light and sound. Such poetry helps convey the overwhelming power of the divine, with angels as participating agents in this cosmic theater.

Similarly, the Song of Songs evokes the mystery and beauty of celestial wonders with radiant and musical metaphors that some theologians have read as echoes of angelic praise. These poetic glimpses cultivate an imaginative space in which the angelic realm becomes a living reality, perceived through the senses and experienced emotionally.

By engaging with these metaphors, readers are invited into a transformative encounter that transcends the mere intellectual study of angels. The sensory richness of light and sound metaphors challenges believers and scholars alike to perceive angels as living presences—beings whose arrival is heralded by luminous brilliance and harmonic praise, who light the darkness and fill the silence, beckoning toward a deeper understanding of God's kingdom at the threshold of heaven and earth.**Conclusion: The Enduring Significance of Light and Sound Metaphors in Angelology**In summary, the biblical employment of light and sound metaphors in describing angels operates on multiple levels: as theological affirmations of divine holiness and glory; as symbolic expressions of angelic power and purity; as sensory invitations into a deeper spiritual experience; and as poetic devices that stimulate imagination and worship. The multifaceted imagery not only shapes how angels are understood within the biblical worldview but also influences the devotional and doctrinal appreciation of their role as celestial messengers and ministers.

By focusing on the radiant flashes and fiery brilliance of light alongside the thunderous voices and angelic songs of sound, Scripture offers readers an entrancing glimpse into the heavenly realm that is simultaneously mysterious and accessible. This sensory language bridges the chasm between the infinite and the finite, inviting human beings into a participation in divine revelation and presence. The metaphors of light and sound ensure that the angelic world is not remote or abstract but vividly real—seen in flashes of glory, heard in celestial hymns, profoundly felt in the soul's awakening to the sacred.

Such rich sensory symbolism continues to inspire theological reflection, liturgical expression, and artistic imagination, underscoring the enduring power of biblical metaphor to communicate the transcendent mission and majestic nature of angels. In embracing these luminous and harmonic visions, readers are drawn into a deeper wonder and reverence for the celestial messengers who occupy the liminal space between God and humanity, illuminating the pathway to divine encounter through light and sound.

Gary E. Risenhoover

From Text to Doctrine: Evolving Understandings of Angels

Early Church Interpretations

The dawn of Christian thought found itself deeply engaged with the unseen world, a realm where celestial beings—angels—played indispensable roles not only within scripture but also within the living faith of the early Church. As nascent Christian communities grappled with the mysteries of divine interaction, the figure of the angel emerged as a crucial intermediary, a bridge between the finite and the infinite. The earliest followers of Christ inherited a rich tapestry of Jewish angelology—a multifaceted tradition saturated with images, stories, and hierarchies of angels—and, through their reflection and teaching, began to shape a distinctive Christian understanding. This subchapter traces the development of angelic theology during the formative centuries of Christianity, focusing on patristic writings, where scripture's living words interwove with philosophical inquiry. It lays bare how early Church fathers, theological councils, and prevailing intellectual currents converged to form the bedrock of Christian angelology, a foundation that continues to influence theological discourse today.

The earliest Christian writings beyond the New Testament, emerging from apostolic times into the second and third centuries, reveal a profound interest in angels both as scriptural realities and as doctrinal affirmations. This interest was not merely academic; angels were integral to the spiritual life of Christians, viewed as agents of God's providence, guardians of faithful souls, and participants in the cosmic struggle between good and evil. Yet, as diverse as these early texts are, they share a common impulse to articulate the nature, function, and place of angels within God's salvific economy.**Foundations in Scripture and Jewish Tradition**To understand early Church interpretations, it is essential first to recognize the dual heritage the Church inherited: the Hebrew Scriptures' portrayal of angels and burgeoning Christian revelation. The Old Testament conveys angels as messengers (mal'akhim), warriors, worshippers of God, and sometimes mysterious manifestations of divine presence (theophanies). Notable figures such as Michael and Gabriel begin to take on distinctive identities that later Christian writers would systematically explore. The apocalyptic streams within Judaism, especially those found in the Book of Daniel and extra-canonical works like 1 Enoch and the Testament of Abraham, furnish a highly developed angelology complete with hierarchies and cosmic roles.

The New Testament perpetuates and expands these themes. Angels appear announcing the birth of Christ, ministering after His temptation, standing at His resurrection, and engaging in eschatological activity. The Pauline epistles and the Johannine literature further invite reflection on the angelic realm's proximity to Christian life and divine mystery. Thus, early patristic authors approached angelology rooted firmly in this scriptural foundation but sought to clarify its implications in light of Christ's revelation and the Church's emerging identity.**Philosophical Interactions and the Quest for Ontological Clarity**In the Greco-Roman intellectual context, philosophy was ubiquitous, and early Christian thinkers could not ignore its insights, especially those concerning metaphysics and the nature of spiritual beings. Platonic and Aristotelian ideas about immaterial substances, hierarchies of beings, and the nature of divine providence provided frameworks that early theologians skillfully adapted to interpret the angelic world. The integration of biblical exegesis with philosophical reasoning shaped a uniquely Christian angelology that balanced mystery with rationality.

One of the earliest and most influential of the Church fathers to articulate an integrated angelology was Justin Martyr (c.100–165). In his *Dialogue with Trypho* and *First Apology*, Justin openly affirms the reality of angels as created spiritual beings who serve God and minister to humans. While not extensively systematizing angelic ranks, Justin's apologetic purposes underscore the importance of angels as divine intermediaries, reinforcing Christian claims against pagan and Jewish misunderstandings.

Following Justin, Irenaeus of Lyons (c.130–202) expands the theological horizon by weaving angelic beings into his overarching schema of salvation history. In *Against Heresies*, Irenaeus treats angels as part of the cosmic order crafted through God's wisdom. He emphasizes their role in mediating divine revelation and sustaining the created order, viewing angels also as guardians who combat the forces of evil. Irenaeus' perspective introduced an ethical dimension to angelology: angels were not static entities but active participants in God's redemptive plan.**Origen: The Intellectual Pioneer of Christian Angelology**A towering figure in the evolution of early angelic thought is Origen of Alexandria (c.185–254), whose prolific works dramatically influenced both theology and biblical interpretation. Origen's extensive commentary on scripture and his speculative theology ventured boldly into the nature of angels, their origins, and their relation to humanity.

Origen viewed angels as spiritual substances created by God out of nothing (ex nihilo), possessing intellect and will, thus capable of both good and rebellion. He distinguished between various degrees of angelic beings, albeit without rigid hierarchies, and proposed that angels, alongside human souls, pass through purification processes, underscoring the dynamic characteristic of spiritual beings.

Moreover, Origen introduced the idea that angels might function as guardians to human souls, anticipating later medieval developments. While speculative, Origen's theology foregrounded angels as crucial players in the cosmic drama of salvation and echoed Plato's influence on creaturely hierarchies.**Development of Angelic Hierarchies: Dionysius the Areopagite**Perhaps the most systematic and enduring presentation of angelic orders comes from Pseudo-Dionysius the Areopagite, whose works appeared near the close of the fifth or beginning of the sixth century but drew on earlier traditions and philosophical categories. His *Celestial Hierarchy* differentiates angels into three triads, each composed of three orders: the highest triad—Seraphim, Cherubim, and Thrones; the middle triad—Dominions, Virtues, and Powers; and the lowest triad—Principalities, Archangels, and Angels.

Dionysius' synthesis combined biblical references with Neoplatonic metaphysics, portraying angels as lights reflecting divine brilliance in gradations, mediating God's presence and governance across creation. His influence on medieval scholastics, notably Thomas Aquinas, was monumental, embedding angelic hierarchies firmly into the theology and mysticism of the Western Church.

Although not precisely an "early Church" father in the strictest chronological sense, Dionysius' work represents a culmination of patristic angelology, rooted deeply in the interpretations and speculations of earlier centuries.**Jerome and Augustine: Biblical Exegesis and Doctrinal Development**Two other giants of the early Church, Jerome (c.347–420) and Augustine of Hippo (354–430), made significant contributions to angelic theology through their biblical translations and theological treatises.

Jerome's Latin Vulgate translation of the Bible provided the textual foundation that shaped Western Christian reflection on angels. His scholarly commentaries often drew attention to angelic appearances and symbolic meanings, reinforcing the textual authority for doctrinal development.

Augustine, in particular, undertook a comprehensive theological synthesis that integrated biblical, philosophical, and pastoral concerns. In *The City of God* and numerous sermons, Augustine articulated angels as both spiritual beings and as servants of God's justice and mercy. He grappled extensively with the problem of evil, interpreting the fall of angels as a moral event rooted in free will, thus expanding the understanding of demonology within angelology.

Augustine's nuanced distinction between good angels and fallen ones, and his reflections on their roles in salvation history, profoundly influenced subsequent doctrine and popular Christian imagination.**Councils and Ecclesial Affirmations**While no early ecumenical council explicitly defined angelic doctrine per se, angelology was implicitly affirmed within broader Christological and Trinitarian declarations. The Council of Nicaea (325) and the Council of Chalcedon (451), by safeguarding the divine-human nature of Christ and affirming the Trinity, also framed the theological context in which angels functioned as distinct created beings yet ministering in service to the one God.

Moreover, the affirmation of spiritual realities such as resurrection and eschatological judgment implied the involvement of angelic agents, lending ecclesial weight to patristic angelology. Liturgical practices and creedal formulations made references to angels more frequent and solemn, integrating them into the lived faith of the Church.**Angels in the Life of the Early Christian Community**Beyond theological speculation, angels were woven into the devotional and liturgical fabric of early Christianity. They were invoked in prayers, depicted in iconography, and understood as protectors and guides. Early Christians, often under persecution, found comfort in the belief that angels ministered to them and the Church itself.

Hymns and doxologies from this period evoke angels adoring God and interceding for humanity. Liturgical texts such as the *Gloria* praise "the hosts of heaven," reflecting a cosmic dimension to worship that included angelic beings. The veneration afforded to angels, carefully distinguished from worship reserved for God alone, established a spiritual framework that shaped Christian piety and praxis for centuries.**Conclusion: Foundations for a Living Tradition**The early Church's interpretations of angels represent a profound interplay between scripture, philosophy, and lived faith. From Justin Martyr's affirmations to Augustine's theological profundity, patristic writings furnished a coherent and compelling picture of angels as real, created spiritual beings engaged in God's salvific plan. The gradual elaboration of angelic hierarchies, the reflection on their nature and roles, and the integration into worship and doctrine created a foundation for subsequent theological reflection.

These early interpretations did not exist in isolation; they interacted dynamically with the unfolding Christian tradition, responding to heresies, contextual challenges, and spiritual needs. The early Church fathers bequeathed a rich legacy that enables contemporary believers and scholars to appreciate the angelic realm not as an abstract curiosity but as a vital component of the Christian vision of God's kingdom.

In tracing this formative period, one discerns not only the intellectual rigor but also the spiritual depth that marks the early Church's angelology. Their efforts transformed biblical texts into living doctrine, shaping an enduring understanding of angels that continues to illuminate the Christian faith across ages.

Medieval Angelology and Mysticism

The medieval era stands as a pivotal chapter in the unfolding story of angelology—the study of angels—where angelic beings transcended their biblical portrayals to become integral components of theology, mysticism, and popular piety across Europe. Between roughly the 5th and 15th centuries, scholars and mystics alike sought to deepen understanding of angels, embedding these celestial messengers within complex intellectual frameworks and spiritual practices that reflected the culture and concerns of medieval Christendom. This subchapter delves into this rich tapestry, tracing how scholastic theologians crafted systematic angelologies, how mystics encountered angels as embodiments of divine light and grace, and how the angelic realm infused not only intellectual discourse but also the devotional life of medieval Christians.---### The Intellectual Fertile Ground: Historical Context of Medieval Angelology To appreciate the medieval development of angelic thought, one must situate it within a broader historical and cultural milieu shaped by the synthesis of Christian doctrine, classical philosophy, and evolving social structures. Following the collapse of the Western Roman Empire, Europe found itself in a fragmented yet spiritually vibrant world. The Church emerged as a unifying institution, wielding immense influence in shaping not only religious life but also art, education, and governance. Sanctity, divine order, and cosmic hierarchy were foundational concepts that permeated medieval worldview.

Angels, as intermediaries between God and humanity, naturally invited profound theological exploration. Their biblical appearances, often brief but striking, provided a scriptural foundation; however, the Bible's relatively sparse detail propelled medieval thinkers to seek a more detailed, systematic understanding. In this search, the rediscovery and integration of Aristotelian and Platonic philosophy profoundly influenced angelology. The conflation of scripture and philosophy produced a sophisticated intellectual environment where angels were no longer mere narrative figures but active, essential participants in the celestial order.

This era was also marked by the burgeoning of universities, where theology became the "queen of the sciences." Angelology found a natural home in these scholastic institutions, where careful logic, metaphysics, and careful commentary on patristic authorities gave rise to elaborate treatises on the nature, essence, and hierarchy of angels. Parallel to this academic enterprise was the vibrant world of mystical experience, where saints and visionaries articulated angelic encounters steeped in symbolism and spiritual yearning for union with the divine.---### Scholastic Angelology: Systematizing the Celestial Hierarchy The scholastic method—the hallmark intellectual approach of medieval Europe— greatly shaped angelology by applying rigorous analysis to theological questions. Among the numerous scholastics who wrote extensively on angels, Thomas Aquinas (1225–1274) stands out as a towering figure whose synthesis continues to influence Christian thought.

Aquinas's treatment of angels in his monumental work, the *Summa Theologiae*, offered one of the most comprehensive and systematic accounts of angelology. Drawing upon Aristotle's metaphysics, Pseudo-Dionysius the Areopagite's hierarchy, and Augustine's theological reflections, Aquinas elaborated a precise ontology of angels. Unlike physical creatures, angels were pure spirits—immaterial, indivisible, and possessing intellect and will without bodily constraints.

Aquinas maintained that angels are individual substances—each angel unique and created directly by God—endowed with exceptional knowledge and power, yet subordinate to God's will. This intellectual freedom allowed angels to be perfect messengers and agents of divine providence. Central to Aquinas's conceptualization was the idea of a structured angelic hierarchy, rooted in Pseudo-Dionysius's influential classification, itself descending from earlier Christian and Neoplatonic thought.---#### The Nine Choirs: Angelic Orders and Their Functions A crucial contribution to medieval angelology was the delineation of the angelic hierarchy into nine distinct orders or "choirs," arranged in three tiers of three. Each choir possessed specific roles and attributes, reflecting a divine ordering of the cosmos that paralleled earthly hierarchies and suggested a cosmic harmony. The nine choirs are traditionally grouped as follows:**First Sphere: Closest to God**1. **Seraphim** — Burners or "the burning ones," Seraphim were described as beings of intense love and purity, perpetually praising God and enflamed with divine zeal.2. **Cherubim** — Known for their vast knowledge and wisdom, the Cherubim symbolized the fullness of divine insight and guarded holy mysteries.3. **Thrones** — Representing God's justice and authority, Thrones were envisioned as symbols of divine stability and cosmic order.**Second Sphere: Heavenly Governors**4. **Dominions (Dominations)** — Functioning as celestial governors, Dominions regulated the duties of lower angels and ensured the cosmos remained aligned with God's will.5. **Virtues** — Associated with miracles and grace, Virtues were believed to dispense the strength required for the natural world's operation.6. **Powers** — Defenders against evil, Powers maintained the balance of power within the spiritual realm and fought against demonic forces.**Third Sphere: Messengers and Guardians**7. **Principalities** — Guardians of nations and groups, Principalities oversaw earthly realms and institutions, guiding leaders and peoples.8. **Archangels** — The best-known class, archangels served as chief messengers involved in key salvific events (e.g., Michael, Gabriel).9. **Angels** — The lowest choir, individual angels were closest to human beings, acting as personal protectors and messengers.

This divine ordering resonated deeply in medieval imagination, prompting theological reflection on the function and activity of angels both in heaven and on earth. Artistic depictions, liturgical texts, and sermons often illustrated these cosmic ranks, reinforcing the vision of a heavenly court that mirrored earthly order but extended infinitely in glory and perfection.---### Mystical Angelology: The Angelic Light in the Contemplative SoulWhile scholastic theologians elaborated angelology chiefly through intellectual inquiry, medieval mysticism offered a complementary perspective—one rooted in personal experience, vision, and ecstatic union with God. For mystics, angels were not only theological entities but living realities encountered in the inner spiritual journey. They functioned as guides, protectors, and symbolic figures representing stages of spiritual ascent.

Among the most influential mystical voices was Hildegard of Bingen (1098–1179), a German abbess whose prolific visions included vivid angelic presences. Hildegard depicted angels as radiant lights and forces of divine harmony, integral to cosmic balance and intimately involved in human salvation. Her visions reflected a universe suffused with sacred energy, with angels acting as luminous messengers bridging the gap between God and creation.

Similarly enriching was the spirituality of Meister Eckhart (1260–1328), a Dominican friar whose contemplative sermons emphasized the indwelling of God within the soul. For Eckhart, angels symbolized pure intellect and the soul's capacity to receive divine illumination beyond the distractions of the material world. Although more abstract and philosophical in tone, Eckhart's insights contributed to an angelology that was as much about internal spiritual transformation as about external beings.---#### Angelic Visions and Devotional Practices Mysticism often involved direct experiences of angels as part of broader visionary and devotional phenomena. Saints such as Catherine of Siena and Bernard of Clairvaux reported encounters that reinforced angels' roles as spiritual companions and intercessors. These visions, sometimes recorded in hagiographies and mystical treatises, offered emotional and symbolic depth to the notion of angels.

Popular devotion also embraced the angelic realm, with prayers, feasts, and iconography devoted to angels flourishing throughout medieval Europe. The feast of Michaelmas, celebrating the Archangel Michael's triumph, became a significant liturgical event. Angels were invoked as protectors—especially as guardians of the soul at death—and as advocates before God's throne. The Angelus prayer, commemorating the Annunciation, became a daily devotional practice that underscored the mystery of angelic mediation in salvation history.

This widespread devotional attention attests not only to the theological importance of angels but to their pervasive presence in the lived religious consciousness of medieval Christians.---### Symbolism and Imagery: Portraying the Divine Messengers Medieval art and literature contributed significantly to shaping the popular imagination of angels, embedding symbolic meanings that conveyed theological and mystical truths. Illuminated manuscripts, frescoes, stained glass windows, and sculpture depicted angels with distinctive iconography that reflected their nature and roles.

Seraphim, for instance, were often illustrated with six fiery wings, inspired by Isaiah's vision, manifesting the consuming love that characterized their eternal praise. Cherubim, with multiple eyes and a complex, awe-inspiring form, represented divine wisdom and vigilance. Thrones were portrayed as majestic wheels or luminous orbs, symbolizing God's unshakable justice.

Angels were frequently shown wielding instruments such as trumpets or swords, denoting their functions as heralds of divine revelation or as cosmic warriors battling evil. The Archangel Michael, clad in armor and brandishing a lance or sword, iconically embodied the triumph of good over evil.

Literary works such as Dante Alighieri's *Divine Comedy* immortalized angels within a poetic schema that integrated scholastic theology and medieval spirituality. Dante's vision of Paradise features angels arranged in celestial spheres, blending Angelology's intellectual categories with vivid imaginative power. The symbolism went beyond mere representation—it functioned as a theological language that communicated the mysteries of divine order to the medieval mind.---### The Angelic Influence on Medieval Thought and Culture The integration of angels into medieval theology and spirituality was not an abstract or isolated development. Instead, it permeated many aspects of society, influencing moral teaching, ecclesiastical authority, and even political ideology. Angels as agents of divine justice, guidance, and protection reinforced the Church's claim to spiritual authority and the sanctity of rulers consecrated by God.

The concept of guardian angels, for example, underscored a personal relationship between the sacred and the individual, assuring believers that divine care extended intimately to each soul. This belief fostered ethics centered on obedience, vigilance, and repentance, qualities necessary for maintaining the soul's alignment with angelic guardianship.

In the realm of education, angelology was a standard subject among theologians and students, representing a critical element of the broader quest to understand God's creation and providence. The elaborate classifications and metaphysical reflections demonstrated the medieval aspiration to order the cosmos through knowledge and faith.

Beyond academia and the church, angels inspired poetry, drama, and popular stories. They appeared as characters in morality plays, symbolizing virtues, or guiding protagonists toward salvation. Their presence in cultural expressions affirmed the pervasive medieval conviction that the spiritual world was alive and active—a realm where the human and divine intersected continually.---### Challenges and Critiques in Medieval Angelology Despite its widespread acceptance, medieval angelology was not without debate and critique. Some theologians questioned the extent to which angels could be known or depicted, cautioning against excessive speculation. Others expressed concern over popular practices that might border on superstition or diminish the sole worship due to God.

The rise of nominalist philosophy toward the late medieval period also introduced shifts in metaphysical assumptions about angels and spiritual beings. Questions arose about how angels, as purely spiritual, could interact with the material world and human bodies, provoking ongoing theological reflection and refinement.

Nevertheless, these challenges did not diminish the central role of angels—they rather highlighted the dynamic nature of medieval theology, ever attuned to the tension between mystery and understanding, faith and reason.---### Conclusion: The Angel's Evolving Face in Medieval Christendom The medieval era's angelology and mysticism unveil a world where angels transcended textual references to become multidimensional figures embedded deeply within theology, spirituality, and culture. The scholastic endeavor provided a robust intellectual framework that ordered the angelic host into coherent hierarchies and clarified their metaphysical nature. Simultaneously, the mystic tradition illuminated the experiential and symbolic dimensions of angels, presenting them as radiant companions on the soul's journey toward God.

Popular devotion and artistic expression further animated these ideas, embedding angels in the collective imagination of European Christendom. Across centuries, angels were envisioned as fiery seraphim, vigilant cherubim, mighty archangels, and tender guardians—a spectrum reflecting divine attributes and human hope.

In this fusion of doctrine, experience, and art, medieval angelology emerges as a vibrant testament to the enduring human fascination with the celestial realm and its messengers. It bridged the divine and the earthly, the seen and the unseen, offering medieval Christians a glimpse of the divine order that sustained and animated their world. The angel's face in medieval Christendom was thus ever-changing, a kaleidoscope of light and mystery, inviting believers to contemplate the heavenly and strive for holiness amid the challenges of mortal life.

Modern Perspectives and Interpretations

In the vast tapestry of biblical interpretation, angels have always occupied a distinct and compelling space—entities that bridge the divine and human realms, messengers of God's will who inspire awe, wonder, and sometimes profound fear. While traditional understandings have long been rooted in scriptural exegesis, ecclesiastical teaching, and doctrinal formulation, the contemporary landscape presents a more varied and dynamic engagement with angels. The modern world, shaped by advanced scholarship, diverse spiritualities, and the pervasive influence of popular culture, invites fresh perspectives on angelic beings that both challenge and enrich the classical paradigms. This subchapter seeks to explore these evolving attitudes, highlighting how modern theology, cultural expressions, and spiritual curiosity contribute to a renewed fascination with angels, while maintaining an openness to the mystery that surrounds these celestial figures.---**Theological Reflections in a Postmodern Age**Modern theology, unlike its traditional predecessors, often approaches angels not merely as static doctrinal fixtures but as living symbols embedded in a broader existential and relational context. The twentieth and twenty-first centuries have produced a wave of scholarship intent on re-examining angelic references within scripture under the light of contemporary hermeneutics. The rise of historical-critical methods, literary analysis, and comparative religious studies has encouraged theologians to probe the socio-cultural milieus that shaped biblical descriptions of angels, as well as the theological intentions behind these portrayals.

One important shift is the move away from purely literal interpretations toward more nuanced, metaphorical, or existential readings. For instance, some theologians argue that angels in scripture often function not simply as external beings but as symbolic representations of God's presence, guidance, and transcendence—figures that communicate the intersection of the divine mystery with human experience. This perspective aligns with the broader theological trend of emphasizing God's immanence and relationality, seeing angels as a bridge not solely between God and humanity, but also between the seen and the unseen dimensions of reality.

Furthermore, in ecumenical dialogues and interfaith conversations, there is greater recognition that angelic figures are not unique to Christianity but appear in various forms across Judaism, Islam, and other traditions. This comparative approach encourages scholars to look beyond confessional boundaries, appreciating the shared motifs while respecting distinct theological nuances. Angels thus become a point of intersection—an opportunity for mutual understanding in a pluralistic religious landscape. It also prompts a reconsideration of angelic attributes, roles, and hierarchies, contextualizing biblical angels within a broader spiritual ecology.

Modern theology also wrestles with questions about angels in light of contemporary scientific worldviews. Skepticism regarding supernatural entities, informed by rationalism and empiricism, often invites believers and theologians to reframe angels in ways that resonate with faith and reason. Some theologians propose that angels function as "signs" of God's ongoing involvement in the world rather than as autonomous, independently existing spirits. From this vantage, angels perform a hermeneutical role—inviting believers to discern God's action amidst the complexities of life and history. This reframing does not diminish the awe inspired by angelic appearances but situates them within a carefully balanced theological framework that respects both faith commitments and intellectual inquiry.---**Spirituality and the Angelic Experience in Contemporary Faith**Beyond academic theology, angels hold a vital place in the lived spirituality of many Christians and seekers today. Contemporary spirituality often reflects a heightened openness to personal and mystical experiences, including encounters with angels. This is evident in popular devotional materials, prayer movements, and testimonies wherein angels are portrayed as compassionate guides, protectors, and bearers of divine encouragement. Such experiences are frequently described within the language of comfort and healing, emphasizing angelic involvement in the practical realities of human suffering and hope.

This trend is particularly visible within charismatic and Pentecostal circles, where angelic phenomena such as visitation, miraculous intervention, and prophetic messages are embraced with enthusiasm and seriousness. These communities often interpret angelic encounters as affirmations of God's immediate nearness and power. Moreover, the angelic presence serves as a tool for spiritual empowerment—encouraging believers toward moral courage, perseverance, and deeper intimacy with the divine.

At the same time, a variety of spiritual movements outside traditional ecclesial structures have adopted angels as central figures in their worldview. New Age spirituality, for example, often reimagines angels in syncretistic ways, borrowing from Christian angelology but inflecting it with ideas drawn from Eastern religions, esotericism, and metaphysical teachings. Here, angels are sometimes conceptualized less as divine messengers than as personal guides, teachers, or energy beings, overseeing individual growth and cosmic harmony. While such portrayals diverge significantly from orthodox Christian understandings, they reflect the enduring human aspiration to connect with transcendent forces that offer meaning and support.

This plurality has sparked lively discussions within Christian circles about the theological boundaries and pastoral implications of angelic devotion. Questions arise concerning discernment—how to distinguish authentic spiritual experiences from illusion or deception. Pastoral guides caution against excessive fascination that distracts from the centrality of Christ, urging believers to prioritize scriptural grounding and ecclesial wisdom. Yet many also acknowledge that a vibrant angelic spirituality can enliven faith, nourish hope, and deepen worship when embraced within a balanced, Christ-centered framework.---**Angels in Popular Culture: From Sacred Messengers to Cultural Icons**Perhaps nowhere is the modern reshaping of angelic imagery more visible than in popular culture. Literature, film, television, visual arts, and music have all contributed to a rich and complex tapestry of angelic representation that both draws from biblical tradition and innovates boldly in new directions. This cultural phenomenon reflects society's enduring fascination with the mystical, the moral, and the transcendent, using angelic figures as a means to explore profound themes such as good and evil, innocence and corruption, justice and mercy, and the quest for meaning in an often chaotic world.

In literature, angels have sometimes appeared as intermediaries grappling with their own identity and purpose. Works of fiction ranging from classic novels to contemporary fantasy often portray angels in humanized terms—beings with emotions, doubts, and moral dilemmas—

thus inviting readers to ponder their own spiritual journeys. This personification makes angels accessible, relatable, and emotionally engaging.

Cinema and television feature angels in a remarkable array of narratives, from inspirational dramas highlighting divine intervention to action-packed series depicting angels as warriors combating evil. Examples include popular movies where angels guide protagonists toward redemption or offer protection in moments of crisis, as well as television shows that blend theological elements with thriller or mystery genres. These portrayals both reflect and shape public perceptions, fueling renewed interest and dialogue about angels' role in the spiritual lives of people today.

Visual arts continue to use angelic imagery as symbols of transcendental beauty, hope, and the sacred. Angel motifs appear in contemporary sculpture, installation art, photography, and digital media, often reinterpreted to address current social issues such as peace, justice, and human dignity. Through such works, angels become not only theological entities but also cultural icons—emblems of humanity's aspiration toward goodness and divine connection.

Music, too, plays a part in popular angelology. Numerous songs across genres reference angels, whether celebrating their comforting presence or lamenting their absence in times of struggle. These musical expressions resonate with audiences by articulating universal yearnings for protection, healing, and spiritual reassurance.

The widespread cultural engagement with angels inevitably leads to a complex interplay between imagination, belief, and myth. While this can sometimes blur theological clarity, it also contributes to a vibrant cultural conversation about the significance of angels as symbols and realities. Popular culture, in effect, serves as a contemporary folklore, transmitting and transforming angelic themes to speak meaningfully into the present moment.---**Angelology and the Digital Age: Connectivity and New

Expressions**The digital era amplifies the reach and diversity of angelic discourse. Online platforms, social media, podcasts, and streaming services allow for the rapid dissemination of angel-related content, connecting global audiences in unprecedented ways. Enthusiasts share personal encounters, theological reflections, artistic creations, and spiritual practices centered on angels, facilitating community formation around shared interests.

This digitally mediated landscape encourages a democratization of angelology: expertise is no longer confined to academic institutions or religious authorities but is available to anyone with internet access. This openness is double-edged, fostering creativity and inclusivity but also the spread of misinformation and superficial readings. Nevertheless, the Internet provides valuable resources for those seeking deeper understanding, including access to ancient texts, scholarly debates, and interreligious perspectives.

The interactive nature of digital media also invites participatory experiences of angels. Virtual prayer groups, meditation apps featuring angelic themes, and multimedia storytelling immerse users in angel-centric spirituality. These tools can help individuals cultivate a sense of divine companionship and guidance, echoing the biblical tradition of angels as active participants in human life.

Moreover, digital art and virtual reality open new horizons for experiencing and imagining angels. Artists create immersive environments where viewers can engage with angelic symbolism in multisensory ways, blending ancient motifs with modern technology. Such innovations suggest that angelic imagery will continue to evolve alongside technological progress, adapting to new cultural languages and aesthetic sensibilities.---**Challenges and Controversies in Modern Angelology**With the resurgence of interest in angels comes certain challenges. One is the risk of commodification or trivialization. The proliferation of angel-themed merchandise—from jewelry and home décor to self-help books and workshops—sometimes reduces these profound celestial beings to mere decorative or commercial elements. This risks detaching angels from their scriptural grounding and theological depth, presenting them as generic symbols of positivity rather than as complex agents of divine will.

Another challenge lies in navigating the boundaries between legitimate spiritual experience and potential deception or psychological vulnerability. The popularity of "angel healers," channelers, and mediums who claim angelic communication raises important ethical and doctrinal questions. Pastoral sensitivity and critical discernment are essential to ensuring that individuals seeking angelic encounters are protected from exploitation or false teachings.

Additionally, as popular portrayals often blend diverse religious and cultural ideas, tensions arise among those committed to confessional purity and those embracing a more inclusive spirituality. Some Christian leaders express concern that syncretistic angelology dilutes core doctrines about Christ and the role of angels, while others advocate for engagement and dialogue that acknowledges the evolving spiritual landscape.

Despite these challenges, the renewed interest in angels also offers opportunities. It invites contemporary believers and seekers to reclaim a rich heritage, to integrate angelic themes into ethical and theological reflection, and to foster spiritual practices that nurture hope, compassion, and reverence for the divine mystery.---**Toward a Contemporary Theology of Angels: Hopeful Openness**As the modern world continues to change, the figure of the angel endures as a source of intrigue, inspiration, and spiritual significance. Contemporary scholarship and spirituality increasingly recognize the need for a theology of angels that neither rejects the supernatural nor succumbs to naïve credulity but maintains a posture of thoughtful openness.

This contemporary theology acknowledges the ancient roots of angelology while embracing the questions and insights brought about by modern contexts. It recognizes angels as more than mythic beings or psychological archetypes, affirming their role within a living faith that encounters God's active presence in history. At the same time, it respects mystery—the recognition that angels, by nature, transcend full human comprehension and invite continual contemplation.

Hope remains central to the angelic narrative in modern thought. Angels symbolize God's steadfast care amidst turmoil, the possibility of redemption, and the promise of ultimate justice. Their presence encourages believers to remain attentive to the subtle ways grace operates in daily life and in the course of world events.

Ultimately, the modern perspective on angels calls for intellectual curiosity balanced with devotional sensitivity. It invites readers to explore the intersections of scripture, tradition, culture, and personal experience without shortcutting the complexity of these encounters. In doing so, it fosters a renewed appreciation of the multifaceted roles angels play as messengers, protectors, and reminders of the divine mystery that continues to shape human existence.

In this spirit, angels remain not relics of a distant past but vibrant figures who challenge, console, and inspire—a celestial language that speaks into the hopes and fears of contemporary humanity and points beyond to the eternal. This hopeful openness to ongoing discovery ensures that the study of angels is not only a scholarly endeavor but a living journey of faith and wonder.

Gary E. Risenhoover

Angelic Encounters: Personal and Communal Experiences

Testimonies through the Ages

Throughout the tapestry of human history, countless voices have risen to recount moments when the veil between heaven and earth seemed to part, allowing a glimpse of the divine through angelic presence. These testimonies—scattered across ages and cultures, yet rooted deeply in the biblical tradition—carry the luminous imprint of encounters that transcend ordinary experience. They are stories whispered in quiet prayers, shouted in desperate pleas, or sung in joyful celebration—each one bearing witness to a reality often unseen yet deeply felt. As we immerse ourselves in these sacred recollections, we step into a world where the ethereal touches the earthly, surprising the soul with wonder, solace, and purpose.

The ancient records of Israel's history preserve some of the earliest and most compelling testimonies of angelic visitations, tales that have been passed down through generations as beacons of hope and divine intervention. Consider the account of Hagar in the wilderness, a woman enveloped by despair, yet suddenly met by an angel whose words breathed new life into her spirit. The angel's voice was both gentle and authoritative, declaring, "Return to your mistress and submit yourself under her hands; for the LORD hath heard thy affliction." This encounter, recorded in the book of Genesis, illustrates how angels function as messengers of God's care and guidance, bridging moments of anguish and abandonment with the assurance of divine presence. Hagar's testimony is one of pain transformed into faith, a luminous moment that continues to inspire those wrestling with isolation and fear.

Across centuries, prophetic figures likewise shared experiences that revealed the multifaceted roles of angels—warriors, guides, and agents of God's judgment and mercy. The prophet Elijah, fleeing danger and despair, finds himself under an angel's care, dining on food delivered to him in the wilderness, sustained not merely physically but spiritually for the perilous journey ahead. This intervention, tender yet vital, conveys the nurturing aspect of angelic ministry, revealing that their roles include sustaining the fragile human spirit in times of great trial. Elijah's testimony speaks volumes of the angelic assurance that even in moments of exhaustion and desolation, God does not abandon His servants.

The New Testament further enriches this cascade of testimonies, unveiling angelic encounters that stir the heart with awe and mystery. Zechariah's encounter in the temple, the annunciation to the Virgin Mary, and the comforting presence at Christ's resurrection are among the most renowned moments when heaven touched earth. Take Mary's experience, for example: the angel Gabriel's visit was at once startling and overwhelming, yet filled with gentleness and clarity. The celestial messenger announced a divine purpose that would shift the course of human history, evoking a response that mingled fear, wonder, and faith. Mary's testimony invites readers to contemplate the paradox of angelic appearances as both disruptive and inviting, shaking the foundations of comprehension yet opening the doors to salvation's unfolding.

But these encounters are not confined to biblical times alone. Throughout history, saints, mystics, and ordinary believers alike have reported experiences that echo the ancient testimonies, revealing that angelic presence remains an active, vital force in the contemporary human journey. The writings of saints such as Teresa of Avila and Padre Pio abound with references to angelic beings who appeared to guide, protect, and even engage in mysterious interactions that deepened their faith and strengthened their resolve. Teresa spoke of a seraphic angel whose fiery love pierced her soul, a symbol of divine intimacy that transcends human understanding. Padre Pio's many reported encounters with guardian angels echo the biblical assurance that each believer is assigned these heavenly protectors, who guard the body and soul from harm. These accounts, while rooted in personal mysticism, provide a resonant continuity with the scriptural narratives, affirming that angelic ministry—though often unseen—remains an abiding reality.

Laypeople's testimonies offer equally vivid and profound insights, bringing the presence of angels into the everyday fabric of life. One might consider the story of a young soldier during the turmoil of war, surrounded by chaos yet inexplicably shielded from harm. Recounting the sensation of a protective presence, the soldier described feeling hands that guarded without violence and an overwhelming peace that settled amid the storm. Many such wartime experiences are chronicled in memoirs and oral histories, testimonies that disclose the angelic role as guardians amid human conflict. These stories illuminate the paradox of war's brutality contrasted with moments of supernatural mercy, inviting reflection on how angelic beings might serve as instruments of peace even amid discord.

Other testimonies reveal angelic presence as a source of comfort and guidance in moments of profound sorrow or uncertainty. Consider the account of a grieving mother who, after losing her child, encountered a radiant figure during a solitary walk. The angel's silent embrace conveyed a peace beyond words, easing the crushing weight of loss with a balm known only to the heart that grieves. Such experiences, often shared in quiet communities or private prayer circles, testify to the tender mercy angels extend to the brokenhearted, embodying the biblical affirmation that "the angel of the LORD encamps round about them that fear him, and delivers them" (Psalm 34:7). In these intimate moments, angelic presence becomes a living symbol of the hope that transcends grief.

In contemporary times, reports of angelic sightings and experiences continue to emerge, often accompanied by profound spiritual transformation. Within global communities touched by crisis or natural disasters, survivors speak of luminous figures who aided escape, offered warning, or provided inexplicable assistance. An example is found in the testimonies following the 2010 earthquake in Haiti, where numerous survivors described fleeting moments when angelic beings seemed to offer guidance amid rubble and despair. Whether these accounts are recognized strictly as divine intervention or interpreted through varying cultural lenses, their emotional and spiritual impact is undeniable. These narratives resonate with the ancient biblical themes of deliverance and divine accompaniment, reaffirming the continuity of angelic interaction across time and space.

Transformative encounters often parallel narratives of angels appearing as bright light or radiant figures, experiences suffused with both fear and fascination by those who behold them. Some witnesses recount a moment when the ordinary world suddenly shimmered with otherworldly brilliance, their senses overwhelmed by a presence that communicated without words. These moments often leave a lasting imprint—a profound shift in perspective or a renewed commitment to a life aligned with divine will. The testimonies of such encounters reveal the transformative power of angelic visitation: not merely as a supernatural curiosity but as an invitation to deeper spiritual awakening.

Conversely, many accounts emphasize the quieter, gentler nature of angelic interaction—angelic presences that comfort without spectacle, guide without fanfare. One not uncommon testimony is that of a person who, amidst the loneliness of illness or despair, senses an unseen companion whose presence provides steady reassurance. These experiences may be subtle—a sudden warmth in the room, a whispered sense of encouragement in the soul, or a fleeting shadow that seems both near and beyond. Such moments carry a profound truth: that angelic ministry is not confined to dramatic manifestations but often dwells quietly in the daily rhythms of faith and hope.

Throughout these testimonies—whether ancient or modern, grand or humble—a consistent thread emerges: the angelic presence calls forth a response that is deeply emotional and spiritual. Fear often intermingles with awe, yet is quickly replaced by peace; confusion gives way to clarity; despair is transformed into hope. Witnesses frequently describe feelings of overwhelming love, protection, and an unshakable sense of being held within the embrace of divine care. These dimensions underscore the theological and existential significance of angelic encounter—moments when the invisible becomes visible, when heaven's messengers affirm the tender mercies of God in human experience.

Indeed, such testimonies challenge us to expand the horizon of our spirituality, to remain open to the mysterious ways in which God's presence manifests. By listening to these narratives, readers are invited into a shared sacred space where the boundaries between the seen and unseen grow permeable. Each story becomes a luminous thread in a vast tapestry—threads woven through time by countless generations whose lives have been touched by angels' grace.

In reflecting on these testimonies, it is essential to recognize their diversity: angels may appear in many forms, serve many purposes, and engage with humanity in ways as varied as the human story itself. Some encounters are charged with urgency—a call to action, a warning, a commissioning—while others are suffused with consolation and healing. Some are marked by dazzling light and celestial presence; others are enfolded in quiet darkness and silence. Yet all share the hallmark of an encounter with the sacred, a moment where human beings come face to face with a mystery that exceeds understanding yet invites faith.

One must also acknowledge that such testimonies often emerge from contexts of great vulnerability, a twilight where human finitude meets the infinite. It is in moments of fear, sorrow, joy, or wonder that angelic visitations seem to flourish, reminding us that the spiritual realms are not distant abstractions but active realities intersecting the fabric of human existence. Through these encounters, witnesses are renewed, tasks are affirmed, and lives are set on paths shaped by divine purpose.

A notable reflection appears in the life of the mystic Julian of Norwich, whose visions of angels accompanied her profound revelations of God's love. Her writings convey an understanding of angels not merely as individual beings but as participants in the intimate relationship between God and humanity. Julian's testimony enriches our exploration, showing how angelic presence can open windows into divine truth, inspiring hearts to trust in mercy above all. Her gentle and poetic language invites readers to linger in the glow of these moments, to listen with open hearts to the silent songs angels sing in the soul's deepest chambers.

Moreover, the testimonies of children often carry a special poignancy, their unguarded wonder and simplicity offering a unique lens on angelic presence. Incidents of children describing visits from angels who comfort or guide them have been reported through the centuries and across cultures. These accounts frequently reflect themes of innocence, trust, and the gentle care of heavenly protectors. Perhaps it is their unfiltered openness to the spiritual world that affords children a particular sensitivity to angelic ministry, reminding adults of the faith that Jesus himself extolled as essential for entering the kingdom of heaven.

Encounters with angels have also inspired artistic and literary expressions that echo their emotional and spiritual power. From medieval iconography to contemporary music and poetry, these works embody the testimonies' essence—capturing the mystery and majesty of angelic encounter in ways that stir the imagination and uplift the spirit. The arts become a bridge connecting the experiences of witnesses to the hearts of others, preserving and renewing the sacred stories through creative expression.

Yet, as we cherish these testimonies, it remains important to approach them with discernment and respect—acknowledging the mystery that surrounds angelic phenomena while guarding against sensationalism or reductionism. The richness of angelic testimony invites a balance of wonder and wisdom, where the divine mystery is honored without succumbing to skepticism or credulity. The testimonies stand not merely as proofs or curiosities but as invitations—to deepen our faith, to cultivate openness to the unseen, and to recognize that angels continue to walk alongside us on life's journey.

In summation, the testimonies through the ages form a breathtaking chorus that resonates with the recurring reality of angelic visitation. From biblical patriarchs to contemporary believers, from saints to unknown souls, the stories reveal a heavenly dance within human history—a continuous unfolding of grace and presence. They invite all who hear them to be attentive to the ways angels manifest, to ponder the meanings of their appearances, and to embrace the profound spiritual transformation that angelic encounter can provoke. Through these living memories, the age-old truth is reaffirmed: angels are not mere myth or legend but genuine messengers of God's love, tirelessly bridging heaven and earth with light, comfort, and hope.

Communal Angelic Experiences

Throughout the tapestry of biblical history, encounters with angels are often depicted as deeply personal moments—intimate dialogues between an individual and the divine messenger. However, the phenomenon of angelic visitation is not confined solely to solitary experiences. Time and again, Scripture reveals episodes in which entire groups, communities, or assemblies witnessed the presence, intervention, or unfolding work of angels. These communal encounters open a distinct dimension to angelic manifestations, where the spiritual and social realms intersect, providing fertile ground for understanding the broader cultural and theological repercussions of angelic activity.

The communal angelic experience, as witnessed in both the Old and New Testaments, reveals how angelic appearances often function beyond individual edification, impacting collective consciousness, faith identity, and worship practice. Such episodes challenge the notion that angelic revelation is exclusively a private matter; rather, they remind readers that angelic intervention frequently addresses corporate needs, ranging from protection and guidance to validation and encouragement of a community's spiritual journey.

One of the earliest and most compelling examples of a communal angelic encounter arises from the account of the Israelites wandering in the wilderness. As the people journeyed toward the Promised Land, the Lord provided a divine guide for their protection and instruction—a practice that the biblical narrative associates with angelic guardianship. Exodus 23:20-23 explicitly mentions the Lord sending "an angel before you to guard you on the way and to bring you to the place I have prepared." This angel was not a transient messenger for an individual but a perpetual protector of the entire nation.

The presence of this angelic guide was more than symbolic; it was an assurance to the community of God's intimate involvement in their collective destiny. The Israelites' awareness of this angel contributed significantly to their communal identity as chosen people, under divine supervision and care. This angelic accompaniment was a sustaining reality during the trials of the desert wanderings, embedding a conviction that the community was always under heavenly protection.

Likewise, the narrative of Jacob's ladder in Genesis 28 offers a vision where angels ascend and descend between heaven and earth. While the vision is presented as Jacob's private experience, its implications ripple into the community's understanding of divine communication channels. This image has historically shaped Jewish and Christian conceptions of angels as intermediaries dynamically engaged with the world, serving not only individuals but the cosmic order that includes the entire people of God.

Communal angelic visitation reaches a dramatic zenith in the battle narratives found within the Old Testament. The incident in 2 Kings 6:8-17 is striking: Elisha's servant is frightened by the enemy army encamped against them, only for Elisha to pray that his eyes might be opened. When this prayer is answered, the servant beholds the mountain "full of horses and chariots of fire all around Elisha." The passage clearly describes a heavenly army—angelic beings—arrayed in protection of the prophet and by extension, Israel itself. Though the vision is experienced by two individuals, the implication is that angelic forces are actively involved on behalf of the entire nation.

Similarly, the angelic deliverance recorded in Daniel 6, during the deliverance of Daniel from the lions' den, while centered on an individual, speaks to the community's faith in the divine protection extended through angelic mediation. Daniel's survival amid national persecution serves as a testament to God's sovereign power, articulated through angelic agency. The story's communal impact is highlighted by its place in the canon as an encouragement to the exiled Jewish people, reinforcing their hope in divine intervention for the nation.

The New Testament continues this theme of collective angelic involvement, often within the context of the early Christian community. A notable example occurs in Acts 5:17-20 when an angel releases the apostles from prison and instructs them to continue their mission of preaching in the temple courts. This miraculous event is not merely the liberation of a few individuals; it is a direct heavenly endorsement of the burgeoning church's communal mission. The angel's appearance energizes the entire group of believers, signaling divine approval and protection over their collective activity.

Moreover, Pentecost—though not explicitly described as an angelic event—serves as a foundational communal spiritual experience where the Holy Spirit descends upon the gathered believers. Within this sacred moment, the role of angelic beings as messengers who prepare or assist in divine manifestations becomes an underlying theological assumption, connecting angelic and pneumatological realities. The collective reception of the Spirit's power and the accompanying signs suggest an environment where heavenly and earthly realms simultaneously converge for the edification of the community.

The Book of Revelation offers perhaps the most vivid portrayal of communal angelic interplay with spiritual realities, describing multitudes of angels accompanying God's final acts of judgment and redemption. The participation of angelic hosts in worship scenes before the throne of God, as depicted in Revelation 4 and 5, foregrounds their role as celestial beings facilitating communal praise and intercession. These heavenly assemblies serve as prototypes for earthly worship communities, demonstrating that angelic involvement encompasses not only protective or emissary functions but also liturgical and cosmic worship roles.

Beyond the biblical text, communal angelic experiences have permeated the liturgical and visionary traditions of various faith communities throughout Christian history. Ecclesial celebrations, such as the feast of the Guardian Angels or the commemoration of archangels Michael, Gabriel, and Raphael, reflect long-standing acknowledgment of angelic presence within the gathered body of believers. These communal observances affirm the conviction that angels are active participants in the life of the Church, interceding, adoring, and ministering to the faithful as a collective.

Historical accounts of angelic interventions in communal crises further illustrate this phenomenon. For example, various traditions recount angelic appearances during times of communal danger, such as in medieval Christian Europe, where reports of angelic armies aiding cities under siege reinforced a shared spiritual identity and fortified communal morale. These narratives, while sometimes bordering on the miraculous, serve an essential function: they embed the tangible presence of celestial allies within the collective memory, encouraging perseverance and unity.

Similarly, visionary experiences recorded by mystics and saints frequently describe angelic encounters where the visionary is not alone but part of a larger assembly, or where the angelic presence addresses an entire congregation. The spiritual writings of figures such as Hildegard of Bingen and John of the Cross include testimonies of collective angelic visitations, underscoring a correlation between sacred vision and communal awakening. Such experiences elevate the collective spiritual consciousness and offer a tangible link between the divine realm and earthly communities.

Miraculous healings and deliverances attributed to angelic intervention often become communal testimonies, passed down as formative stories that shape a community's self-understanding and identity. The sharing of these experiences within congregations serves not only as evidence of God's active involvement through angels but also fosters communal faith and hope. The phenomenon of angelic-related miracles validates a group's belief in the ongoing reality of divine agency that transcends individual lives and encompasses the entire faith body.

Theologically, communal angelic experiences invite reflection on the interplay between the invisible spiritual realm and visible social reality. Angels, as messengers and agents of God, signify the transcendent breaking into the immanent world, not merely for isolated individuals but for entire communities positioned at the crossroads of history and salvation. This interplay fosters a sense of spiritual solidarity, as the community recognizes itself as part of a larger divine narrative, one in which angels play indispensable roles.

Moreover, communal angelic encounters can be understood as manifestations of God's covenant faithfulness, reinforcing collective obedience and inspiring hope. In times of persecution, exile, or trial, the presence of angels serves to remind a community of their divine election and protection. These interventions validate the community's perseverance and encourage continued fidelity to their faith commitments.

From a liturgical perspective, angelic participation deepens communal worship and reinforces the cosmic dimension of praise. The biblical imagery of angels worshiping alongside the faithful invites assemblies to view their gatherings as extensions of heavenly worship. This realization not only enriches the community's experiential awareness but also cultivates a profound sense of unity that transcends earthly divisions.

Symbolically, angels in communal experiences represent the bridge between divine mystery and human history. Their presence signifies that God's involvement in human affairs is neither distant nor abstract but immediate and personal, reaching into the collective lifeblood of a people. The social dimension of angelic encounters highlights how spiritual realities are lived out in the public sphere, affecting culture, tradition, and communal norms.

In summary, communal angelic experiences recorded in Scripture and echoed throughout the history of faith communities demonstrate that angels move beyond solitary encounters into the realm of collective spiritual life. These appearances and interventions serve multiple functions: protection and guidance, encouragement during crises, theological confirmation of divine presence, and enhancement of communal worship. By expanding the scope of angelic interaction beyond the personal, these episodes enrich our understanding of the relational and corporate nature of spiritual realities, underscoring that the work of angels is integrally linked to the destiny and life of the faith community as a whole.

Recognizing this broader canvas compels believers not only to seek personal encounters with the divine but also to be attentive to the ways in which God's messengers operate within and for the community. Communal angelic experiences challenge modern readers to reimagine the spiritual dynamics of their faith traditions and to remain open to the possibility that angelic activity is not a relic of ancient history but a continuing aspect of God's engagement with His people.

In fostering this awareness, communities today may find renewed confidence and inspiration, perceiving themselves as participants in a cosmic drama where angels serve as both protectors and heralds of God's kingdom. Such comprehension invites the faithful to embrace a more expansive spirituality—one that honors the intersection of heavenly grace with earthly fellowship and envisions the Church as a living space where human and angelic collaboration shapes the unfolding story of redemption.

Interpreting Angelic Presence

Interpreting Angelic Presence Throughout the rich tapestry of biblical narrative, angelic encounters hold a distinctive place—both as divine manifestations and as profound moments of spiritual significance. These appearances, at once awe-inspiring and deeply mysterious, invite not only narrative appreciation but also interpretive engagement. How, then, are we to understand the presence of angels in scripture, in tradition, and in personal or communal experience? This question lies at the heart of interpreting angelic presence, necessitating a careful balance between reverence for the ineffable and rigorous reflection grounded in theology, psychology, and faith.

At the threshold of this exploration, it is essential to acknowledge the liminal nature of angelic encounters. Angels by their nature, as depicted in biblical texts, are otherworldly beings—messengers from the transcendent God to humanity. As such, their presence often defies ordinary explanation, hovering on the border between the seen and unseen, the material and spiritual realms. This ambivalence presents both a challenge and an opportunity: a challenge to interpretation that seeks clarity and coherence, and an opportunity to cultivate openness to mystery and transcendence that lies beyond human comprehension.

Theologically, angelic presence underscores the dynamic relationship between God and creation. Angels serve as intermediaries, bridging the infinite holiness of the Creator and the finite vulnerability of human life. This intermediary role situates them uniquely as both divine emissaries and empathetic companions. In biblical accounts—from the sending of angels to protect, warn, guide, or announce pivotal revelations—we observe a divine economy that affirms God's active engagement with the world. Interpreting these encounters involves recognizing that angels are never mere folkloric embellishments or symbolic devices but genuine participants in the unfolding drama of redemption.

At the same time, theological interpretation invites reflection on the nature and function of angels within the broader framework of Christian doctrine. Traditionally, angels have been understood as created spiritual beings, endowed with intellect and will, created before humanity yet distinct in purpose and essence. Their presence in scripture reflects divine priorities—mercy, justice, worship, and protection—all of which are mirrored in their roles and missions. Thus, to interpret an angelic encounter is to discern not only the literal event but also the theological truths such an event reveals about God's character and intentions. For believers, these truths affirm the continuity of divine care, the reality of spiritual warfare, and the ultimate sovereignty of God over all creation.

Yet, the interpretive endeavor does not stop at theological abstraction; it extends profoundly into the lived experience of individuals and communities. Angelic encounters, biblical or contemporary, are often accompanied by transformative effects on faith, hope, and understanding. The angelic presence becomes a tangible sign of God's nearness and love, a catalyst for spiritual renewal and moral courage. Interpreting these encounters thus involves a nuanced appreciation of their existential impact. They invite believers to reimagine their relationship with the divine, to see their lives as embedded within a sacred cosmic order, and to participate actively in God's ongoing work in the world.

In this vein, psychological perspectives offer illuminating insights into how angelic encounters are experienced, processed, and remembered. The human psyche, with its capacity for symbolism, archetype formation, and transcendental experience, plays a crucial role in shaping the perception of angelic presence. Carl Jung, for example, appreciated angels as archetypal figures representing the Self's bridge to the divine, the anima or animus's guiding force, and ultimately, the integration of consciousness with the numinous. From this viewpoint, encounters with angels may be understood as profound moments of psychological awakening or spiritual breakthrough, where the boundaries between the conscious and unconscious dissolve, revealing a deeper dimension of reality.

Complementing this understanding, the field of transpersonal psychology explores angelic experiences as manifestations of spiritual phenomena that transcend individual ego boundaries. Angelic figures may appear in visions, dreams, or waking experiences that communicate guidance, reassurance, or healing. In such cases, interpretation shifts toward discerning the personal and collective meaning embedded within these experiences. They may serve as symbols of inner growth, vehicles for coping with trauma, or invitations to engagement with the sacred mystery of existence. The angel, therefore, functions doubly: as both a personal psychological symbol and a doorway to transcendent reality.

Caution, however, must accompany psychological interpretation, lest the richness of angelic presence be reduced solely to subjective projection or neurophysiological anomaly. While understanding the cognitive and emotional dimensions of angelic experience is indispensable, it is equally necessary to embrace the theological affirmation that angels exist as real spiritual beings who participate in God's providential plan. The mystery of angelic presence resists simple reduction, inviting instead a hermeneutic marked by humility, wonder, and openness to multiple levels of meaning.

Moreover, communal frameworks of interpretation deepen our grasp of angelic encounters by situating them within the life of the believing community. In the history of the Church, angels have been venerated not only as sentinels and warriors but also as companions in the journey of faith. Liturgical traditions celebrate angelic beings in hymns, prayers, and feast days, integrating their presence into the rhythm of worship. The collective memory of angelic interventions—whether in scriptural history, the lives of the saints, or contemporary testimonies—anchors these experiences in the communal consciousness. This communal dimension suggests that angelic presence is not merely an individual phenomenon but a shared reality that shapes ecclesial identity and spiritual formation.

Within this communal context, discerning the meaning of an angelic encounter entails openness to the interpretive wisdom of tradition, pastoral insight, and scriptural grounding. It requires dialogue between personal experience and communal faith, so that individual interpretations are enriched, validated, and corrected by the broader body of believers. This interplay fosters a balanced perspective that avoids extremes of fanaticism or skepticism. It also encourages the cultivation of discernment—the spiritual practice of testing the origin, content, and fruit of a perceived angelic experience in light of biblical truth, ecclesial teaching, and prayerful reflection.

This brings us finally to the responsibility placed upon those who encounter or interpret angelic presence. The encounter with an angel according to biblical pattern is never a casual event; it demands a response of humility, obedience, and transformation. The angelic messenger issues an invitation—to trust, to repent, to rejoice, or to act. Thus, interpreting the presence of angels involves listening attentively to the message and living in fidelity to its implications. It calls for integration of the encounter into daily life, so that the experience becomes a source of sustained spiritual growth rather than ephemeral fascination.

Equally important is the embrace of mystery that remains at the core of angelic encounters. No interpretive system, be it theological, psychological, or communal, can exhaust the depth of their significance. Indeed, the very essence of angels as spiritual beings assigned to the service of the divine mystery means that they always point beyond themselves—

to God's unfathomable majesty, love, and purpose. Thus, interpreting angelic presence must honor this dynamic tension between revelation and concealment, between knowing and marveling. Such interpretive humility nourishes faith and wonder, inviting believers to remain open to God's ongoing revelation in ways both surprising and profound.

In closing, the interpretation of angelic presence emerges as a multifaceted endeavor—one that enriches our understanding of divine-human interaction and deepens our appreciation of the sacred mysteries. It is a journey that weaves together scriptural insight, theological reflection, psychological awareness, and communal wisdom. By approaching angelic encounters with discernment and openness, readers are encouraged to explore their own experiences and the experiences of others not simply as curiosities but as genuine windows into the transcendent. This exploration nurtures a spirituality that embraces both the certainty of God's faithful involvement in the world and the wonder that accompanies every brush with the heavenly realm.

As the study of angels continues to unfold, so too must our curiosity and reverence. Each encounter—whether ancient or contemporary—beckons the faithful to listen deeply, reflect prayerfully, and respond faithfully. Angelic presence thus remains an enduring source of inspiration, a celestial signpost pointing toward the mysterious purposed heart of God, inviting all who seek to grow in faith to welcome the light and love that angels, as God's messengers, faithfully convey.

May this invitation to interpret angelic presence inspire ongoing openness to the transcendent, a deepening faith that finds joy in mystery, and a sustained wonder that welcomes the divine into the very fabric of our lives.---Interpreting angelic presence is not merely an academic exercise; it is a living dialogue between the seen and unseen, between human yearning and divine revelation. Through this dialogue, the faithful participate in the sacred economy where heaven and earth meet, and where the story of God's redemptive love is continually enacted in the lives of individuals and communities. The angel remains at once a bearer of divine message and a beacon of hope—proof that in every age, the divine extends its hand in compassionate care and powerful guidance. To interpret their presence is to open oneself to this enduring mystery and to embrace the radiant possibility that no journey of faith is ever walked alone.

Living With Angels: The Ongoing Significance in Faith and Worship

Angelic Presence in Prayer and Devotion

In the vast tapestry of Christian spirituality, the presence of angels weaves a subtle yet profound thread throughout the fabric of prayer and worship. Though often unseen, these celestial beings are intimately connected to the life of faith, serving as messengers, protectors, and worshipers themselves. For believers, the awareness of angels can bring an enriched dimension of devotion—one that deepens the sense of divine closeness, invites reverence, and nurtures spiritual awareness. This exploration invites you to consider how angelic presence both grounds and elevates Christian prayer and devotional life, drawing on biblical foundations and unfolding into contemporary practices that embrace the luminous grace angels embody.

At the heart of Christian prayer lies an invitation: to commune with God in honesty and openness. Recognizing angels in that sacred space does not replace our direct relationship with the Divine but rather enhances it, reminding us that our prayers transcend the earthly realm, engaging the vast heavenly host. Scripture offers glimpses into this interplay between human supplication and angelic ministry, a partnership that continues to inspire worshipers across centuries.

In the Old Testament, angels frequently appear as agents of God's will, intervening in moments of peril and revelation. Consider the story of Daniel in the lion's den, where an angel shuts the mouths of the lions to protect the faithful servant (Daniel 6:22). This narrative highlights not only divine deliverance but also the angelic role as guardian, a protector engaged in the unseen spiritual dimension surrounding believers. When incorporated into prayer, such biblical images invite us to perceive angels not as distant mythic figures but as active participants in the believer's spiritual journey.

In a similarly profound passage, Psalm 91 beautifully captures the assurance of angelic guardianship: "For he will command his angels concerning you to guard you in all your ways; they will lift you up in their hands, so that you will not strike your foot against a stone" (Psalm 91:11-12). This poetic promise has long nourished the devotional life of the faithful, affirming that prayer appeals not only to God's protective power but also to the ministry of guardian angels, who surround and uphold the believer. When invoked with heartfelt faith, these verses become a wellspring of comfort and courage, transforming prayer into a lived experience of celestial fellowship.

Transitioning to the New Testament, the role of angels in the life of Jesus and the early Church deepens this spiritual dynamic. Angels announce Christ's birth to the shepherds in radiant proclamation (Luke 2:8-14), reminding us that worship itself is a shared enterprise between heaven and earth. Angels minister to Jesus in the wilderness after His temptation (Matthew 4:11), signifying divine sustenance and support in moments of trial—this conveys a profound truth for prayer: angels attend not only joyful occasions but moments of spiritual wrestling and growth.

Revelation, the apocalyptic book replete with vivid angelic imagery, frequently depicts angels as worshipers before the throne, praising God incessantly (Revelation 4:8). This heavenly worship scene invites earthly believers to join in a cosmic chorus, blending human voices with those of angels in adoration. The knowledge that our prayers are echoed and augmented by angelic worship adds a radiant dimension to spiritual practice—it elevates personal devotion into a shared celestial liturgy.

Beyond biblical texts, Christian tradition has long embraced the role of angels in prayer and devotional life. From the early Desert Fathers to contemporary spiritual guides, there is a rich legacy of seeking angelic companionship in silent meditation, petition, and praise. Engaging with this tradition invites modern believers to approach prayer not in solitude but in an intricate community of the visible and invisible—an assembly of saints and angels alike.

One powerful way belief in angels enriches prayer is through the practice of invoking the guardian angels. The Catechism of the Catholic Church underscores the ancient tradition of guardian angels assigned to each believer, entrusted with watching over and guiding (CCC 336). Calling upon one's guardian angel in prayer channels a tender intimacy— the angel becomes not an abstract symbol but a personal companion, nurturing a relationship grounded in trust. This practice often appears in short, simple prayers like the "Angel of God" prayer, memorized by children and adults alike, anchoring prayer in a daily, tangible sense of protection and divine closeness.

Contemporary Christian spirituality continues to expand upon this foundation, integrating angelic presence into guided meditations and contemplative prayer. One such approach involves visualizing the presence of angels as surrounding light or gentle voices of encouragement during moments of quiet reflection. This form of imaginative prayer invites the practitioner to feel enfolded in a sacred embrace, a spiritual atmosphere charged with celestial peace. It creates space for ethical introspection and transformative insight, as the angelic presence is felt not only as protector but as inspirer—urging the soul toward holiness and compassion.

Another avenue through which angels inspire devotion is the angelic liturgy. Many churches and Christian communities incorporate hymns, prayers, and readings that celebrate angels, fostering a sacred rhythm attuned to the heavenly realm. For example, hymns like "Angel Voices Ever Singing" or "Holy, Holy, Holy, Lord God of Hosts" echo the biblical praise of angels, aligning earthly worship with the eternal chorus. Participating in these musical offerings broadens the believer's awareness of being part of a community that transcends time and space, flowing seamlessly into the worship of angels around God's throne.

Angelic symbolism also ventures beyond structured liturgy into personal devotional expression. Artistic representations — icons, stained glass windows, sculptures, and paintings — serve as focal points that draw the heart toward contemplation and prayer. Encountering an angelic figure in a sacred space can stir a sense of wonder and awe, reminding the faithful that the divine realm is near and active. Such visual aids act as portals into prayer, inviting the believer to step beyond the immediacy of daily life and enter a world suffused with divine light.

Stories of angelic encounters throughout Christian history and contemporary testimonies further enrich prayer life by providing authentic narratives of divine-human interaction. While acknowledging the mystery and humility with which these experiences are approached, such accounts foster a tangible hope that angels walk alongside believers, accompanying their prayers and offering visible signs of God's loving presence. Reading or hearing these stories can energize one's devotion, encouraging boldness in prayer and a heightened receptivity to grace.

Reflecting upon the ethical dimension, angels function as models of obedience, purity, and relentless praise, attributes that inspire believers to mirror these virtues in their spiritual growth. The awareness of angels as moral exemplars encourages the faithful to approach prayer as a transformative discipline, not merely a habitual recitation. Angels' steadfast loyalty to God and their ceaseless worship demonstrate the ideal posture of the believer's heart—one of surrender, dedication, and joyful service.

In daily life, this means that invoking angelic presence in prayer is more than seeking protection or assistance; it is an invitation to align oneself with the divine will as faithfully and fully as angels do. Prayers asking for angelic guidance help cultivate discernment, especially when faced with ethical dilemmas or moments of spiritual dryness. The belief that angels can illuminate the path toward righteous decisions infuses prayer with a practical, hopeful dimension.

To integrate angelic understanding into one's spiritual journey practically, consider establishing rituals that consciously welcome their presence. A simple practice might involve beginning prayer with a moment of silent invitation: "Come, holy angels, minister with me in this sacred time." This brief invocation can become a gentle habit, opening the heart to angelic ministry throughout the day. Similarly, journaling prayers or reflections with the awareness that angels accompany your thoughts invites a more mindful and sacred approach to spiritual writing.

Guided meditations can further deepen this connection. Visualize an angel standing beside you, radiating warmth and light, gently supporting your breath as you pray. Imagine the angel whispering words of encouragement or offering quiet strength to face challenges. Allow this imagery to nurture a sense of peace and confidence that transcends circumstance, weaving angelic grace into the fabric of daily faith.

Moreover, engaging in communal prayer that acknowledges angelic presence can cultivate a profound sense of unity and support. Sharing prayers that include angels re-centers worship around the heavenly realm, reminding the community that their devotion is woven into a larger cosmic reality. This awareness has the power to transform group worship into a rich encounter with the divine order.

It is important to approach these devotional practices with the balance of reverence and humility, recognizing that angels serve God and mediate God's will rather than being objects of worship themselves. The Christian tradition is clear that all prayer ultimately ascends to God through Jesus Christ, with angels acting as ministers, not principals, in worship. This theological clarity prevents misunderstandings that can distract from the central focus of Christian prayer while still leaving room for joyful appreciation of angels' role.

Incorporating angelic presence in prayer also enhances spiritual resilience. When trials or doubts surface, affirming the reality of guardian angels' watchfulness can instill courage. Memorized prayers asking for angelic protection can become spiritual armor that bolsters faith in moments of uncertainty. Additionally, contemplations on angelic worship can reorient the believer's focus from personal anxiety to the eternal praise of God, renewing hope and perspective.

In conclusion, the presence of angels in prayer and devotion enriches Christian spirituality in multifaceted ways. Rooted deeply in biblical testimony, these heavenly messengers accompany the faithful on their journey through life, prayerfully bridging earth and heaven. Their ministry invites believers to engage prayer not merely as a personal dialogue with God, but as part of a communal and cosmic worship that includes unseen hosts. Through scriptural foundations, traditional practices, and modern spiritual creativity, integrating angelic awareness into prayer invites ethical inspiration, spiritual growth, and a daily experience saturated with divine grace. Let this understanding transform your moments of devotion, making each prayer a sacred encounter blessed by the gentle accompaniment of God's celestial messengers.

Angels in Liturgy and Church Tradition

The presence of angels within the life of Christian worship is both profound and pervasive, spanning liturgical texts, hymns, sacramental rites, feast days, and devotional practices. From the earliest days of the Church, angels have been recognized not merely as biblical figures or theological abstractions but as active participants in the spiritual life of believers, functioning within the liturgy as messengers, protectors, and celestial worshipers. This subchapter embarks on an exploration of how angels feature within formal worship, tracing the evolution of their veneration in Christian tradition and the theological implications woven into the fabric of liturgical expressions.### Angels as Participants in Divine WorshipAt the heart of Christian liturgy lies the attempt to replicate or join in the celestial worship described in Scripture, wherein the throne room of God is encircled by angelic hosts. The biblical vision of angels, especially as seen in the heavenly worship scenes of Isaiah 6 and Revelation 4-5, strongly influenced the shape and tone of Christian liturgical prayer. These passages depict angels as worshipers of God, singing "Holy, holy, holy" and casting their glory before the divine presence—a dynamic that Christian worship seeks to emulate.

This heavenly model served as a theological foundation for understanding the role of angels in the liturgy: not only are humans joining the angels in praise, but the angels themselves are imagined as participants in the earthly worship, bridging heaven and earth. Early Christian writers and Church Fathers articulated this understanding, emphasizing that the sanctuary was a place where the celestial and terrestrial realms intersected, supported by angelic beings who help carry prayers to God and mediate divine grace.### Angelic Hymnody: Voices of Glory The hymnic tradition of Christianity is rich with references to angels, serving both celebratory and contemplative functions. One of the most iconic hymns encapsulating angelic worship is the *Sanctus*, sung as part of the Eucharistic Prayer in both Eastern and Western rites. The *Sanctus* derives its text directly from Isaiah 6:3 and Revelation 4:8, proclaiming, "Holy, holy, holy Lord God of hosts. Heaven and earth are full of your glory." This declaration is explicitly connected to the choirs of angels who eternally praise God. By singing the *Sanctus*, congregants join their voices with those of seraphim and cherubim, participating in the timeless liturgical reality of heaven's praise.

Beyond the *Sanctus*, many hymns address or celebrate specific angelic figures, often Gabriel and Michael, who hold important places in Christian devotion. In the Byzantine tradition, troparia and kontakion dedicated to archangels abound, reflecting the ancient practice of invoking angels as protectors and intercessors. In the Western Church, particularly within the medieval period, hymns such as "Te Splendor Angelorum" (You Light of the Angels) articulate theological reflections on angels, inviting the faithful to contemplate their purity and closeness to God. These hymns operate on multiple levels, simultaneously praising angels and inviting believers to emulate their obedience and holiness.### Prayers and Liturgical InvocationsPrayer remains one of the most direct and intimate means through which Christians engage angelic presence. Within the liturgical cycle, numerous prayers invoke angels—asking for their protection, guidance, and aid. Many Christian traditions incorporate angelic invocations into daily prayers, the Divine Office, and special liturgical moments.

A prime example is the "Angel of God" prayer, a cherished devotional prayer taught from childhood, asking one's guardian angel for protection and guidance. Although this prayer is predominantly devotional rather than liturgical, its ubiquity marks the angel as a perennial companion within the personal piety of the faithful—a reflection of angels' liturgical significance as spiritual guardians.

Within the Mass and Divine Liturgy, angels also inform the words and gestures of the celebrants. The Roman Rite, for instance, includes the Prayer over the Offerings in which the priest prays that "our sacrifice may be acceptable to God the Father almighty, in union with the whole Church, in heaven and on earth: with the bishop, the clergy, and all his servants, living and dead; and in spirit with the angels and archangels..." This explicit inclusion attests to the belief that the angelic hosts join the earthly Church in offering worship to God, uniting the cosmic Church in a single act of praise.

Moreover, the inclusion of angels in blessings and exorcisms — rituals integral to the life of the Church — emphasizes their role as protectors and warriors against evil. In the Sacramentals, such as the blessing of a home or individual, prayers often call upon the archangels Michael, Gabriel, and Raphael for guardianship against spiritual harm, indicating their continuing active ministry in Christian life.### Feast Days Dedicated to AngelsThe liturgical calendar houses specific solemnities and memorials dedicated to angels, revealing how their place in worship extends beyond hymns and prayers into the full rhythm of ecclesial time and communal celebration. These feast days honor the glory and service of angels, inviting the faithful to reflect on their enduring spiritual presence.

One of the most prominent is the Feast of the Archangels Michael, Gabriel, and Raphael, celebrated in the Roman Catholic Church on September 29th (formerly known as Michaelmas). This celebration traces its origins back to early Christian veneration of Michael as the leader of the heavenly host, defender of the Church, and a mighty warrior against evil. Gabriel, the herald of divine messages, and Raphael, the healer and guide, also receive honor on this day, underscoring the diverse roles angels fulfill. The feast is marked by special Mass texts, prayers, and often public blessings invoking the archangels' protection.

Eastern Christianity similarly observes the Synaxis of the Archangel Michael and the Other Bodiless Powers on November 8th, a major feast that involves elaborate liturgies, iconography, and communal festivities. This liturgical honor highlights the protective and intercessory functions of angels and presents them as exemplars of purity and service, inspiring the faithful to emulate their virtues.

In addition to these major celebrations, numerous local traditions commemorate guardian angels or angelic apparitions, often associated with shrines, monasteries, or miraculous events. These celebrations serve as tangible expressions of the angelic presence within particular communities, reinforcing the ongoing relationship between humans and their celestial protectors. ### Ritual Symbolism and Angelic Imagery The integration of angelic imagery and symbolism within liturgical spaces— church architecture, art, vestments, and sacral objects—reflects theological truths and enriches worship with layers of meaning. Churches have long been adorned with depictions of angels, serving as visual reminders of the unseen realities that permeate the liturgical encounter.

Frescoes, mosaics, and stained glass windows often portray angels as majestic beings surrounding Christ, the Virgin Mary, or saints, participating in divine mystery. From the soaring arches of Romanesque cathedrals to the intricate iconography of Orthodox churches, the angelic form conveys transcendence, holiness, and the mystery of God's kingdom. These images also symbolize the presence of angels as protectors and guides, creating a sacred atmosphere that bridges the spiritual and material worlds.

Liturgical objects likewise incorporate angelic motifs. Chalices, patens, altar cloths, and even vestments frequently bear the iconography or embroidery of angels, emphasizing their role in sanctifying the Eucharistic celebration. For example, in the Byzantine liturgy, the priest's vestments are often adorned with images of seraphim and cherubim, recalling the heavenly worship at God's throne and reminding the celebrant that he shares in this cosmic liturgical reality.

Incense, an essential element of worship that evokes sanctification and prayer ascending to God, is also richly associated with angelic symbolism. The fragrant smoke is seen in Scripture as symbolic of angelic activity (e.g., Revelation 8:3-4) and functions liturgically to signify the presence of the divine and the participation of angels in the prayer of the Church.### Theological Reflections on Angelic Worship The liturgical veneration of angels embodies profound theological insights about the nature of worship, the communion of saints, and the order of creation. It underscores the Church's understanding of itself as a cosmic entity, a mystic body that encompasses heaven and earth.

The participation of angels in worship reflects their vocation as messengers and servants who glorify God unceasingly yet also assist humanity's redemption. This dual role elevates the liturgy from a mere human action to an event of cosmic significance, where the visible Church unites with the invisible hosts in an eternal hymn of praise.

Moreover, the inclusion of angels in liturgy reveals the Church's acknowledgment of the spiritual battle inherent in the Christian journey. Their protective presence and triumph over evil inspire hope and spiritual vigilance, encouraging the faithful to persevere in faith with the confidence that unseen forces stand with them.

The consistent invocation of angels in prayer and ritual also reflects the doctrine of the communion of saints, linking believers not only to the departed but also to the angelic realm. This holistic vision of communion enriches worship and supports the believer's confidence in the interconnectedness of creation and salvation history.### Angels in Contemporary Worship and Ecumenical Perspectives In modern Christian worship, angels continue to feature prominently, though the emphasis and style vary across traditions. Roman Catholic, Eastern Orthodox, Anglican, and some Lutheran liturgies maintain rich angelic imagery, incorporating traditional prayers and feast days. Pentecostal and charismatic communities may emphasize angels' active ministry in spiritual gifts, deliverance, and divine guidance.

Ecumenically, angels provide a point of shared heritage and devotion, bridging diverse theological perspectives. While interpretations of angels' nature and role can differ, the acknowledgment of their presence in worship fosters unity in the celebration of God's eternal kingdom.

Additionally, artistic and musical expressions within contemporary worship often draw upon angelic themes to evoke awe and transcendence, signifying the desire of human communities to glimpse the heavenly reality beyond the visible.### Experiencing the Angelic Presence in Communal Life Beyond formal liturgical frameworks, the veneration and recognition of angels permeate Christian communal life, shaping rhythms of prayer, personal devotion, and sacred art. Celebrations of guardian angels, processions, and the recitation of angelic prayers cultivate an awareness of divine companionship that sustains believers through life's challenges.

The emphasis on angels within worship also invites the faithful to deeper spiritual attentiveness—a posture of openness to grace, protection, and divine communication. By engaging with angelic presence, worshipers partake in the mystery of God's kingdom, anticipating the eternal liturgy of heaven toward which all earthly worship strives.

In conclusion, the manifold appearances of angels in Christian liturgy and tradition reveal a vibrant and dynamic reality. They are not relics of the past, but living participants in the Church's sacred mysteries. Through hymns, prayers, feast days, symbolic arts, and theological reflection, angels draw the faithful into a deeper experience of the divine, enriching communal worship and sustaining the connection between heaven and earth—a testament to the enduring significance of these celestial messengers in the life of Christian faith.

Contemporary Spirituality and Angels

In the vast tapestry of human spirituality, angels have maintained a compelling presence — not merely as ancient scriptural figures but as dynamic agents within contemporary faith expressions. This enduring fascination reflects more than just nostalgia for biblical narratives; it reveals a profound thirst in the modern soul for connection to the divine and the unseen realms. As we navigate the complexities of twenty-first-century spirituality, believers increasingly look to angels not only as theological entities rooted in scripture but as vibrant companions in daily life, sources of comfort, guidance, and awe. This evolving relationship, shaped by diverse cultural forces and theological reflections, invites us into fresh encounters with the angelic realm, prompting both renewed reverence and practical engagement.

Modern perceptions of angels are remarkably pluralistic, shaped by an interplay of traditional Christian teachings, popular culture, personal spiritual experiences, and interreligious perspectives. Unlike purely academic or dogmatic approaches, contemporary spirituality often embraces a more experiential and relational understanding of angels. Believers today tend to see angels less as distant and intimidating heavenly sentinels and more as accessible guardians — loving presences who walk alongside humans through the challenges and celebrations of everyday life.

This shift owes much to the widespread influence of popular culture and media. From best-selling books and television dramas to movies and new age spirituality, angels have become prevalent symbols—sometimes sanitized, sometimes sensationalized, but always captivating. These portrayals often emphasize angels as messengers of hope, healers, and protectors whose intervention punctuates human history and personal stories alike. The proliferation of angel-themed literature, both fiction and non-fiction, has introduced countless individuals to angelic concepts beyond church pews and academic study, democratizing access to these celestial beings in ways unimagined in previous centuries.

Consider, for example, the astounding popularity of works like P.L. Travers's "Mary Poppins," the television series "Touched by an Angel," or spiritual classics such as Eileen Elias Freeman's writings on angels in everyday life. These cultural phenomena have helped popularize the idea that angels are intimately concerned with human welfare and remain actively engaged in the modern world. They embolden believers to seek angelic presence not only at moments of crisis but also amid ordinary routines. This popular cultural lens does, however, present challenges: it can blur doctrinal clarity, foster romanticized or overly sentimental images of angels, and sometimes encourage uncritical acceptance of unverifiable claims. Nonetheless, it's undeniable that such cultural integration ignites curiosity and reverence for the angelic, setting fertile ground for more robust theological reflections.

Simultaneously, contemporary theology has been grappling with how to uphold the biblical seriousness of angels without dismissing or denigrating the genuine spiritual experiences of individuals who seek connection with these messengers. Mainline Christian denominations tend to approach angels cautiously, emphasizing their biblical roles as God's servants and messengers, avoiding speculative or mystical excesses. Yet within Pentecostal, Charismatic, and many evangelical circles, a renewed interest in angelic activity flourishes, often alongside charismatic gifts and spiritual warfare teachings. Here, angels are perceived as active participants in God's ongoing salvific work — ministers to the saints, warriors against demonic forces, and heralds of supernatural encounters.

Theologically, angels continue to be understood as created beings, distinct from God yet empowered by Him to execute divine will. Contemporary scholars stress their nature as spiritual, immortal servants tasked with worship, guidance, protection, and revelation. Such theological clarity serves as a necessary corrective to any tendencies that might equate angels with independent spiritual authorities or deify them. Nonetheless, theology also opens space for appreciating angels as conduits of grace, reminding believers that spiritual realities transcend human comprehension and invite ongoing wonder.

Personal spiritual practices surrounding angels have likewise diversified, reflecting a deepening engagement with angelic companionship. Prayer toward or through angels, once a practice marginal within orthodox Christianity due to concerns over idolatry or distraction from Christ, now finds more widespread expression in carefully nuanced forms. Many believers speak of angels in their private devotions — asking for guidance, protection, or intercession, always bearing in mind the primacy of God as the ultimate source of grace. Angelic imagery adorns homes and worship spaces, fostering a palpable sense of the sacred that bridges heaven and earth.

Moreover, angelic subjects feature prominently in spiritual retreats, contemplative exercises, and guided meditations. Practices rooted in ancient Christian mysticism, such as the Angelic Liturgy of the Hours or the use of angel prayers developed by various saints, resonate with many seeking depth and transcendence. New approaches, including contemplative visualization and journaling about angelic encounters, allow modern seekers to explore their own narratives of divine companionship. These personal experiences, while subjective, often become powerful testimonies to the presence of something beyond the visible, nurturing faith and hope.

Meanwhile, the popularity of angel astrology, angel oracle cards, and workshops on angel communication illustrates how some spiritual seekers draw upon angelic symbolism and perceived energies outside traditional church settings. While these modalities sometimes venture beyond orthodox definitions and warrant discernment, they underscore the universal human desire to experience comfort, clarity, and a glimpse of the divine through angelic intermediaries. For many, these practices catalyze spiritual reflection and open vistas toward the greater mystery of God's creation.

At the heart of these multifaceted contemporary engagements lies a common thread: the ongoing mystery and fascination with angels reflect humanity's deep-seated yearning for transcendence and assurance of God's presence. Angels function as liminal figures bridging the seen and unseen, providing tangible signs of divine care in a world often marked by uncertainty and suffering. They encourage us to remember that faith is not a sterile intellectual exercise but a living journey interwoven with moments of wonder, protection, and revelation.

Importantly, the contemporary angelic encounter need not undermine Christian doctrine but can enrich it. When understood in grounded theological frameworks, angelic ministry invites believers to embrace a spirituality that recognizes God's agency operating through multiple dimensions. It serves to remind the faithful that the divine realm continually intercedes in human affairs, not as frozen history but as vibrant reality. Angels, therefore, become spiritual road markers—signs that God's kingdom is already present and unfolding in myriad mysterious ways.

In worship contexts, the presence of angels is frequently acknowledged through hymns, liturgical prayers, and iconography, evoking the biblical vision of the heavenly host singing praises around God's throne. This liturgical remembrance preserves the angelic narrative as integral to Christian hope — a hope that extends beyond death to eternal communion with God's creation. Churches that cultivate angelic symbolism invite congregants to participate in this cosmic chorus, reinforcing the conviction that angels serve God's glory and human salvation.

Yet contemporary spirituality also challenges faith communities to discern carefully the balance between fascination and fanaticism, between genuine spiritual experience and escapism or superstition. Pastoral sensitivity plays a pivotal role in guiding believers who report angelic encounters, ensuring their experiences lead to deeper trust in God rather than distraction or fear. Spiritual directors, clergy, and theologians are increasingly called upon to offer frameworks that affirm the reality of angels while situating them holistically within the Christian narrative of redemption centered on Christ.

Finally, the ongoing dialogue between biblical tradition, theological investigation, personal spirituality, and cultural expression enriches the contemporary understanding of angels. Each believer — whether a scholar, a casual seeker, a worship leader, or someone simply curious — is invited into a shared adventure of discovery. Angels, as living, breathing symbols of God's presence, continue to inspire, illuminate, and guide. They challenge us to stand with awe before the mysterious interplay of heaven and earth and to cultivate a faith that is adventurous, open, and deeply rooted in divine intimacy.

In embracing angels today, therefore, we embrace a dynamic corridor to the sacred, one that calls us beyond the mundane into the radiant light of grace. We are reminded that the angelic reality is not a relic of the past confined to dusty manuscripts but a living, active means by which God communicates love, protection, and purpose. May this knowledge inspire each of us to open our hearts more fully, to listen more attentively, and to walk with courage—knowing that we are never alone. The celestial messengers who once moved across the pages of ancient scripture now move alongside us, inviting us into the ongoing mystery of God's unfolding kingdom. Their presence is a sacred reassurance that the divine is intimately near, ever-watchful, and endlessly compassionate.

As readers close this exploration, may they be encouraged to see angels not merely as distant myths or abstract theological concepts but as genuine, present companions on the spiritual journey. This ongoing discovery of angelic presence beckons us all to deepen our faith, heighten our awareness, and embrace a life animated by the sacred communion between heaven and earth. In doing so, we open ourselves to new realms of divine intimacy, finding in angels a mirror of God's unwavering love and care, a reminder of the transcendent beauty awaiting those who faithfully seek.

The Celestial Canvas: Art, Music, and Angels

Visual Arts: Painting and Sculpture

From the dawn of artistic expression, angels have served as profound muses, their ethereal forms bridging the earthly and the divine with a power that transcends mere depiction. The visual arts—painting and sculpture foremost among them—offer a rich canvas upon which these celestial beings have been imagined, reimagined, and immortalized throughout centuries. This subchapter embarks on a journey through iconic representations of angels, tracing their portrayals from biblical origins to the modern era, revealing how artists have harnessed light, color, and form to reveal angelic majesty, mystery, and theological significance.

The earliest biblical texts describe angels in terms that evoke awe, power, and sometimes terror; they are messengers, guardians, and agents of God's will. Yet in visual art, these descriptions have been translated not only into literal representations but also into symbolic forms that reflect the evolving theology, cultural contexts, and aesthetic sensibilities of artists and their audiences. From the majestic cherubim guarding Eden to the luminous archangels leading heavenly legions, the artistic vision of angels encapsulates a wide spectrum of divine attributes—holiness, grace, protection, judgment, and revelation.

In the ancient world, the iconography of angels took shape alongside emerging religious art. Early Christian catacombs in Rome, dating from the 2nd to the 4th centuries, provide some of the earliest known depictions of angelic beings. These figures often appear as youthful, winged messengers, draped in classical robes, embodying a humanity touched with the divine. Their wings symbolize swift transit between heaven and earth—a motif adapted from pagan imagery, yet transformed through Christian theological lenses.

As Christianity gained imperial favor, angelic imagery expanded dramatically in mosaics, frescoes, and sculptures adorning churches. By the Byzantine era, angels were often portrayed with solemn, hieratic expressions, their golden halos and richly patterned robes radiating divine light. A striking example is found in the mosaics of the Basilica of San Vitale in Ravenna (6th century), where angels flank Christ in majesty, their solemn faces and outstretched wings representing the celestial court. These figures express a theology emphasizing order, sacred authority, and the mystery of the heavenly realm. The use of tesserae in gold and vivid colors captures the transcendent light believed to emanate from the divine, a luminous backdrop that envelops angelic figures and invites contemplation rather than earthly engagement.

Moving westward in the medieval period, angelic art diversified both in form and symbolism. Gothic cathedrals, with their soaring vaults and stained glass windows, transformed both the spiritual experience and the visual language of angels. The angelic figures carved into stone capitals, flying buttresses, and portals reflected local artistic traditions and theological emphases. For example, the sculpted angels on the Chartres Cathedral in France are not merely decorative; their youthful faces, dynamic poses, and elegantly crafted wings engage the viewer directly, evoking the presence of the heavenly hosts safeguarding the sacred space.

Stained glass brought a new dimension of color and luminosity to angelic imagery. The vibrant reds, blues, and greens filter sunlight into kaleidoscopes of divine light, with angels rendered as radiant figures amid brilliant geometric patterns. These images invite worshippers to glimpse the transcendent mystery of angels as intermediaries between God and humanity. In these windows, light becomes a theological metaphor itself—angelic radiance shining through earthly materials, a vivid emblem of spiritual illumination.

In parallel with architecture and stained glass, illuminated manuscripts became another crucial medium for angelic representation. The Book of Kells and other medieval gospel books depict angels with intricate interlacing forms and stylized wings, conveying their otherworldly nature as well as the reverence accorded to their celestial missions. The angels in these manuscripts often frame biblical scenes or text, performing the dual role of divine messengers and guardians of sacred scripture, blending artistry with devotion.

The Renaissance ushered in a profound transformation in the portrayal of angels, driven by humanist ideals, renewed interest in classical antiquity, and advancements in artistic techniques such as linear perspective and chiaroscuro (the dramatic interplay of light and shadow). Artists sought not only to capture the spiritual essence of angels but also to render their forms with naturalistic beauty and emotional depth.

One of the most celebrated Renaissance examples is Raphael's "Sistine Madonna" (1512), wherein two cherubs rest dreamily beneath the figure of the Virgin Mary, their chins propped on cupped hands, gazing outward with innocent, contemplative expressions. These cherubs have transcended their original religious context to become universal symbols of childhood innocence and celestial joy. Raphael's mastery of form and expression, combined with soft coloration and delicate modeling, invites viewers to apprehend both the humanity and divinity that angels symbolize.

Elsewhere, Michelangelo's monumental "The Last Judgment" fresco in the Sistine Chapel (completed 1541) teems with angelic figures depicting apocalyptic themes. Here, angels carry the instruments of Christ's passion, wield trumpets to herald the resurrection, and engage in the battle between good and evil. Michelangelo's dynamic composition pulses with muscular energy and intense emotion, reflecting both the majesty and cosmic significance of angels as participants in divine judgment.

Color takes on profound theological meaning in such works. The heavenly blue of the sky, the gold glints on wings, and the ruby tones of martyrdom robes are employed not merely for aesthetic appeal but to symbolize divine truths—pure devotion, sacred glory, and celestial power. The contrast between light and shadow shapes the angelic body into something at once tangible and transcendent, embodying the tension between earthly form and heavenly spirit.

Baroque art, characterized by drama, movement, and emotional intensity, elevated angelic depictions to new heights of theatrical splendor. Artists like Gian Lorenzo Bernini in sculpture and Peter Paul Rubens in painting exploited dynamic compositions and expressive gestures to convey angels as fiery agents of divine intervention. Bernini's "Ecstasy of Saint Teresa" (1647–1652), while centered on a human saint, features an angel whose delicate yet impassioned pose communicates the intimate and overwhelming presence of divine love. The marble angel, with its flowing drapery and finely crafted wings, embodies both spiritual beauty and corporeal grace, inviting viewers into a moment of ecstatic encounter between heaven and earth.

Rubens' angels, by contrast, often descend in swirls of robust movement, their robust physiques and reddish tones conveying vitality and divine power. His painting "The Annunciation" pulses with light streaming from the angel Gabriel as he announces to Mary the coming incarnation of Christ. Here, light is not a static attribute but an active force, bathing the scene in a supernatural glow that suggests revelation and hope.

In parallel with painting, sculpture throughout the Baroque period embraced similar motifs. Angelic statues adorned cathedrals, public squares, and private chapels, crafted with lifelike realism and dramatic expression. This tactile immediacy reinforced theological ideas about angels as active participants in human affairs rather than distant, abstract concepts. The sculptures became embodiments of prayer and protection, physical reminders of the angels' ceaseless guardianship over humanity.

The Romantic era witnessed a shift toward subjective spirituality and emotive symbolism in angelic art. Artists like William Blake infused their works with visionary intensity, blending biblical references with personal mysticism. Blake's angelic figures, often depicted amidst flames or ascending in visionary spirals, reflect an inner spiritual journey as much as scriptural narratives. Light, in this context, becomes a symbol of insight and imaginative revelation, illuminating hidden divine truths.

In the 19th century, angelic imagery also engaged with cultural anxieties and aspirations. The Victorians' fascination with the afterlife is captured in the serene, mournful angel statues commonly found in cemeteries, their downcast eyes and folded wings evoking consolation and hope amid grief. These sculptures, often crafted from marble or alabaster, combine delicate detail with a poignant sense of stillness, communicating theological beliefs about resurrection and eternal life.

The dawn of modernity, with its myriad artistic movements, introduced new challenges and opportunities for angelic representation. Impressionist painters, for example, approached the theme with an emphasis on fleeting light effects and atmospheric color, suggesting the ineffable quality of angelic presence rather than literal form. Artists like Odilon Redon used ethereal hues and dreamlike compositions to evoke mysticism and spiritual transcendence, inviting a meditative experience rather than a clear narrative.

In the 20th century, abstract and expressionist artists pushed the boundaries further, often eschewing traditional iconography to explore angelic themes through dynamic shape, color, and texture. Marc Chagall's stained glass windows, especially those created for synagogues and cathedrals alike, reveal a uniquely poetic and multicultural approach to angelic imagery. His angels float serenely amidst scenes of daily life and biblical stories, their luminous forms integrating personal memory, folklore, and universal spirituality.

Contemporary art continues to reinterpret angels, sometimes merging traditional symbolism with new media, conceptual frameworks, or social commentary. The angelic figures may appear as monumental installations, minimalist line drawings, or digital projections, reflecting an enduring fascination with these celestial messengers in a rapidly changing cultural landscape.

Throughout this vast artistic history, certain elements remain constant in the portrayal of angels. Wings, foremost among these, symbolize more than mere physical attributes; they express theological truths about transcendence, speed, protection, and spiritual elevation. The use of light—whether through gilded halos, radiant backgrounds, or vibrant color contrasts—is central to communicating the divine origin and purity of angels. Form and posture convey hierarchy and function: archangels are often majestic and authoritative, cherubs innocent and playful, guardians gentle yet vigilant.

The artistic interplay of light, color, and form thus becomes a language through which profound theological themes are made tangible. Angels stand as embodiments of God's presence, intermediaries who bridge the infinite and the finite, the spiritual and the material. Their visual representations invite viewers not only to aesthetic admiration but also to spiritual reflection—to consider mystery, grace, and the divine order that undergirds existence.

Moreover, these artistic depictions resonate deeply with the biblical study of angels' roles and significance explored throughout this book. Whether as messengers bearing revelation, warriors triumphing over darkness, or protectors guiding the faithful, angels in art encapsulate the manifold ways Scripture reveals their celestial mission. The symbolism embedded in painting and sculpture enriches theological understanding by rendering abstract doctrines into vivid, evocative images.

In appreciating angelic art across time, one recognizes that these works are not static relics but living traditions. They continue to shape how believers and observers envision the unseen realm, inviting awe and wonder. The enduring creative beauty inspired by angels reflects humanity's ongoing quest to glimpse and express the intangible realities of divine mystery.

In sum, the monumental heritage of angelic painting and sculpture comprises a celestial gallery where artistry meets sacred truth. Each masterpiece, each delicate brushstroke or carved feather, draws us into a deeper contemplation of the ineffable. These visual arts transform theological concepts into radiant encounters with the holy, affirming the angels' profound impact on the spiritual imagination and the Christian faith. Through their forms, colors, and light, angels continue to soar across the ages—messengers not only of God's word but of transcendent beauty itself.

Angelic Music and Hymnody

In the vast tapestry of sacred art and expression, music holds a uniquely transcendent place—an auditory thread weaving the earthly and the divine. Among the many elements that imbue religious soundscapes with spiritual depth, the presence and influence of angels stand paramount. Throughout centuries, angels have been imagined not merely as messengers but as celestial musicians, their voices and instruments resonating with divine harmony. From the earliest chants that reverberated through monastic cloisters to the stirring hymns swelling within modern cathedrals and sanctuaries, the theme of angelic music and hymnody has persisted as both inspiration and embodiment of heavenly worship.

Sound, by its very nature, moves beyond the tangible—it invokes the intangible; it evokes presence, mood, and mystery. The biblical witness offers a foundation for envisioning angels as participants in divine praise, their voices blending into the eternal chorus that surrounds God's throne. This subchapter journeys through the sensory realm of sacred sound, exploring how angelic music has been conceived, depicted, and experienced in sacred traditions, while examining the interplay between auditory artistry and celestial devotion. It affirms that the power of music to articulate the ineffable is inseparable from the angels' role as bearers of divine glory and worship.---Angelic Music in Scripture: The Origin of the Celestial ChoirThe notion of angels as musicians derives predominantly from the biblical portrayal of heavenly worship, where angels stand as principal participants in adoration. In passages such as Isaiah 6 and Revelation 4–5, angels are depicted as singing, praising, and proclaiming God's holiness and reign with voices that shimmer with overwhelming majesty. Isaiah's vision of the seraphim, repeating "Holy, holy, holy is the Lord of hosts; the whole earth is full of his glory!" (Isaiah 6:3), suggests a perpetual hymn echoing through the heavenly realm. Likewise, the cherubim and heavenly elders around the throne in Revelation unite their voices in complex hymns of praise and worship.

These scriptural accounts imply a celestial music that is both ordered and dynamic, combining liturgical repetition with spontaneous exaltation. The recurring sanctus and the doxologies of Revelation give shape to a heavenly liturgy that transcends space and time while infusing earthly worship with a glimpse of eternal adoration. Significantly, these passages do not explicitly name musical instruments, yet the vibrancy of the voices and the imagery of celestial beings in motion call to mind an orchestration beyond mere speech, an angelic symphony resonating in the spiritual realm.

Moreover, the psalms, grounding much of Judeo-Christian worship, include calls to "sing unto the Lord a new song" (Psalm 96:1) and exhortations for the angelic host to "praise him, all his angels" (Psalm 148:2). These inter weavings of human and angelic praise in the biblical text establish a spiritual kinship where music serves as a bridge—human voices aspire to mirror the angelic choirs who eternally sing before God's presence.---The Medieval Celestial Soundscape: Gregorian Chant and Angelic Inspiration In the unfolding history of Christian music, the Middle Ages witnessed a momentous intertwining of angelic imagery and liturgical sound, crystallizing most notably in the form of Gregorian chant. This monophonic, unaccompanied vocal music embodies the solemn, meditative, and ethereal qualities traditionally ascribed to angelic voices. The chant's fluid melodies, free of fixed rhythm, evoke a sense of timelessness and spiritual elevation, inviting listeners into a contemplative space where the earthly and the heavenly seem to merge.

Medieval theologians and composers often reflected on their art as a participation in the celestial praise described in Scripture. The anonymous monastic singers who chanted the psalms and hymns perceived themselves as joining an eternal heavenly choir, their melodic lines connecting the chapel's stone walls with the throne of God. The chant's simplicity and purity were understood to mirror the unblemished, radiant qualities of the angelic realm.

Songs such as the "Sanctus" and the "Gloria" within the Mass Ordinary are laden with angelic references; the "Sanctus" itself declares, "Holy, holy, holy Lord God of hosts," echoing Isaiah's seraphim and creating a liturgical presence of angels in the earthly liturgy. Monastic writers like Hildegard of Bingen, herself regarded as a visionary and composer, explicitly linked her sacred compositions to visions of heavenly music, describing sound as the breath of God's creation and the angelic language of the cosmos itself.

The sound of Gregorian chant achieved a spiritual ideal: to transcend the chaos of worldly distraction through sustained melodic lines, conveying the angelic order and divine harmony. The monochromatic purity of chant suggested not only the voices of angels but their perfect union in a celestial symphony, a continuous hymn inside the walls of God's invisible sanctuary.---Baroque Opulence and the Chorus of Angels As Western sacred music expanded beyond monophony into the rich textures of polyphony and orchestration, the imagery and emotional weight of angelic music found new expressions. The Baroque period (ca. 1600–1750) particularly embraced the dramatic and ornate, creating grand compositions intended to invoke awe and spiritual ecstasy, much like the awe reportedly inspired by the appearances of angels in biblical narratives.

Composers such as Johann Sebastian Bach and George Frideric Handel infused their works with angelic motifs, often directly referencing angels in texts or imagining choruses sung by celestial beings. In Handel's "Messiah," for instance, the "Glory to God" chorus evokes the jubilant praise of the heavenly host announced at Christ's birth, while the "Hallelujah" chorus resonates with triumphant exaltation reminiscent of the angelic proclamations in Luke's nativity account.

Bach's cantatas and oratorios frequently portray the heavenly realm with intricate choral fugues and soaring soprano lines representing the purity and radiance of angelic voices. The complexity of counterpoint mirrors the ordered majesty of the celestial order, while the harmonic progressions suggest the dynamic interplay of divine love and glory. These works not only sought to uplift the spirit but to recreate in sound what the Scriptures suggest the choir of angels might sing continually before God's throne.

The period's fascination with the "angelic" was also evident in the use of suddenly appearing vocal and instrumental effects—soloists symbolizing angelic messengers, trumpets representing the heralds of divine revelation, and shimmering string passages conveying heavenly light. Such musical gestures were designed to draw listeners into a sensory experience that touched, if only partially, the ineffable beauty of the celestial sphere.---The Angelic Chorus in Hymnody: Voices Raised in Devotion Beyond the grand stages of cantatas and oratorios lies a rich tradition of hymnody that has perpetually invoked angels as part of communal worship. Christian hymn writers through the centuries have included angelic imagery to underscore the sacredness of song and the unity of all voices—human and heavenly—in worship.

Classic hymns such as "Holy, Holy, Holy! Lord God Almighty!" by Reginald Heber and "Angels, from the Realms of Glory" by James Montgomery integrate visions of angelic praise within the experience of earthly congregational singing. They remind worshippers that their voices participate in a cosmic chorus, echoes of the perpetual angelic hymns described in biblical visions. "Angelic hosts adore Thee," one stanza of Montgomery's famous Christmas carol proclaims, positioning angels not only as messengers of good news but as fellow worshippers calling humanity to join in glorifying God.

This sense of shared song between the choir of heaven and the assembly on earth continues in modern hymnody and worship songs, where references to angels often encourage spiritual attentiveness and awe. The concept that singing becomes a conduit joining mortal voices to the unending praise of angels transforms the act of hymnody into an encounter with the divine.---Contemporary Worship and the Continuation of Angelic Sound In the realm of contemporary Christian worship, the motif of angelic music persists, adapted to new musical languages and cultural contexts. Modern worship songs frequently evoke images of angelic praise as a means of emphasizing God's glory and power. Lyrics celebrating "the angels joining in the song" or calling down "heavenly choruses" reinforce the spiritual reality beyond the sensory experience of worship music.

Moreover, contemporary composers and worship leaders often describe the experience of musical worship as engaging with the spiritual realm, perceiving the music as "heaven touching earth." In this, the angelic is not merely poetic imagery but an experiential reality—musical worship as a portal to divine encounter, where the sound waves become carriers of spiritual presence and divine majesty.

The incorporation of ethereal harmonies, layered vocal effects, and echoing instrumental textures in contemporary worship music serves to create an ambient soundscape that suggests the enveloping nature of a heavenly choir. Such musical choices foster a space where congregants sense that their praise is joined by unseen angelic hosts, an idea tracing back to the biblical foundations of angelic worship.---Sound as a Manifestation of Spiritual Realities At the heart of angelic music and hymnody lies a profound theological assertion: sound possesses the capacity to manifest spiritual realities. The act of singing or listening to music becomes more than entertainment or ornamentation—it becomes an experience where the sacred breaks into the mundane.

Theologians such as St. Augustine reflected on music as a pathway to divine truth, remarking that harmonious sound reflects eternal order. This eternal order is precisely what the biblical angels symbolize—agents maintaining cosmic harmony and continually declaring God's authority through melodious praise. Through sacred music, humans glimpse and participate in this heavenly harmony.

The sensory richness of angelic music involves not only the sound itself but the emotional and spiritual resonance it evokes. Music's ability to move hearts, to quiet anxieties, to kindle hope and wonder, echoes the angelic mission to inspire and uplift. The auditory experience, therefore, is a sacramental encounter, where the immaterial and invisible become tangible and perceptible in human experience.---Music as Language Beyond Words Angelic hymnody also points to an understanding of music as a language surpassing the limits of human speech. Sacred sound, particularly in the angelic context, communicates mystery, reverence, and joy in ways that words alone cannot capture. This idea is reflected in the biblical descriptions of heavenly praise as a continuous song, an eternal utterance without end or need for translation.

The very nature of hymnody is to articulate divine truths and mysteries through melody and rhythm, to encode theology in sonic patterns that stir the soul. The angelic choir thus symbolizes the perfect expression of adoration and glory—infinite, beautiful, and yet intimately approachable through music.

The mystical qualities of angelic music serve as a reminder that worship transcends intellectual understanding and enters the domain of experience and encounter. When music lifts human voices toward the heavens, it participates in the angelic ministry of revealing God's glory through sound.---The Intersection of Music, Devotion, and Angelic Imagery In devotional practice, the invocation or remembrance of angels within musical settings encourages believers to situate themselves within a divine cosmic order. Singing or hearing music associated with angelic themes shapes the imagination to perceive the presence of the sacred and the transcendent realities that surround human life.

In many traditions, angelic music is believed to intercede, assist, and empower worshippers. The auditory element of prayer and hymnody thus connects the faithful not only to God but to the angelic realm that mediates divine grace. This connection bears witness to the ancient conviction that music can embody spiritual truths and open doors to heavenly realities.

Theologically, the intertwining of angelic imagery and music underlines the communal nature of worship that extends beyond earthly participants. With angels as fellow worshippers, hymns become more than a human endeavor—they become a cosmic and eternal act of praise.---A Multisensory Encounter with the Divine Finally, the presence of angels in music reminds us that the experience of worship is inherently multisensory. While visual arts depict angelic beings in radiant imagery and devotional iconography, music summons the invisible realm through sound, enveloping worshippers in an immersive spiritual atmosphere.

The auditory experience of angelic music thus complements and completes the "celestial canvas" of Christian worship, where art and sound together draw the believer into the mystery of God's presence. The sense of listening to or singing with the angelic choir cultivates an awareness of the sacred beyond words and images, a sacred harmony that suffuses body and soul.---In sum, the theme of angelic music and hymnody resonates deeply across biblical texts, historical musical traditions, and contemporary worship. Angels, in their celestial role as divine singers and praise-givers, inspire human musicians to reach beyond the limitations of earthly sound, to create music that aspires to heaven itself. Through these sacred sounds, believers hear echoes of the eternal hymns sung before God's throne, participate in the cosmic chorus, and experience the transformative power of the divine manifested in melody and song.

The angelic dimension of sacred music is thus both a theological vision and a living reality—a sonic bridge uniting creation and Creator, humanity and the heavenly host, earth and heaven. It invites every listener and singer to embrace music not only as art but as an offering, a form of worship, and a gateway into the celestial realm where, forevermore, the angels sing the praises of God.

The Continuing Artistic Inspiration

Throughout history, the figure of the angel has sparked an unquenchable flame within the human spirit, inspiring artists, musicians, poets, and creators of every era and culture. The angel, as an emblematic bridge between the earthly and the divine, embodies the mystery of transcendence, and it is this mystery that continues to captivate and challenge the imagination. In this continuing dance between heaven and earth, angelic motifs reign as timeless muses, their presence echoing through galleries, concert halls, and the pages of literary masterpieces.

The endurance of angelic inspiration lies not merely in their visual or auditory appeal, but in what angels represent on the deepest level. They are the intermediaries of grace and revelation, the bearers of messages from beyond the veil, and guardians whose gestures evoke protection and hope. Artists, whether consciously or instinctively, tap into these meanings, channeling the ineffable qualities that angels symbolize into tangible forms. With brushstroke and melody, sculpture and verse, they construct windows through which glimpses of the divine can pass, inviting observers to contemplate the sacred dimensions that permeate existence.

In the vast expanse of visual art, angels have been rendered in myriad styles—each epoch and culture refracting their essence through its own lens. Gothic cathedrals in medieval Europe celebrate angels with soaring arches and intricate stained glass, filling sacred spaces with luminous colors that seem to harness heaven's own light. Renaissance masters imbue angelic figures with ethereal beauty and human grace, their carefully crafted compositions balancing naturalism with spiritual transcendence. Through baroque exuberance, romantic reveries, and modern abstractions, angels extend an enduring invitation for viewers to engage with the mysteries beyond the tangible world.

Yet, beyond the evolution of styles lies an unaltered core: the angel as a symbol of the divine encounter. Each depiction acts as a silent sermon, a visual theology that speaks to universal yearnings for connection, comfort, and revelation. The wings of angels are not only anatomical features but metaphors of ascent, freedom, and the soul's passage between realms. Faces imbued with compassion or solemnity become mirrors of divine empathy and judgment. In this way, art transcends mere representation, becoming an act of devotion and dialogue, drawing both creator and viewer into a shared spiritual journey.

Music, too, resonates with angelic inspiration, transforming the intangible light of the heavens into the flowing currents of sound. Angelic motifs abound in sacred and secular compositions, from choral hymns that echo the celestial choirs of scripture, to symphonies that strive to capture the vastness and mystery of the divine. The notion of the angelic voice, pure and unearthly, has propelled countless composers to craft melodies that seek to reflect that sweet, transcendent sound. Throughout the ages, the invocation of angels in musical works serves as an auditory reminder of the unseen realities that hover just beyond human perception.

Moreover, the symbolic power of angels in music extends beyond religious settings, permeating genres such as opera, folk, jazz, and contemporary popular music. These genres embrace angelic imagery as metaphors of hope, salvation, struggle, and transformation. The angelic figure adapts fluidly, capable of embodying a guardian's compassion or a beacon of change amid human turmoil. The persistent recurrence of this symbol across musical landscapes underscores the depth of its resonance within the collective human psyche.

Literature and poetry expand this creative spectrum, employing angelic imagery to explore profound theological and existential themes. Writers have long grappled with what angels represent—not only as heavenly messengers but as symbols of human aspirations, fears, and moral reckonings. From biblical verse and medieval mysticism to modern novels and poems, angels populate narratives as catalysts of change, guardians of lost souls, or enigmatic figures whose presence invites reflection on the nature of good and evil, destiny, and divine justice.

In particular, poetry harnesses the ethereal quality of angels to give voice to the ineffable. The angel becomes not just a figure but a motif of mystery itself, a parable written in light and shadow. Poets craft images of wings brushing the sky, voices that pierce the silence, and eyes that see beyond earthly sight, weaving these into metaphors of hope, dread, and transcendence. This lyrical tradition demonstrates how angels inspire language to stretch beyond the limits of everyday experience, ascending toward the realms of spiritual insight.

Modern and contemporary art forms continue to find in angels a wellspring of creative possibility, even as interpretations become increasingly complex and nuanced. Today's artists often interact with angelic motifs layered with historical, cultural, and personal meanings. The angel can appear in unexpected places—graffiti murals, digital imagery, film, and performance art—each iteration inviting new dialogues about what it means for humanity to seek the divine in a rapidly changing world. These contemporary expressions confirm that the angel remains a potent symbol, adaptable to the times while holding fast to its spiritual roots.

Technology, too, shapes the continual reinvention of angelic inspiration. The ability to manipulate light and sound with unprecedented precision allows artists to conjure immersive experiences that evoke celestial realities. Virtual reality exhibitions, interactive installations, and multimedia performances extend the boundaries of traditional art, crafting environments where audiences can feel enveloped by the sublime presence angels represent. In doing so, art becomes not only a mirror reflecting divine mystery but a transformative doorway inviting active participation in the encounter.

Underlying all these expressions is the profound human desire to bridge the gap between temporal existence and the eternal. Angels, as messengers and manifestations of divine will, embody this yearning. By giving form, sound, and narrative to the angelic archetype, artists offer a language through which the sacred can be apprehended, albeit partially and imperfectly. This creative dialogue affirms that the pursuit of understanding the divine is inseparable from the impulse to create—a testament to the interconnectedness of faith, art, and imagination.

In contemplating the continuing artistic inspiration drawn from angels, one perceives a tapestry woven with threads of light, hope, and mystery. It is a tapestry not confined to distant religious or historical contexts but vibrant and alive in the cultural imaginations of today. This ongoing dialogue between the celestial and the earthly invites us to recognize in each artistic expression a flicker of the divine—a reminder that, through creativity, humanity participates in a sacred storytelling that stretches across time and space.

The angel's presence in art and music affirms the enduring human conviction that there is more to reality than what meets the eye, and that in glimpsing the angelic, we glimpse a truth both ancient and ever-renewing. As muses of divinity, angels continue to inspire creators to reach beyond the ordinary, to translate the whispers of heaven into forms we can behold, hear, and feel. Through this sacred inspiration, the invisible becomes visible, the silent becomes song, and mystery is rendered momentarily tangible.

Thus, this celestial influence illuminates not only individual works of art but the collective imagination, urging us toward wonder and reverence. It challenges us to embrace the infinite possibilities of the spirit and to honor the divine spark kindled within creativity itself. In this way, angelic imagery and symbolism transcend their biblical origins to become a living, breathing force within the human journey—an everlasting beacon casting light upon the path where heaven and earth converge.

As we close this chapter, we are invited to celebrate the angelic muse in all its facets: as a guardian of inspiration, a symbol of the divine encounter, and a catalyst for transformation. The artistic legacies forged through angelic themes remind us that creativity is a sacred act—a bridge from the mortal to the eternal. Whether through the fragile stroke of a brush, the soaring crescendo of a symphony, or the delicate cadence of a poem, angels continue to beckon us toward the mysteries that lie beyond, urging us to lift our eyes, open our hearts, and soar on wings of imagination.

May this enduring artistic inspiration inspire us, as readers and seekers, to perceive the angelic in our own lives—not only in the masterpieces crafted through time but in the moments when the divine breaks through the mundane, inviting us to experience the wonder, beauty, and mystery that transcend human understanding. In recognizing angels as celestial messengers and muses, we affirm a profound truth: that art, forever entwined with the sacred, serves as a luminous thread connecting earth to heaven, forever carrying the human spirit toward the light.

231

Thanks for Riding the Wave!

Wow, what a journey! If you've made it this far, kudos to your brave and adventurous spirit. This book was crafted to be more than just words on paper—it's an experience, a rollercoaster of thoughts and emotions that I hope left you buzzing with excitement.

Thank you for trusting me enough to embark on this wild ride. Your curiosity and openness made this entire voyage worthwhile. It's readers like you who breathe life into the stories and ideas shared within these pages.

As you close this book, carry with you the sparks of inspiration, the bursts of creativity, and maybe even a fresh perspective or two. Let these pages be a reminder that exploration never truly ends—it just pauses until the next great adventure calls.

Keep questioning, keep dreaming, and above all, keep pushing the boundaries of what you believe is possible. This book is just a stepping stone to your own incredible journey.

So until we meet again, stay fearless, stay curious, and never stop turning those pages of life. Here's to the countless adventures that await you!

With heartfelt thanks and endless enthusiasm

Gary E. Risenhoover